A STATE OF HEAT

GROSSET & DUNLAP
A National General Company
Publishers   *New York*

1/94 GIFT

*Some of the names and places have been changed
to protect the guilty.*

Contents

CHAPTER 1

A State of Heat

I am no longer young, but I am still told I am attractive. "Smashing," claimed Patrick McGoohan when I interviewed him recently. Young men still desire me, they still want to take me to bed, they still seek my companionship. They say they find me fascinating.

It may sound conceited, but it is the truth. I have had —and still have—all the men I have ever wanted, all the sex experience I have desired, success in my career, money, fame, great love, proposals by the score, and hundreds of propositions.

Only last week a man who lives near me in London became hot and bothered when I told him I'd written this book. We bumped into each other at Harrods, and he insisted on carrying my packages. He leaned against the railing of my front garden while I told him about *A State of Heat*. I could see the steam rising. I thought he was planning to become a permanent fixture. I did not ask him in. It was before noon and I was not in the mood for a tussle. The morning is for fantasies, not real sex. Besides, he always wore jet-black glasses, indoors and out, and I would never go to bed with a man whose eyes I could not see. I might dream of being taken by a man in black glasses; it was mysterious and somehow wicked. But I would never enjoy it in real life.

Looking back, the total of my experiences has added up to a wonderful life. I have used my femininity to the hilt, and it has worked.

From my early twenties I have lived like a millionaire. Rolls Royces and Cadillacs have always been at my disposal. I get the best theater seats at Broadway first nights and sit in the royal circle for film premières in London. People in the entertainment, literary, and business worlds have listened attentively to me. I have eaten the finest foods in the best restaurants. I have been treated like a queen by airline executives. I have not had to wait in line for anything.

I have a few pieces of jewelry that I like; otherwise I do not care for jewels—bits of glass. My small collection started with a brooch—a gold spray tied with five emeralds—from Howard Hughes, joined by a string of pearls from a young New York theater producer, a Tiffany brooch from a New York millionaire, and an exquisite diamond and platinum watch from another millionaire admirer.

But I have achieved far more than material success. Men have provided me with all the experiences a woman yearns for. I will never forget Scott Fitzgerald and what loving him taught me. After his death, when I married for the second time and had children, an admiring colleague in Los Angeles exclaimed, "Now you have everything, don't you?" But there was more to come, a son-in-law, a daughter-in-law, and a grandchild I enjoy even more than I did my own children. I have even known what it is like to have a woman make love to me —though I never wanted to repeat the experience.

When I was sixteen my mother told me I would be ruined if I had sex before marriage, but she did not tell me of the power of sex, how it could fill the hours with longing and pleasure. Or that a woman could use sex to get what she wanted. Where would we be if men did not want to make love to us?

I don't understand the fuss over women's liberation. I accept my role as a woman and use it to get the most out of life. I have never wanted to be a man. Men are frequently emotionally superior. But not mentally. Men are not stupid, but they *are* simple. The dumbest blond can make mincemeat of them.

Women think faster than men. They are trickier and more dishonest. They have learned to get what they want by quick thinking and devious methods. The clever woman allows the man-monkey to pull the chestnuts of life from the fire. She eats them while he toils and normally dies an earlier death than the mate he supports.

Even in the business world we can outwit men by judicious use of our femininity. I sold my first article to a newspaper editor showing a fair amount of crossed leg, at which he glanced from time to time as he listened to my eager babble. When I was threatened with a lawsuit because of some remarks on my radio show, I went to the lawyer who was planning to serve me with the papers and wept copiously until he declared, "I don't care what my client says, I'd like to have dinner with you tomorrow." The next day he had second thoughts and his secretary canceled the date, but I was never served with those papers.

Who would want to lift a fifty-pound load in a factory or carry a heavy suitcase around an airport when the strong arms of any adjacent man can do it for you? I always act weak and helpless under such conditions. If they don't offer to carry my burdens, I ask them. So far I've never been refused.

Women have always led men by the nose. We do not need the label "equality." Not all men are born equal, and unless we systematically breed Amazons, women can never be the physical equals of men.

I have been married three times and am sometimes asked if I would marry again. "Perhaps," I answer. "It would be nice to have someone always there to carry the packages and be with me at night." Yes, I am a weak woman, and I need help. But only physically. All my life I have searched for a man who is emotionally stronger than I am. I might have given up my career if I could have completely trusted the men who were offering me an annuity via marriage, or a trust fund. But in every relationship save one I have been the dominant partner. I had to be. But I have always been a feminine woman. Why act like a man? What does it accomplish?

Men—I have learned much from them: how to please them and how to get them to do as I wish by acting the role of devoted slave. I was always ready to be a slave for the man I adored, and it usually worked both ways.

The trick is to be desirable all your life. I was and still am. "Desirable" was how Randolph Churchill described me when we were young and he was the handsomest man in London. He still found me desirable when many years later we renewed our friendship in Hollywood. He invited me to his suite at the Beverly Hilton Hotel. No longer the beautiful boy of his youth, he'd grown fat, and at the moment was very drunk. He greeted me at the door, looking disheveled and wearing a bathrobe. We'd hardly said hello before he was chasing me around the living room, breathing heavily. I was literally saved by the bell—the arrival of the committeewoman who had arranged for him to lecture in Pasadena the next day.

When I first went to Hollywood, a group of actors, including Leslie Howard, Errol Flynn, and Ronald Colman, was discussing desirable girls. Afterward, Bill Grady, who was casting director at MGM, confided to me: "The majority vote for 'The Girl I'd Most Like to Sleep With' was you." With all those gorgeous actresses around, I was surprised—and flattered. I have never been insulted if a man wants to have sex with me. I have been annoyed if he persists when I do not want him, but I have always found it pleasurable to be desired.

Can desirability be acquired? Any woman can be desirable. It takes a little practice, a little faking at first, and then it will come instinctively. The author of *The Sensuous Woman* offered some much-talked-about advice, but I don't agree with her methods. If she spent so much time masturbating, she wouldn't have time for satisfying sex with a man and might not even want it.

The complete woman will always have a man to fulfill her sex needs. If she uses her sex to envelop herself and her man in a state of heat, she can win almost any man and use him to get what she wants from life. In the following pages I've drawn on my own experiences and those of others—successes and failures—to show you how to develop this all-powerful "state of heat."

CHAPTER 2

Sitting on the Grass in Wimbledon Common in a State of Heat

I was sitting on the grass in Wimbledon Common, wondering if anything would ever happen to me. I was fifteen but looked thirteen. I was like a cuddly baby, round, with a cherubic smile. I smiled a great deal. I smiled when I was pleased. I pouted or wept when I was not. My body was swelling toward adulthood, but my emotions were those of a child. I had recently left an orphanage, and I expected stupendous happenings in the "outside" world.

My mother had been a widow since I was ten months old. She had been very ill, with one serious ailment after another, ever since my father had died. I had been sent to the orphanage when I was six years old, as soon as they could accept me.

At fourteen I was offered a scholarship that would have taken me to high school and college, but because of my mother's illness there was no chance for higher education. I was needed at home to do the shopping and the housework.

Far from being disappointed, I was somewhat relieved. I might not have won the scholarship, although all my teachers believed I would. But who wanted to be a dry old stick of a teacher and spend your life in stuffy class-rooms when all the wonder of the great outside world beckoned you and where all the excitement was, the rich life I saw in the movies and in books by Charles Garvice.

So far, nothing had occurred, except a job stamping tin plates at the Addressograph Company in Shoe Lane, a narrow street near Fleet Street. About a hundred girls and women worked in an enormous room—each girl at her own awkward-looking machine. All day long the bang and clatter of stamping the plates reduced the conversation to a shouting minimum.

In the lunch break there was a rush to a nearby sandwich shop. Being timid, I was usually the last to be waited on. I took my ham roll to a seat in a nearby churchyard and ate slowly, making it last as long as possible, before returning to the factory. Four other girls had been hired at the same time as I was, and like sheep in the cold, they huddled together in the breaks and formed a small group of their own. But I was too shy to join them. Most of them lived in the East End of London—Bow, Stepney, or in the even drearier neighborhoods of Lambeth and the Elephant and Castle.

An operator aged about twenty-eight—she appeared middle-aged to me then—who wore a dilapidated seal coat with a big black velour hat, summer and winter, sometimes gave me the time of day, and imperceptibly I became a part of the older group. Their high-pitched conversation was pierced with shrieks of laughter as they told stories about their experiences with men. I strained to understand their stories, and afraid to be conspicuous, always joined in the laughter.

The one thing I really desired above all else was to be part of the crowd, to be accepted as one of them. I had been a leader at the school, both in class and on the playing field. Now I was feeling my way cautiously in this new world, fearful of making a mistake, anxious to seem like everyone else, not a girl for whom everything was strange and rather wonderful.

One day the woman in the seal coat told a story about an experience with a man, and as usual I laughed with the others. "I betcha didn't understand a word I was saying," said the older woman, fixing her dark brown eyes on me. I felt like a cornered rat.

"Oh, yes, I did," I said, blushing deeply. Why did I always give myself away with a telltale blush?

"Nah," said the other—the rest had drifted back to their machines. "I betcha," she said, looking at me critically, "I betcha don't even know how babies are made."

At school I had not thought much about babies; there were none around, and the youngest inmate was six years old. As for where they came from, God sent them.

Once I was walking with an older girl to the cake shop in the High Street, where I spent my weekly allowance of a penny on two currant buns. I was startled and intrigued when my companion exclaimed, "How shocking! That woman is going to have a baby!" I looked around quickly, but the woman had disappeared.

"How did you know?" I asked. The girl looked mysterious and said nothing.

There had been a joke at the orphanage about fat cooks. The girls giggled but did not explain. I know why cooks are fat, I thought contemptuously; it's easy—they're always tasting the food they're cooking. Why was it funny to be a fat cook? Why did they always laugh when they talked about boys? Perhaps now I would know.

"All right," said the seal woman, "How *are* babies made?" I thought hard. I must come up with an answer, or I would be exposed as a girl who knew absolutely nothing. They would exclude me from the jokes. I would be an outsider. I had recently asked my mother this very question. She had answered sternly, "Never ask that, especially if people are present." How were babies made? In the movies a baby sometimes appeared after the girl had sat on a man's lap.

"I think you have to sit on a man's lap," I said cautiously. "Also, I think you have to kiss him," and blushed deeply. The woman laughed. It was her duty to enlighten this ignorant girl: she must be warned. She explained in detail how babies were made. "You know that a man has a ——." She pointed quickly to the inside top of her legs. Oh, yes, I knew that. I had sometimes seen boys widdling in the street. "Well," said the woman—she was somewhat embarrassed talking this way to a child, but I was hanging on every word—"he puts that into yours." And again she made the brief gesture. I was amazed, and at first skeptical. How could a baby come from where I go to the lavatory? It was a put-on.

No that's where they came from all right, one of the other more knowing of the new girls assured me when I waylaid her as they were all hurrying to catch their buses and trains. Well, imagine that. What a strange way for babies to be born.

I thought about the process of birth all the way home in the underground, and looked furtively at the men and boys in the crowded train, wondering if they knew.

Now I started looking at boys in a new way. One of the mechanics who fixed the machines when they jammed or went on a mad rampage of stamping the plates was always watching me and making me blush. He was young—about nineteen—with a round face and a cockily turned-up nose. He usually brushed my arm as he passed the machine where I sat for hour after hour, stamping the bright tin plates with addresses and numbers.

Then, one day, my machine balked. I will always remember the fast beating of my heart as he hurried over to fix it, breathing close to my face while he turned his screwdriver and undid part of the machine. He took a long time, and my face was burning. I hoped my machine would break down again, but it didn't. I was desolate when he went on vacation. There was an emptiness in the room and in my heart.

Addressograph operators were often sent in pairs to work on the premises of the customers who required large quantities of the thin plates stamped with the addresses of their clients. I was working with an older girl at Colnaghi's, the important art dealers on Bond Street. Anne was twenty-one years old, but working together every day for three months in an isolated room at the back of the art gallery, we became friends. Anne had a real boyfriend. His name was Martin Bolls, and she called

him Marbles. I was sure that I would never have a boyfriend of my own; I would always look too young, with
my thick ash-blond hair tied in a bow at the back of my
neck. I was not very pretty now, although I did look
much better than I had at the orphanage, where I usually
had a cold, chilblains, and eczema, and until I was
twelve, my hair was cropped close to my skull.

Barbie, my close friend at the school, was pretty, with
curling brown hair, a faint smell of wax in her ears, and a
petulant smile. I wished I could look like her. Years
later I heard that Barbie had become a prostitute.

When I won my first prize at the school, an older girl,
pointing a finger at me, said, "You wouldn't think to
look at her that she was clever." I knew too well how I
looked—homely. But I was always at the top of my class.
And I clung to this fact and worked harder at my studies
and at hockey, cricket, and basketball until I became
the very best at everything in the whole school. Younger
girls admired me, and I became haughty and egotistical.
But in the outside world I was a grain of sand on a vast
beach. I longed for attention, I longed for boys to notice
me, and yet I was afraid of them.

Marbles was in Scotland on business, and Anne was
lonely. She asked me to lunch on Sunday at her home in
Wimbledon. There was roast beef, Yorkshire pudding,
roast potatoes and Brussels sprouts, hot apple pie, two
dim parents, and a young brother who left before we
did.

"Let's walk to the common," Anne suggested. Now that
lunch was over, I was aware that she didn't know what
to do with me. In the common we could sit on the grass
and maybe get off with some boys.

It was a beautiful day in early spring. The fresh buds,
wet and sticky, and the smell and color of the new grass
made us both restless. When Anne lay down, I copied
her, looking dreamily at the pale blue sky with the white
clouds playing hide and seek with the sun. It was warm
until the clouds drifted over the sun. We sat up and
looked around.

I could guess what Anne was thinking: "It's been a month since I've seen Marbles, and I want to be kissed. Why did I bring her? She looks like a kid. I'd have done better alone." Anne was sure she was a good girl, but there was something about the soft day.

Most of the men walking on the common were in pairs or with a girl. Here and there a man was alone. Anne was pretty in a sharp, thin, blond, English way. She had high color in her cheeks, and her eyes were sky blue.

Everyone said I was going to be plump if I didn't watch out. The red woolen sweater I wore over my brown cotton dress accentuated the curve of my burgeoning breasts, already more noticeable than Anne's.

"Why am I bigger here than you?" I said to Anne, cupping my breasts.

"Yours are too big. Mine are just right," she said, looking at me sharply. Did I think my breasts were prettier than hers? No, there was no fear of competition with me. My green-brown eyes were on the small side, my hair was thick and untidy. I had a good mouth. I was to hear "You have a lovely mouth" many times in my life. But I was dressed atrociously.

Anne turned away, a complacent half-smile on her face which I saw and understood. I was more perceptive than I appeared to be. Very early in my life I developed the habit of studying people, wondering what they were thinking. This was useful when I became a journalist. Now I longed for someone to fall in love with me, to tell me I was beautiful, to touch me, a hand to linger on my body. I had accepted the strange method of making babies, and the thought of such close contact excited me very much.

Recently I had experienced a totally new sensation when my mother was fitting me for a pair of panties and accidentally touched the inside area between my upper thighs. When she touched me, I had stood absolutely still while my face flamed. I wanted her to touch me again, but she didn't, and my blood cooled and the feeling went away. But in bed that night, trying not to listen to my mother tossing restlessly from side to side, I thought of it again, and by pressing my thighs together, the feeling almost returned. Whenever I thought of it, I pressed my thighs together and experienced a warm spiraling sensation that stopped short of a climax.

I thought of it now, sitting on the grass, legs hunched up, my arms around my knees, watching a group of men playing football on the common a hundred yards away. One of them was staring in our direction, and we both sat up more alertly. Who was he looking at? I knew I should not put on my glasses, but I had to make sure. He was looking at Anne. I hastily removed my glasses and put them back in my handbag. I felt flat. Who would ever look at me? Would it always be only a hand on my groin in the dark of a cinema?

One Saturday afternoon I had gone to the cinema alone, and at first I wasn't sure and moved my leg away and became absorbed again in the film. Norma Talmadge was fighting for her honor, which was obviously very precious to her, but I hoped the man would have his way and crush her in his arms. A hand was suddenly squarely on my crotch. I leaped up—I thought I would go to the ceiling—and ran out of the theater. All my life I would react to the music tinkling away at the time on the unseen piano, and it would always give me a sensation of pleasure.

I had returned to the cinema on other Saturday afternoons, hoping it would happen again. Sometimes it had, and I had pretended not to notice for a few blissful minutes before changing my seat. It was excitingly dangerous, but not entirely what I wanted. I wanted a boy to say "I love you" as they did in the films and the books.

Now I yawned, stretched, and looked fleetingly at a man and a woman nearby, lying on the grass, facing each other in a tight embrace. Quite unashamed. I could never do that. People were passing. How could she? Serve her right if she had a baby, I thought, pursing my mouth virtuously. What a chance the girl was taking.

What did it feel like, lying there with a man's body pressed so close? It must be thrilling, and I was on fire again, longing to be held by a faceless man, to have a voice say "I love you; will you marry me?" Because you would never give in unless he had married you. Mother says no one will ever marry you unless you are a good girl, and you will be a sour old maid unless you marry a man who will love you, and support you, and give you a home of your own. No, I would never take a chance on having a baby and being an outcast forever.

Two pimply young men passed by, and one said, "What's up, girls?" They laughed loudly and hurried on.

"Silly arses," Anne shouted after them, and returned to her *Picturegoer* magazine.

I picked a buttercup and held it to my chin. They said if your skin turned yellow it proved you liked butter. A lean young man with a loose lock of dark hair across his forehead paused briefly in front of us, glanced at Anne, and walked on. His indifference banished me to the cradle. He had seemed nice. Ah, if he had sat down beside me . . . Anne would understand the situation and walk away.

Gently, without my realizing, he was drawing me back-ward on the grass. We were lying close together, face to face, his right arm wrapped around me. It was so tight that I could hardly breathe. "I love you," he murmured. "I have been searching for you all my life. I have tons of money; will you marry me?" I was aware that his other hand was moving quietly up inside my skirt, reaching the apex, giving me the exquisite sensation that was almost pain. This time I didn't move away. He unbuttoned his trousers and put his thing just on the edge of my thing. No, no further please, not until after we are married. . . .

Without being aware, I had stretched out my legs and was pressing them together, closer, closer, until the tops of my thighs were one. I could not stop now if I had to die for it. My breath came in short, accelerated gasps; my cheeks flamed. Something indescribable had occurred. My shoulders relaxed. I was suddenly depressed and wanted to cry. Had anything really happened? I looked guiltily at Anne, but she was still absorbed in the *Picturegoer.*

Four years later, when a girl talked about a friend who had put a candle up her vagina and it melted, I heard the word "masturbation" for the first time in my life, and I realized what had happened on the grass in Wimbledon Common.

CHAPTER 3

Johnny

I was delighted when I married Johnny. Now I could find out what sex was all about. We met when I went to work as a saleswoman in his small office. He was twenty-five years my senior, but he was a handsome ex-major, and we fell in love almost immediately.

I married Johnny secretly on a Saturday morning at the Marylebone Registry Office in London, with two cleaning women acting as witnesses. He was worried about his sister's reaction. He planned to tell her afterward and she'd have to accept the fact. But to her dying day she never forgave him. She had not married until she was forty-three, and when her husband was in his cups he complained to Johnny that it would require gunpowder or a hammer and chisel to enter the fortress. She adored her handsome brother, and his desertion to me, the common little girl in his office, was unforgivable.

It was a bright morning in April, and I was happy. The sun always makes me feel that the lark's on the wing and all's well with the world. I smiled lovingly at my husband during the train trip to Brighton. I was actually on my honeymoon. I was married, and I was not yet of age. I could not stop smiling. I promised myself I would soon chase away the small furrow of worry on my husband's brow. My husband . . .

15

We traveled first class, and I was pleased with his extravagance. He had booked a double bedroom high up at the Metropole Hotel overlooking the English Channel.

"Alone at last," he said, trying to be facetious, but he was nervous. He wanted me desperately, and I was eager for the experience. The bellboy had been tipped, and we were alone in the bedroom.

Ah, here it comes, I thought, wondering how many clothes I should remove. It was three in the afternoon, and the Easter sun was flooding the room. It seemed almost indecent.

"I'll undress in the bathroom," he said, resolving the problem. I waited for him to close the door, then hastily removed my dress, slipped off my shoes, stockings, and underwear, retaining my bra to give me a feeling of not being totally naked. I rushed to hide my clothes in a drawer before he returned, then scrambled under the bedclothes, and waited in a glow of fearful anticipation.

In the months before our marriage, he had kissed me passionately whenever we were alone. I had gone sometimes to his flat in the evening, and after kissing me gently on the mouth he had suddenly sunk to his knees, his head under my skirt, and rather awkwardly kissed me. I was startled, but I enjoyed the sensation and was sorry when he stopped, gagging with some hair down his throat. He had almost had an orgasm.

He was a dark and handsome forty-three. "I did not kiss a woman until I was twenty-nine," he confessed. He believed it was a sin to have carnal knowledge of a woman before marriage, especially if she were a virgin. A decent man did not take advantage of a virgin. But he longed to possess me—a pretty, vibrant girl whom he loved desperately. I would give him new energy; together we could conquer the world. We were both optimists, and nothing could stop us.

In the year before my marriage, nearly every man I met had wanted to kiss me. Some of them forced my lips open and their tongues wallowed inside my mouth until, afraid of suffocating, I pushed them off. One man bit my teeth, a grating experience. Ever since I realized that kissing does not produce babies, I enjoyed being kissed. It gave me a sensation of floating in warm water. But when a boy from the Palais de Danse in Hammersmith took me home and tried to put his thing into mine outside my door, I wriggled free. I would not go that far. It was dangerous. Kissing was fun. And when I liked the boy, it was thrilling, but when I didn't, there was no sensation at all. You had to like him or it was nothing. I longed for the night when I would be initiated into all the mysteries of sex, but I was determined never to allow this until I was married. It would have to be my husband.

And now I was in bed on my honeymoon, with my husband sleeping in the bright afternoon, snoring softly beside me in the double bed.

When he had come in from the bathroom I was waiting, tense and expectant, the blanket held modestly up to my chin. I saw that his penis was very small. I waited for it to harden as I had felt them harden when the various boys with whom I "necked" had pulled them out for me to fondle while they kissed me.

His penis remained semisoft and quite small, although he breathed hard as he tried desperately to push it inside the willing area between my legs. His sperm, a thin gooey trickle, dampened my upper thigh. He had not quite made it.

All those stories and jokes about the wedding night came flooding into my mind. He had gone to sleep, and I was feeling flat and sticky. Is this what those indescribable feelings amounted to? The longing to be held, the burning anticipated pleasure. If this were all, what a fraud. The whole business was a fraud. I hated that snoring man; why didn't I first find out what it was all about?

I was a virgin, but this inept man didn't know the difference. I married a man I thought I had loved. Now I was sure I didn't. I sat up and studied his face dispassionately. He looked sad now, with the corners of his mouth relaxed. Weak. But he was handsome; his forehead was wide, with dark hair growing low. I brightened, remembering that he was a marvelous dancer. Tonight we would dance in the big ballroom at the hotel. We might even win some competitions. We would dance our way through life. Perhaps it was the excitement of being married that had made his organ so limp.

I slipped out of bed and dressed in the bathroom after taking a cold shower. I felt considerably better. Johnny was still sleeping, but had turned over and was lying in the slight hollow where I had been. I went to the window and lifted the blind, and he awakened.

"Oh, you're dressed," he said, yawning. Suddenly he remembered. "I was too excited. I'll do better next time. I'll dress, and we'll go for a walk on the pier."

Did I want a next time, I wondered while we crossed the road and my husband paid the entry fee to the pier. An artist drew our silhouettes. Johnny bought me some caramels coated with chocolate, which I munched as we walked up and down the pier. He talked. I thought. Perhaps it was better to stay calm and not get all worked up, only to be left hanging in midair, with not even the satisfaction I had when I pressed my thighs together. If it happens again, I promised myself, I'll squeeze my legs together, and that will satisfy me. He might get better, and then he could penetrate me, and even if I had a baby, it wouldn't be so awful. I would not be an outcast, but I didn't want a baby. I wouldn't know how to look after it. What I wanted was someone to look after me.

My husband was no more successful financially than sexually. He was an agent for all sorts of things—bricks for buildings; ingots of iron that came by something he called F.O.B. from Antwerp; Suji-Muji, a polish for cleaning cars; false pearls; lace tablemats; clocks; lamps that lit with a battery concealed in the base; and Turkish delight. I had worked as his only saleswoman, but during the year I was in the office I had never heard of him selling anything except the lamps via mail order. He had a large staff for this nonexistent business; in addition to me there were two typists and an office boy. Before he told me of his sister, I had no idea of how he lived. He should have taken a job, but he preferred the make-believe of having his own company.

There seemed to be no shortage of money—there

never is when people don't have any. Johnny's suits came from Savile Row; his shirts were made for him by Turnbull and Asser. It was a pleasure to walk with him, and how I wished my friends from the East End and the Addressograph Company could see me now with the handsome gentleman I had captured for my very own.

Back in London I was soon bored with a life of leisure, and since his sister no longer provided funds, it was imperative that one of us earn some money. He had a brilliant idea. "You must go on the stage," he insisted enthusiastically. "With your personality, you are bound to be a success. You're so pretty, all of London will be at your feet." "Do you really think I'd be good?" I asked doubtfully.

He went to the moneylenders—perhaps this was the first time—and enrolled me in the famed Royal Academy of Dramatic Art, where the top actors and actresses on the London stage had trained. He also hoped I'd lose my double-jointed vowel sounds and improve my speech, which was liberally sprinkled with "oo-ers" and "fancy that!"

But I left after one term at RADA. My husband ran out of money, and I'd shown absolutely no acting talent. I was too self-conscious and uncomfortable in all the courses except the miming classes, when I could really let myself go as the hind legs of a donkey.

I hoped this would be the end of Johnny's acting aspirations for me, but there was still the musical stage. "When you sing and dance, they will all be in love with you," he declared with his never-failing enthusiasm for everything that concerned his young wife or his own future prospects. He lived in a dream world, never facing reality, forever expecting something marvelous around the corner, refusing to accept the hard facts of earning a living, always hoping that his inadequate lovemaking would satisfy his inexperienced wife.

I have always tried to change a situation if it is unsatisfactory. I read some books on sex. I crept into one of the questionable shops on Charing Cross Road—those that display trusses in the window and carry books with lurid covers as well as sex manuals with titles in big black letters: *What the Married Woman Should Know, What the Married Man Should Know, Should the Virgin Be Told!, Aphrodisiacs for the Impotent Man.*

The salesman wrapped the book in a plain cover. I avoided his eyes, feeling that mentally he was stripping me. As I read the book on a seat in Hyde Park, I was excited sexually, but after a few chapters I felt nauseated and left the book on the seat. I wouldn't want anyone, certainly not my husband, to know I had read such a book, although he might have benefited from the contents.

Later when we were in Paris for a weekend, I wandered over the bridge to the Left Bank, paused at the bookstalls, and bought what the bookseller cheerfully assured me in heavily accented English was a "feelthy" book.

While my husband—the Mr. Micawber of my life—was transacting some mythical business certain to make our fortune, I took the book to the Tuileries Gardens. It was hot stuff, all right. The man was always flinging the maid onto the bed and tearing off her dress and underwear, but never the stockings. "He took out his prick, which was like the Rock of Gibraltar, and thrust it deep into her cunt." All the words were there, and I masturbated in the usual way, pressing the inside of my upper thighs close together. The sensation soon reached a climax. But then the chapters became repetitious and disgusting. I dropped it into a trash can.

But I had learned something from the book. In one chapter the girl did all sorts of things to the man. She had not lain there like a lump waiting for him to have his orgasm and be gone. She had put his John Thomas into her mouth. She had heaved and rolled around and said coarse words, some of which I did not understand, but now I knew what "Fuck me, fuck me" meant.

I determined to help my husband to be a good lover. I knew he was worried about his inability to make love. He had visited his doctor for advice. "You must give her satisfaction," the doctor warned him, "or she will go off with someone else. It's bad for her nervous system to be excited and unsatisfied." "Ah," Johnny sighed to me, "if only you were Spanish. Spanish women excite me tremendously."

It must be my fault that our sex life had added up to zero. But now that I knew more about sex, I would do my part. One Sunday afternoon I produced some fragrant Havana cigars—he loved cigars but could not afford them; I had taken the money from his change on top of the bureau. To complete the seduction scene, I added a bottle of champagne. I had heard a joke about dry old Mumm, but this was Piper Heidsieck. We drank the champagne, he smoked a cigar, and I caressed his penis while we undressed. I felt it getting bigger and shouted "I love you" over and over again and once "Fuck me" in a shrill falsetto. He tried his damnedest to put it inside me, but he couldn't. We gave up after an hour of sweating, rubbing, and pushing, and were so exhausted from the hot exercise and champagne drinking that this time we *both* fell asleep.

We never tried again. But I loved him and he loved me. It was enough to sit on his lap and be cuddled. In bed his arms held me close. It was like sleeping with my mother when I was small—safe, warm, and cozy.

But I was still yearning to experience real sex. . . .

CHAPTER 4

A School for Sex

Dickens had his school for pickpockets. I had my school for sex—the stage. "Don't put your daughter on the stage, Mrs. Worthington," sang Noël Coward. He could have added: ". . . not if you wish her to remain innocent."

The musical-comedy stage as I knew it in London during the late twenties and early thirties was a great school for learning about sex. The music and dancing engendered excitement. You were on show. Who knew how many men in the audience wanted you.

I, who had been excluded from the lowest dance classes at school because I was clumsy, who was so shy I almost fainted when asked to make a speech to the class, who had a nice little singing voice, but nothing more, was in 1928 propelled onto the stage with the highest standard of musical revue in London, the Pavilion. I was one of eight chorus girls in Charles B. Cochran's *One Damn Thing After Another.* We were chosen more for our pretty faces and figures than for ability as singers and dancers.

Cochran was the Ziegfeld of London, and his girls were as famous in England as the Follies girls were in the United States. "The chorus will be a small one," Mr. Cochran, a florid, smiling entrepreneur, informed me, following my quavering rendition of "Rose Marie, I Love You" and an embarrassing one-two-three kick. As I mounted the stage I wanted to run back into the street, but I have rarely run away from anything. The more frightening the experience, the more I had to go through with it, mesmerized by the childish superstition that if I backed away I would never do anything.

There were thousands of girls who could sing and dance, but the Cochran girls in the late twenties had sex appeal. They were a draw for the Oxford and Cambridge undergraduates, the young bloods in the Guards regiments, and the lecherous millionaires of the business world whom Cochran needed to finance his productions.

In spite of my secret marriage, I was still naïve and still a virgin when I was signed to be what the producer euphemistically called a "Cochran Young Lady." A bit of class made the chase more exciting for the moist men of Manchester and Birmingham.

The Young Ladies and the bit players were a mixed bunch, but all of them had obviously been around. One tough brunet had been to Hollywood and regarded us with contempt. A bit player was married to a brigadier general, had two children, and lived in Kensington.

Elsa Lanchester was among the group. She had recently starred in an A. P. Herbert production at the Hammersmith theater and was bitterly disappointed at the meager bits apportioned to her in the revue. She did not stay long.

For a girl who had lived in the East End of London for four years preceding my marriage, it is hard to believe that the strongest language I had ever understood was "damn." As a Cochran Young Lady I heard all the four-letter words from "cock" to "cunt" and learned what they meant.

I knew how babies were made, and I had kissed a great deal. I loved to be held closely and cuddled, but I was still out of my depth when they discussed matters of sex. I was a sensitive square and could feel the derision beneath the surface politeness. Where I had come from a "cunt" was called a "pussy cat" and a "cock" was a

"John Thomas," although I had not yet read *Lady Chatterley's Lover.*

And now I heard this new word, "fuck." I looked up from the intense business of putting black dobs on the tops of my eyelashes and asked, "What does 'fuck' mean?" There was an astounded silence.

"Fuck, fuck, fuck," I repeated. I realized I was trapped, but could not stop. "Is it a dirty word, or is it the same as 'damn'?"

"No, it isn't," said Lorne flatly. Lorne was an assistant to Noël Coward, and she could not understand why "Cockie" had hired me. I was pretty, but such an obvious misfit. I did not belong in a sophisticated revue. When she learned that I was popular with the male customers and was receiving flowers and gifts, she said in wonderment, "I have a cunt too, but no one is sending *me* presents."

This was lesson number one for me in this interesting university. Lorne was very efficient. Men seemed less inclined to send presents to efficient women. They preferred to subsidize the helpless-looking girls. I was too intelligent ever to be really helpless, and more organized than people would give me credit for. But I would always give the impression that I needed help. This has stood me in good stead over the years. Whenever I am in a jam I become bewildered and helpless, and men or efficient women take over the problem. Now, doing my best to keep my emotions in check, I was feeling my way cautiously in this exotic new world.

I controlled my fears when I was with the girls or on the stage, but when I was at home, the nervous tension often exploded in a storm of tears, and my alarmed husband enfolded me in his arms and rocked me like a baby.

Unexpectedly, I had blossomed into a beauty. I still have the London Theatre Beauty Trophy to prove it. I was not the classic beauty, some of my features were irregular, but the mouth "that never counted costs" (Kathleen in *The Last Tycoon*) invited kisses, my teeth were excellent, and my smile knocked the aging men off their seats in the stalls.

My husband prophesied I would be a great star. I was eager to believe him, although I had never before thought of being an actress. I was too self-conscious. And yet being on the stage in the full glare of the warm footlights excited me tremendously. It was like stripping naked before the world. I *would* be a great star. I *would* justify my husband's faith, which was as childlike as my own. As soon as the show opened I asked the stage manager if I could understudy Mimi Crawford, one of the two leading ladies; Jessie Matthews was the other. He knew I was not a good dancer, but he was a victim of my smile.

A few months after the revue opened to great acclaim, Miss Crawford fell ill. I was rushed literally into her shoes.

"The audience was captivated by her fair beauty and charming voice," a kindly critic enthused in print. Afterward, with my husband prodding in the wings, I cornered Mr. Cochran and asked for promotion from the chorus. "I have an offer to play a leading part on tour," I lied, "but I'd rather stay with you." To my astonishment, he said, "Of course, my dear," and promised I would be a featured player in his next revue, *This Year of Grace.*

Cockie was a shrewd evaluator of female flesh. He knew my eager helplessness appealed to men with money to spend, men who had experienced every kind of sophisticated sex, who would welcome the untrained young beginner in the field.

The producer was married and adored his wife. He also adored a succession of Young Ladies. His permanent mistress was a beauty of the English-rose variety, long straight blond hair, the creamiest of complexions, a swanlike neck, and high color in her cheeks, caused, I was told, by her recurring tuberculosis. Eileen was untalented but had her own dressing room and lived in an expensive flat in Mayfair.

I was new to the business of bartering sex for comfort, and I shuddered at the thought of being a man's mistress. He would soon get tired of you, I was sure, and throw you to the white slavers, waiting to ship you to the Argentine. I had not read the *News of the World* all those years for nothing. But Eileen seemed to be getting away with it. Who was right? Who was wrong? I was glad I was married and could never be a man's mistress.

One evening Sybil was absent from the show. She was ill. When she returned a week later, pale and thin, she told us she'd had an abortion—she had been two months pregnant. The job was badly performed, and she had hemorrhaged and been rushed to the hospital, where they took out some further bits and pieces.

"I nearly died," she told us dramatically. "It was a ghastly experience. There were three people in an office —two men and a woman. The men were awful. One of them examined me and afterward dragged me down on the floor and fucked me. He said it might bring on the period. But it didn't. He took me into another room with a table and clamps for my legs. I was terrified. The other man was there, and the woman. They said I could not have a proper anesthetic, just a whiff of gas, as they never knew when the police would come and everybody would have to run. It hurt like hell. I screamed, and the woman quickly put her hand over my mouth and told me to shut up. Did I want to bring the cops?" Sybil paused, gulped, and continued, "The sweat poured off me. I could see them all in a haze, and the man doing the operation said, 'Someone must have frightened her.' Frightened me? I was petrified. It seemed to take ages. Afterward they said I could rest only for a few minutes. They got me a taxi, and I went home to my mother. I was bleeding like a stuck pig, and she called an ambulance. It was almost too late."

One of the girls said she had thought she was knocked up and when her period finally came she had rushed to the nearest Boots chemist shop and gasped, "A packet of Modess, thank God." They roared. I wondered how they could laugh at such frightening matters. Sex could be dangerous. I hoped I would never get pregnant. It seemed you could have affairs, but don't get caught.

Although Dan, the choreographer, was a severe taskmaster, he could have his pick of the girls. Not all of them—certainly not Marjorie Robertson, who changed her name to Anna Neagle and became a famed star of the stage and screen—but others would have gladly have had an affair with him, for love or career, or both. Dan was very masculine and simply oozed sex appeal.

The smell of sex was always backstage. Dan alternated between Nancy and Rosemary. I would find Dan and Nancy on the narrow landing leading to the dressing rooms, locked in each other's arms, breathing heavily, Nancy giggling when I passed, tossing her dark hair as if to say, "You are too much of a sissy to let yourself go like this." She was to commit suicide many years later.

Rosemary was cleverer and more demure than Nancy. She was less free with her kisses and would never embrace a man in public. She became engaged to Dan, who helped to advance her career, but she married someone else.

As Ziegfeld had the Winter Garden in New York, Cochran had the Pavilion in London, straddling the west side of Piccadilly Circus. The opening night of a Cochran revue was the most glamorous in the world. The Prince of Wales, his brother Prince George, and the richest and most important people in London were crowded into the stalls, the boxes, and the royal circle, a blur of bare shoulders and blazing jewels, white ties and tails, soft male conversation and laughter. Sometimes the lower boxes were filled with men only, and they talked to us as we whirled around the stage, asking to take us to supper, telling us how pretty we were. I thought this was living life to the full, smiling at the white ties and tails. I found the Pavilion's atmosphere of flamboyant unashamed sex dazzling.

Many famous figures of the day visited the Pavilion. Through Mr. Cochran I met Arnold Bennett, A. P. Herbert, Bernard Shaw, H. G. Wells, G. K. Chesterton, Margot Asquith, Lady Diana Cooper, Frederick Lonsdale, Diaghilev, Nijinsky, Fokine, the great dress and stage designers—Idare, who designed the silvery dress I wore when I won my cup for beauty (I was always sure it was the dress that won)—Doris Zinkeisen, Oliver Messel, Hannen Swaffer, the acidulous critic, and all the interesting people floating around the theater in a bright panorama that was a rather alarming fairyland for a girl from a drab orphanage. What could I say to them? I listened and learned.

I was marked for early slaughter. My freshness was a challenge for the dirty old men as well as the young. On Saturday night there was usually a party somewhere in Mayfair, with a blanket invitation for Mr. Cochran's Young Ladies. I was invited with the rest, but I usually declined. I was afraid they might drug me and then do what they wanted with me; I would be pregnant and have to have an abortion. I was glad to go home to my husband and find comfort in his platonic arms. I was always tired, and he sometimes took me to bed as though I were a kitten, propelling me forward with his teeth softly in the nape of my neck.

Some of the stories I heard in the dressing room on Monday! At one party the host, an aging roué, was the only man present except for his butler. There were girls from other theaters at the party, about twenty in all. At a command from his master, the butler lined up the girls in the drawing room and told them to undress.

When they were all "naked and ready for the hungry shark," they were told to form a circle. Were they going to be whipped? It had happened at other parties. The roué appeared in full evening dress, carrying a long ostrich feather. The butler ordered the girls to gallop in a circle. His master flicked their bottoms with the feather as they ran. After thirty minutes the butler shouted, "Whoa!" The girls dressed, and as they passed him at the door they were each handed a ten-pound note.

I laughed with the rest as they recounted the unusual adventure. Perhaps I should have gone to this one. The ten pounds would have been useful. Was it so awful to do such things? It had not changed the girls. But I had never stripped completely naked in front of anybody, not even my husband. And what if he had used a whip instead of a feather? When I had been struck at the orphanage by a teacher or a girl, I had always hit back twice as hard. I would have taken the whip and hit him across the face with it. No, I could never bring myself to do anything like that.

Next Saturday night there was a party in Great Portland Street. The middle-aged-bachelor host was a business associate of Cochran, and because he himself asked me to attend, I went, reluctantly. I hated parties, especially this kind of party, where men were looking for an easy adventure with an actress. I never quite knew what to say, whether I should pretend to be wicked so that afterward they could tell their friends in the club, "By jove, what a night I had!" or whether I should just sit there saying nothing while they tugged at their cuffs and mumbled inanities.

It was a large house. In those days in prosperous London the rich lived in big houses with numerous servants. We were ushered into a huge drawing room, exquisitely furnished. There were about a dozen men in evening dress. They had attended the show, had a few drinks, and now were crowding around the girls, paying lavish compliments. Mr. Cochran looked like a benevolent shepherd as he introduced his pretty flock.

I was tense and nervous, ready to ward off anything suggestive. But it was quite respectable, even though there were no other women but the Young Ladies. We were treated with such elaborate courtesy that I started to worry. This was the first step in some of the stories I'd read in the cheap magazines. The more polite the men were, the more they meant mischief. I must be on my guard.

The long buffet table was crammed with cold salmon, cold chicken, beautiful china, and gleaming silver. Against a background of popping champagne corks and laughter I began to relax. Then a dissipated middle-aged man sat next to me, held my hand, and sighed longingly, close to my face. He whispered that I was lovely and asked if he could take me home, but his sentence evaporated in the distance I rapidly put between us.

"The girls will now do the cancan," the host announced. "Will the gentlemen kindly sit on the floor." Much giggling and "Oh, my God, I don't have my

panties on" followed. Nancy flicked her skirt to her waist
to give the boys a preview of what was to come. She had
done this before, but I had not; besides, I could not kick
high enough for the cancan, and Cochran would realize I
was a bad dancer.

"I'm not dancing," I said to myself. But how to get
out of it? To make a run for the door would have been
conspicuous and make Mr. Cochran angry. I wished I
had not come. It would have been easy to pretend I was
ill. I still could. "The champagne," I murmured, slipping
into a half-faint. "Please, I must lie down." A girl helped
me stagger upstairs to a bedroom.

Mr. Cochran himself came to see how I was. I had
been wondering when it would be safe to creep downstairs and walk out into the street hoping to find a taxi. It
was late, and I might have to walk all the way to Chelsea,
but the chief thing was to get out without being seen.

I smiled weakly at Mr. Cochran, who asked solicitously, "Are you feeling any better, my dear?" Damn, I
should have gone earlier.

' "A little," I replied faintly. "I'd better go home; I don't
want to spoil the fun."

"My dear, we'd love you to stay, but if you are unwell,
of course, my dear, you must go home." He had a pater-
nal attitude toward his girls, except when he made love to
them. Then he was a perspiring, rather inept tiger. I returned to my husband in the dark green Rolls Royce be-
longing to the man giving the party.

I learned later that my dissipated admirer was a
millionaire from Australia who had crashed into London
society via an imposing house in Green Street, a door
away from Park Lane and Hyde Park. He was short,
squat, and ugly, with a pronounced cockney accent. He
was generous when he wanted something and made no
secret of wanting an affair with me.

"I'll give her a thousand pounds if she will spend one
night with me," he told an intermediary. I was intrigued.
A thousand pounds for one night! That was more than
Johnny and I earned between us in a year. How marvelous to be worth a thousand pounds FOR ONE NIGHT!

I was valuable. I could buy a fur-trimmed coat for myself, a new suit for Johnny. I could pay off his debts, and
when the show closed we could vacation at the elegant
Palace Hotel in Torquay. And I would buy presents for
the girls. I could hear them thanking me and making a
fuss over me. Lorne had a cunt just like mine, but no
one was offering Lorne a thousand pounds for one
night.

But the man was so ugly. I remembered his longing
look and shuddered. No, I could not. What if I had an
affair with him and he did not give me the money? But
I'd ask for it first, rush home to Johnny, give it to him,
and then return to "pay the price," as the girls called it.
But the Australian was a businessman. He would not
give me the money until afterward. I tried to imagine I
had spent the night with him and was holding a thousand pounds in cash.

"Here you are, my dear," he would say after putting
on his clothes and escorting me to his car. His face was
sweaty and his hands were trembling. Never. He was too
awful. I would throw up. I realized, for the first time perhaps, that while it would be marvelous to possess a lot
of money, it meant nothing if a revolting man was tied
to the other end of the string. "I'd rather scrub floors,"
I thought, and felt depressed.

Later, when I wanted to try my luck in the United
States and needed a hundred pounds for the first-class
fare—I learned early always to travel first class; it gives
you the same confidence as wearing beautiful lingerie and
expensive clothes—I went to the man and asked him to
lend me the money. His face with the swollen bags
under the eyes was expressionless, listening to my
stuttered request. When I had come to an embarrassed
stop, he went to a drawer, counted out a hundred pounds,
and gave it to me without making any demands whatsoever. He bade me an impersonal good-bye and said, "I
hope you have a nice time in America." I imagined him
looking at the door for a long time after I left, then
phoning the woman he was keeping.

Johnny, who had gone into bankruptcy soon after our

marriage, the first of many subsequent failures, encouraged me to accept the invitations of rich men. Perhaps one of them would help him. One of them did. A car went with the job, and there were presents for me—jewels, huge baskets of fruit, enormous bouquets of flowers, and a large case of grapefruit from Florida.

I became the pet of a group of rich men about town, one of whom, Sir Robert, unaware of my marriage, wanted to adopt me formally. He invited me for lunch at his exquisitely furnished home in Belgravia and showed me his collection of pornographic prints. You had to look carefully in the rich foliage of the trees to see the couples who were making love, men with women, men with men, and women with women.

I was uncomfortable. I realized now that this sort of thing went on in higher circles, but I was sure that poor people in the East End of London never did such things, nor would they have dreamed of putting it on paper. Had people posed for the artist, or did he do it from memory? What a strange thing to do. I was glad that my marriage made it impossible to be adopted by a man who owned drawings like this.

But the lunch had been delicious—*poussin polonais,* he told me, rolling his tongue lasciviously as he said it. A butler and a maid waited on us. I loved good food. I found great comfort in eating. The memory lasted long after it was eaten—*poussin polonais*, a whole baby chicken baked in butter; asparagus with hollandaise sauce; and strawberries with rich cream. Sir Robert smiled benignly as I mopped it all up. It would be nice to live like the rich, but I did not hanker for it because I knew it was impossible. For all my fantasies of being rich, famous, and admired, I was a very practical down-to-earth girl. You could dream about these things, but in real life certain people had money and others did not. If you could get them to spend just a little of their riches on you, that was fine. But not too much, or they would want too much in return. A thousand pounds for a night indeed.

Prince George was in love with pianist Edythe Baker, a petite American who was one of the stars of the show. I found it thrilling to bump into him on the stairs as he ran up to the lady's dressing room, as I ran down to meet my secret husband. I thought that if Prince George or the Prince of Wales were to fall in love with me I would not ask for a thousand pounds, I would do it for nothing. Just to be loved by such illustrious men would be enough.

I might have ended up badly. My life could have become a shambles, but I had a husband, and I had to go home to him no matter how late I stayed out; I could not spin off into outer space as some of the other girls did—with disastrous results.

Sir Robert took me to Le Touquet for the weekend. My husband gave his permission because he was sure no one would tamper with a girl who had such an innocent face. At the casino I had to show my passport to prove I was more than eighteen, and Sir Robert was delighted to be the escort for a woman with childlike beauty. He stood behind my chair and taught me to play chemin de fer, and the gnarled witches around the green baize table smiled indulgently when, with beginner's luck, I won eighty pounds.

"Do you want to go on, or do you want to cash it in?" Sir Robert asked me. "Cash it in," I answered quickly. This was a windfall, and I hadn't had to do anything except play cards to get it. It would pay some of Johnny's bills. How marvelous to be young and admired, and it seemed to me, living in the dreamy haze of wealth and the theater, that it had always been like this. The bleak years at the orphanage, the Addressograph factory, my mother's death from cancer in our tiny flat, had been someone else's nightmare. I must never be poor again, but I would play it my way, with female trickery and cunning. I would make sure that respectable people liked me. I would work. I would spend my money on whatever I wanted. I had the security of marriage and the freedom to play with the rich and powerful. I would be all things to all men. Sweet and simple with the old ones. Seemingly sophisticated with the undergraduates and the tongue-tied guardsmen, a hard worker in the theater, learning constantly from the clever people surrounding the great impresario.

At night, after the suppers at Ciro's or the Embassy Club, I returned to my sleeping husband and curled up inside his arms. "We're like two spoons," he said. I slept until noon. There was no lovemaking. Except for his orgasm on my thigh on the afternoon of the first day of our honeymoon, he was impotent. I was to learn that Englishmen were bad lovers. Americans were much better.

CHAPTER 5

The Best Lovers

If you are looking for a good lover you won't go wrong if you take an American. He is the best lover in the world, although the American woman is the worst. These are not just idle reminiscences—I know. My own experiences have been chiefly with Americans and Englishmen, but I have listened and learned about the others.

You can dismiss the Italians. They are mama's boys. They really do get sexual satisfaction from pinching bottoms, smiling at every woman they see in the street, and when they are alone with you, looking into your eyes, making flowery speeches, and murmuring, "Bella, bella, bellissima."

Not long ago I met a good-looking, rather short Italian at a dinner party in the restaurant on the roof of the Royal Danieli in Venice. He stared at me like a dog pointing a bird. When he danced with me he was admiring my face so much he stumbled over my feet, but when he asked me in broken English whether he could see me the following night, I agreed.

"Where shall we go?" he asked when we met in the lounge of the Danieli. He was surprised when I said, "Let's take a gondola ride around the canals." I have always wanted to be made love to in a gondola. As he was shorter than I was, to make him feel more comfortable I slid lower in my seat so that our heads were on the same level. He held my hand and sighed passionately. He was about to kiss me, but I had slid too low, and just as his lips neared mine, I crashed to the bottom of the gondola. Embarrassed, we started again from scratch. He was holding my hand. His face near mine. Suddenly a motorboat careened past us, rocking the gondola and drenching us both with rather smelly canal water. Our attempts to laugh it off were unconvincing.

One more try. I was determined to be kissed in a gondola. We were in position again and he was pulling me toward him passionately when a shout from the gondolier startled us apart. He jabbered something angrily in Italian. "What did he say?" I asked irritably. "He said it is against the law to make love in a gondola," my admirer admitted sheepishly. I had had enough. "Let's go back to the Danieli," I said crisply. I don't like men who are put off by trivialities. They are usually bad lovers.

Of course, I am not judging all Italian men by this one, but the final comment seems to be that most of them talk a lot and do nothing except gratify themselves. An artist friend of mine fell in love with a young Italian man. They met on a bridge in Florence where each had an easel and was painting the view. Soon they became friends, and after a few meetings, decided to have an affair.

"Are you a virgin?" the Italian asked anxiously when they were in bed in her *pensione*. He did not want the responsibility of deflowering a virgin. What would mama say? She *was* a virgin. But they had gone too far to draw back. Soon they were very much in love. When the girl returned to the States, the young man followed, took a job near her home in Wisconsin, and they continued their affair. He never quite promised to marry her. He knew his mother would be upset if he married a nonvirgin!

They rented an apartment together. The bedroom had two single beds, close together, to give him easy access into hers. About a week after they moved in, the girl was surprised to find the beds had been moved a foot apart.

Soon his bed was at one end of the room and hers at the other. She demanded an explanation.

"My doctor has told me that it is bad for me to make love more than twice a week," he told the astonished girl. He was twenty-two years old! The affair ended abruptly —although she had expected it would end at the altar. She was not promiscuous and would go to bed only with a man she was in love with.

For a long time she was lonely, and I thought she would never find another man she could love. But she did find one—an American. She told him about her lover, but it did not bother him. They had a beautiful wedding and now have twin boys. She is happy with her husband as a lover and provider. The Italian had borrowed several hundred dollars from her, which, after many stern letters, he paid back. She realizes she had a lucky escape. If she had married him they would have lived in Rome under the shadow of mama, whom, he warned her, he could never leave.

I have teased and flirted with Frenchmen, but I have never wanted to marry or even have an affair with any one of them. For one thing, they don't seem too clean. Then, too, I am embarrassed by their bird dog stares when I sit at an outdoor table on the Champs-Elysées. I used to wonder what would happen if I went off with one of them. They seem evil and degenerate, and I would not dare.

The first Frenchman I knew was after I left the stage in December, 1929. He was a student at the Institut Français in London. I wanted to learn French, which most of my young society girl friends, having attended French finishing schools, spoke as easily as English.

A pale blond, watery-looking young man arrived at my home, and we started on the grammar and a little easy conversation. After three sessions he flung down his pencil, slid to his knees, buried his face in my lap, and groaned, *"Je t'aime, je t'aime."* He swore he would not take money from me because he loved me. I pulled him to his feet, said a sorrowful good-bye—I had been doing well with the French—and without giving the reason, asked the Institut to send me a woman teacher.

A lady of about thirty with huge buck teeth arrived. She smiled all the time. I soon realized that she too was paying too much attention to the verb "to love." She slavered through her teeth and put her face too close to mine. My God, a lesbian! She had to go.

Then I found an unmarried mother who was living in a Catholic convent in London while her baby was being taken care of by her embarrassed mother in Paris. She had become engaged to a French count. A week before the wedding, when her trousseau had been embroidered with her new initials, he had jumped the gun on her chastity. Two days before the nuptials he broke the engagement and little Jacqueline's heart. Even her pregnancy did not move this typical Frenchman: an Englishman might have married her; an American most certainly would.

She was a girl of good family, and the disgrace was almost more than she could bear. She lived with me for several months teaching me French and then returned to her mother and the baby in Paris. Poor Jacqueline. I have often wondered what became of her. In the early thirties a girl was ruined if she had an illegitimate child.

The Frenchman as a lover has his good points and his bad points. When he is with the woman he desires he will not look at other women. He makes her feel she is the only one. He notices small details—hair, hands, clothes —and he is always complimentary. He rushes her into bed. The first French sentence I understood was *"Voulez-vous coucher avec moi?"*—"Will you sleep with me?" He says this immediately. *Soixante-neuf.* Sixty-nine. Invented by the French. *Cinq a sept.* Between five and seven P.M., the hours when the Frenchman visits his mistress. His wife knows, but she is not upset; why should she be? She has probably spent the afternoon in the arms of her lover. She is careful to get home in time to freshen up and get into a pretty gown. She is devoted to her husband.

The Frenchman will sometimes introduce his mistress to his wife. But the wife, unlike the British, will never bring her lover and husband together. The Frenchman talks about his mistress with his men friends and goes into lip-smacking details. Because of his enormous ego he makes sure that the woman is satisfied with his love-making. He takes a long time with presex love play, but soon dashes away after his own orgasm. When the affair is over, he does not see the woman, although he expects her to be eternally grateful. He is stingy. He rarely buys a present for his wife or mistress, except at the duty-free shops at the airport.

The Frenchman enjoys his bourgeois image. There is less divorce in France than in England and America. He likes being middle-class and respectable.

Because I lived in England and because I had a complaisant husband, it is easier for me to assess the merits, but mostly the demerits, of the Englishman as a lover.

On the stage I learned a lot about the Englishman—both from the other girls and from my own experiences. Life with an impotent husband could not satisfy me for long, and our money troubles were mounting.

My ten pounds a week as a Cochran Young Lady didn't stretch far, so I joined the Midnight Follies at the Metropole Hotel. One of the benefits of working in the cabaret was the supper—usually chicken, string beans, potatoes, and ice cream for dessert. Always hungry after the strain of dancing for hours with a forced smile, I cleaned my plate. It was nearly three in the morning when I limped home. My husband was asleep, and I curled into his arms and slept soundly. When I awakened around noon, he was gone.

There were two girls in the cabaret who always had plenty of money. I wondered why they bothered to work when they were so adept at extracting whatever they wanted from their admirers. Gilda was blond, pretty, and petite. Four men were paying for her nonexistent visits to the dentist. "You can always get a man to pay for your teeth," she explained, smiling. Her teeth were perfect, but she pocketed five or ten pounds a week for dental bills. Secretly I was shocked.

Gilda was a small-time operator compared to Priscilla, a stately brunet who one night swept in wearing a magnificent full-length mink coat. Her admirer was an elderly rich businessman with a chain of London jewelry shops. When he died soon after Priscilla quit the Follies, he left her all his money. His two nephews declared they would contest the will. After much legal wrangling they compromised. Priscilla asked for an annuity for life. She was twenty-six, and it would mean a considerable premium. The nephews instead offered her a hundred thousand pounds. She accepted and died three years later. The nephews could never forgive themselves.

I was very naïve, and I wondered whether Priscilla's death was a punishment from heaven. But I soon rejected that idea. It was becoming obvious to me that the girls who gave, got. I had seen Priscilla's admirer in the Rolls Royce meeting her after the show. He was short, fat, and greasy-looking. Why were rich men usually unattractive? I could never indulge in that kind of adventure. I'd have to like the man. I hoped the men I liked would not all be impotent. I loved my husband, but, as the doctor warned him, I was ripe for adventure.

Derek was a naval officer, aged twenty-seven. He had a sweet chubby face and dark hair that even then was beginning to retreat from his forehead. The captain of his battleship at Portsmouth had invited all the Cochran Young Ladies to lunch on the ship, and I drove there through a pea-soup fog in my husband's car.

Derek was immediately smitten with me. "I worship you," he told me, a bit prematurely, while we were taking a turn about the deck. I enjoyed his open admiration and agreed to another meeting. He called for me at the Metropole that evening and kissed me passionately in the taxi on the way home. "I want you, I want you," he murmured over and over. Why not? I asked myself. I like him. I want to know what real love is like. I promised to go to a hotel with him the following night. He didn't seem rich, but I would lie and tell my husband that he was.

"I'll have to be home before morning; my family wouldn't like it if I were out all night," I lied. At my husband's insistence, our marriage was still secret. He thought it would hinder my career and frighten off rich admirers. So I always pretended I was going home to Mum and Dad.

It seemed strange, having a husband and yet dating other men. I realized that my marriage was unusual, but I loved Johnny. He was the father I had never known and gave me a sense of security, even though I was paying the bills. What a silly girl I was!

But because he was impotent, I decided it did not matter whether I had flirtations or even affairs with other men. I was married, but I could enjoy the expensive restaurants and nightclubs with my admirers.

That next night I could barely get through the performance at the theater, and decided to skip the cabaret. I told them I was unwell. My tense excitement was obvious, but as I was often keyed up, it wasn't considered too unusual.

Derek was not in his uniform when he met me outside the stage door. I was disappointed. He was less attractive in civilian clothes and seemed fatter. But that was unimportant. Tonight I would know what it was all about.

He drove with one hand on the wheel, holding mine with the other. He put my hand on his crotch, and I could feel it getting hard. This penis meant business. He wanted to stop the car to kiss, but I urged, "No, let's go on."

He had booked a room in a small hotel in Maidenhead, on the banks of the Thames not far from London. It was winter, just after a heavy snowfall. There was an enormous fire in the bedroom, champagne in an ice bucket, sandwiches on a silver tray, and three beds.

We drank the champagne; his hand trembled as he filled my glass. I nibbled on a sandwich, but my mouth felt hot and dry. Between gulps and bites he kissed me. We were both on fire. He turned off the lights, and we undressed (I retained my bra, my badge of virtue). The light of the flames played erotically on our naked bodies. He rushed me into the large bed, and suddenly his sperm spurted all over my stomach. It was almost funny. I was committing adultery for the first time, and he had come without even touching my vagina. No, it was not funny;

it was awful. Sex was a fraud. It got you excited, and nothing happened. I wanted to cry with frustration. I decided Englishmen were all bad lovers. Then I met Rex.

Rex was an aristocrat. His proud Scottish lineage was etched on his face. He was easy to be with. Nothing seemed to bother him. He could handle any situation with an ease and charm that fascinated me. His father and older brother had been killed in a plane crash, and I imagined this accounted for the sadness in his eyes. He was dark, lean, and handsome and had a laugh that I found irresistible. I met him at a supper party given by the man who wanted to adopt me. My would-be father was disturbed, but proud of me when he saw that Rex was smitten. He watched us closely and must have felt a tinge of jealousy when we went off together.

Rex was a close friend of the Prince of Wales. When he looked at me with his brooding eyes, it was almost like being with the Prince himself. I decided I must be as pretty as they all said to be able to attract such a man. I held my head high and felt I was the most desirable woman in the room. Perhaps Rex would love me so much that he'd want to marry me. Then I would tell him about my marriage, and he'd help me get a divorce. I was sure my husband would understand. He was always assuring me that one day I would be somebody. He was quite clear about the somebody I would eventually be—rich, powerful, titled, and sought-after. Now, caught on the fringe of high society, I was beginning to believe him.

Rex's family moved in royal circles. His brother, the Duke, was a close friend of the King. His mother had long been a lady-in-waiting to the Queen. I indulged myself with a forbidden "coo lummy" at moving in such exalted circles.

In the taxi taking me home Rex gently kissed my eyes and invited me to sup with him the next night. Did I say yes too eagerly? But he was such a prize—the best-looking man I had ever met in my life. The air of melancholy on his ascetic tanned face was, I learned later, not because of the deaths of his father and brother. He was a soldier himself, and death in war was an accepted way of life. The sadness was because Lady X, a woman he had passionately loved, had recently died in a plane crash. She was the daughter of a famous European actress and had married into the British aristocracy. She was still married to her Lord while having an affair with Rex. This intrigued me. In the upper strata of British society, men had mistresses openly, and their wives looked the other way and had their lovers. They were rarely punished. All my mother's warnings about having nothing to do with a boy or he would despise you and leave you with a baby on your hands were wrong. The affairs of the aristocracy lasted as long as the woman wanted it to last, and they remained good friends afterward. In fact, an affair seemed a prerequisite for a good friendship.

Rex had arranged for supper to be served in the sitting room of a suite at the Savoy. I was somewhat apprehensive. Could I manage a man like him? I decided to let matters take a natural course. The naval officer had proved a dud. Rex was different. He was experienced. He was masterful.

We had grapefruit, grilled sole, and an ice. The white wine affected me more than champagne. I was feeling slightly giddy when Rex pulled me gently by the arm into the bedroom and matter-of-factly started to undress. He did not say "Will you?" He took it for granted.

This is the way it is done with the aristocracy, I thought. Hastily I slipped out of my dress and under the cool sheets. Rex was a good lover. He didn't rush. He caressed me, touched me everywhere, kissed my nipples, and waited until he thought I was ready. He took his time with his orgasm. I could feel him inside me, hard as iron. I was too wound up to have an orgasm, although I tried and tried. It would almost happen; then a stray thought of who was making love to me prevented the orgasm. The excitement and awe of having an affair with Rex kept the blood in my head. The harder I tried to reach a climax, the more the orgasm eluded me. I simply could not relax, the key to the whole business. When he finally gasped, "Are you ready?" I whispered yes, panting and making passionate sounds so he would think he'd satisfied me.

Afterward he was tender and didn't fall asleep, but lay with his arms clasped behind his head talking of many things—my revue, a book he had read, a play he had seen, hunting with the Prince. I preferred this to the huffing and puffing. It didn't matter that I was more keyed-up and more unsatisfied than I had ever been in my life. His lean body next to mine was comforting. I wanted to be with him like this forever.

I smiled in the dark of the taxi all the way home, and the next day my husband told me I was smiling in my sleep.

Rex called for me almost every night. Once he took me to his mother's house near the palace and locked the door of his bedroom. We heard his mother come in, and I was worried. Would she try to come in? I barely breathed until it was quiet again. When we were safely outside, we laughed. "I don't think I want to go back there," I giggled.

This new life was delightful. It didn't matter that I seemed incapable of having an orgasm. The affair lasted three months. I loved being with Rex. He knew everyone in London. One night we went to the Embassy Club, and the Prince of Wales was there. The next time I saw Rex, he told me the Prince had asked who I was, and he had replied, "Sir, I'm not going to tell you; I want to keep her for myself." I smiled but was a bit disappointed. This new life was delicious, but I would have liked to have the Prince of Wales in love with me, to be a member of his glamorous circle.

I was getting bolder, and I wanted to spend a whole night with Rex, and not have to get up and dress. "I'm going to Brighton for the weekend," I told him. "Would you like to meet me there?" He thought it was a fine idea. We would stay at the Princess Hotel, a quiet hotel on the sea front where we would not bump into anyone we knew.

I told my husband I was spending the weekend in Brighton with one of the girls in the show. "You've been working hard, and the sea air will do you good," he replied cheerfully. He sometimes wondered what was going on while he pretended to be asleep and I crept into bed at three or four in the morning. But he was afraid he would lose me if he complained. I had become more confident and less helpless now than he was. I was learning the manners and speech of my new friends, and I was not afraid to join in conversation or even to introduce new topics and make jokes about our acquaintances.

I caught the last train to Brighton after the show and took a taxi to the hotel. "Has my husband arrived?" I asked the night porter. We had decided to be Mr. and Mrs. Arkwright. He did not think so, but he had come on only at midnight. "Oh, yes, Mrs. Arkwright, there is a message for you." He handed me a small envelope. Rex had telephoned to say he could not come. There was no explanation. I was bitterly disappointed. I had been too bold in assuming that Rex would follow where I beckoned. I had taken the initiative for the first time. He knew that I was married—I had told him early in our relationship. He claimed it made no difference. Perhaps he was afraid that going away with me might land him in a nasty divorce scandal. I telephoned my husband. "The girl couldn't come," I sobbed. "Will you join me at the Metropole first thing in the morning?" He was delighted. One reason I loved Johnny was that he was always there when I needed him, and he never asked awkward questions. My life would have been different if he had. I would have respected him in addition to loving him. I would not have had affairs with the men I fancied.

Rex drifted away. He left London for a good job in a brokerage house in New York. He telephoned me occasionally when he came to London, but the calls became more and more rare.

Occasionally I had lunch with Sir Robert. He teased me about Rex, but I knew he was jealous. It gave me a feeling of power. The older man, wanting to please me, said he would give me a present worth a thousand pounds. He had never asked me to go to bed with him. As he seemed in love with me, I wondered if there was anything wrong with him. Later I learned that he was a masochist who could not have an orgasm except through physical pain. I was glad he did not attempt to make love to me. I could never have gone to bed with him. There was something about him that frightened me. "Shall I give you the money?" he asked. "Or would you like me to buy you a piece of jewelry?"

"Why not both?" I asked happily. Because I was uninvolved, I could be more daring. "I'd like a watch for two hundred pounds and the rest in cash." But he was an old fox and not to be caught so easily. He bought me a diamond and platinum watch for two hundred pounds, which I soon pawned and gave the money to Johnny. Sir Robert put the eight hundred pounds into a Canadian brewery stock, and each year I received a dividend of forty pounds. I had assumed it was in my name, but several years later when he died there were no more dividends. By that time I was doing so well on my own that I did not realize it until the manager of a London bank sent me the sealed envelope which contained his promise to give me the brewery shares. I tore it up.

There were other English admirers, but I would not again fall into the trap of imagining I was in love. In the early thirties, with the stage behind me, I played squash rackets with a slightly built, gentle, doe-eyed earl. I was astonished that he was in love with me. He was extremely sophisticated. His friends were in the top strata of international society. After cocktails at the club lounge, he asked me for lunch at Boulestin's, one of the best and most sedate restaurants in London. Cochran would approve, I was sure. He liked his girls to marry into the nobility. "Will you come to my flat for a drink?" he asked after paying the bill. I knew it was dangerous to go, but I was enjoying being with him, and I did not want it to end. We sat for a while on the sofa talking. He put his arm around me and kissed me. He was gentle but determined. Should I? My cheeks were burning. The lunch, the wine, the kissing, and the feeling each other culminated in the delicious state of heat. I yielded to him on the sofa. The earl was the only good lover I had in England. He had no thought of wanting to marry me. I was a good companion, he was to say later in an interview. He was too much of a gentleman to say that I was also very good in bed. To be good in bed, you have to like sex. You don't have to go to school to learn; it comes naturally when you like it. If you don't like it, don't have it. Not everyone is born with a built-in state of heat.

After lunch is the best time for sex. The blood is not in your head; it is lower down, with the food. It is more relaxing after lunch than at night. I have never met a truthful woman who admitted to liking sex in the morning, although men do. After a long sleep, men are ready and raring to go. But a woman is cold in the morning, the vagina tight like a sleeping flower, and it usually takes a lot of stimulation to bring the necessary lubrication. In any case, at this time I had never been with a man in the morning, except my impotent husband.

I also met two brothers whose family were rich shipbuilders in the North. The older brother was tall, blond, and rugged-looking, but very pompous. I wondered why I saw him at all; he intimidated me and I could not relax. But if I said no to his invitations to supper at Ciro's or the Savoy, I would have to go home to my kind but impotent husband, and the thought was depressing. He always embraced me suffocatingly in the taxi and was content to have an orgasm on his own. His brother, also tall and blond, was more charming. The older man introduced me to him as a sort of graduation-from-Cambridge present. I might have had an affair with him, but I went to America and learned how satisfying sex could be. After these experiences with Englishmen, excepting the earl, I never wanted to make love with any one of them again, although I did.

But for a few Continental-trained sophisticates, the earl among them, the Englishman is in a hurry to get the thing over and return to whatever he was doing before. He is afraid of a rebuff, and proceeds cautiously, one step forward, two steps back, if the climate is not quite right.

Sex today in England is better than when I was experimenting with it. Young people walk along the King's Road arm in arm, and live together without marriage, practically unheard-of conduct during my time in London. English girls have always been good in bed, giving freely without expecting anything in return. Outwardly, anyway. Perhaps some of this has now rubbed off on the young men. I'm not sure, and I have no intention of finding out. Give me an American every time.

When I returned to England in the summer of 1941 to write articles for my syndicate, the sex situation with the British male was the same, although the women were more promiscuous than ever—like rabbits. "Here's to your whiskey, which is so dear, and to your women, who are so cheap." I doubt whether the American general in England really said this, but it was true nonetheless.

An American woman writer friend of mine married an Englishman during the war. She met him after he returned from the Middle East, where he had been on a special mission for Winston Churchill. At the cocktail gathering in Claridges hosted by a mutual American acquaintance, she could feel his penetrating stare. He offered her a drink, a treat, since liquor was in scarce supply during the war. She refused the whiskey. "I'll have some sherry." He noted approvingly that she did not smoke, either.

He offered to take her back to her hotel. She was grateful for the lift. Taxis were in short supply, and all during the blackout you heard the despairing cry, "Taxi! Taxi!" It was convenient to know someone with a car. When the American told him she was going to Sussex to visit friends, he said, "I can do some business in Sussex. I'll drive you there."

She was tired after the long drive and decided to spend the night in Brighton and take the train in the morning. He wouldn't hear of it. "I'll stay and drive you back in the morning." To justify the extra time, he would call on some government officials and factories on the return trip.

They had separate rooms on different floors. The woman had thought vaguely about whether he would want an affair with her. Probably. But in registering, they each had to show identity cards, so even had they wanted to, they could not have posed as Mr. and Mrs. She was glad.

But she was not surprised when after settling in bed

with a book she heard a soft tapping at her door. He
entered, wearing pajamas under his dressing gown and
with a tense look on his face. He was afraid of being re-
buffed, but she didn't have the heart. They talked for a
while; then he leaned over and kissed her. He was relaxing, and the woman decided, "Why not?" They had gone
this far. They could be killed at any moment if a German
pilot was careless on the way to London.

They were in bed, his penis was hard, and he was
about to enter her when there was a sound of someone
walking in the corridor. His body stiffened while his penis
softened. He jumped guiltily out of bed and rushed to
the door, listening intently to the footsteps. The woman
almost laughed. There is nothing so potent as a laugh to
make a man impotent, as she had learned from a lover in
America. He had had too much to drink and became
angrier and angrier as his penis flopped around. She had
become hysterical with laughter. Not only could he not
function at all that night, but it took months to forget her
laughter, and he could do so only when he was semi-
drunk. So now she did not laugh.

"Come back to bed," she whispered.

"Do you think anyone heard us?" he asked fearfully.

"No, and what if they did!"

"Sh-sh," he admonished when she gasped rather loudly while he had his orgasm in double-quick time. He was
just as fast the second time around. She was not surprised
when he told her she was one of the few "good" women
with whom he had made love. He explained that he did
not want to get entangled with a "good" woman. He did
not want to marry and was afraid a "good" woman might
expect to.

He dated a different girl every Saturday night. He
prided himself on what he called a rota of six beauties.
He was a catch, and each one hoped to break him down
into marriage, but he was careful to kiss them platonical-
ly when they said goodnight, and he never went in with
them even when they lived alone. His sex life was spent
with prostitutes. He picked them up in Leicester Square
and "had it," as he said, as fast as possible. That was why
he was such a quick and bad lover.

"I will make him a better lover," the American decided. She was looking for another husband, and he would
be a good provider. She was not promiscuous, and marriage had been vaguely in the back of her mind when she
had allowed him into her bed. He liked her, she could see
that. He was a solid person, the sort of man who would
make a good husband. He had a good position with the
government and could look after her. But if she were
going to marry him, he must abandon the prostitutes. For
heaven's sake, she didn't want to catch anything from
him.

He was overwhelmed by her warmth, her understanding, and her importance. She wrote for a top magazine in
America. At this time America had not yet entered the
war, and stories in the American press and magazines
explaining the just cause of the Allies were extremely
helpful. I was in England during Dorothy Thompson's
visit. Churchill gave her a private interview, and she had
the cabinet ministers at her feet. I thought they would
give her the country. The same was true for Quentin
Reynolds, who was a frequent guest at 10 Downing
Street. The British loved him for the sympathetic stories
he wrote of the brave islanders fighting alone against the
might of the Wehrmacht.

Before the American lady returned to New York, the
government official asked her to marry him, and she said
"Perhaps." To make sure of her, he gave her a diamond
engagement ring. He had never before met a "good" girl
—by "good" he meant a girl who supported herself
and was accepted in society—who was not only willing to
have an affair with him but made it last so long.

When he had asked her to marry him, he started to
confess all the affairs he'd had and about a girl he had
almost married. She hastily shut him up. "I'm not going
to tell you about *my* past life," she stated. "And I don't
want to hear about *yours*." He was disappointed, and
she had to be very firm, or he would have gone over
every kiss.

When he came to America, they flew to Las Vegas
and were married. He was now a good lover, taking his
time, able to wait as long as she wanted. Her method was

simple. When he gasped that he was coming, or if his rhythm became too accelerated, she moved away from him. He could not come until she allowed him to. She gradually made the intervals longer and longer. She was proud of her pupil. But she did not care for the new trick someone had taught him. He begged her to punch him hard on his bottom while he was thrusting in and out. It was something to do with exciting the scrotum. She hit him as requested the first time, but never again during the four years of their marriage.

I always knew where I was with American men. If they wanted you, they said so. No stealthy creeping up. American men want to look after you. They really do put you on a pedestal—at the beginning, anyway. You are a rare goddess to them.

Except for the rich, dirty old men in England, the American is the more generous. He does not keep his hands in his pockets when the check appears. He is actually eager to pick it up. There are excuses for the English. They are no longer a great power. Since the First World War, poverty among the upper classes has been a virtue. The men who display wealth ostentatiously are considered bounders.

Americans make money easily, and they spend it freely. They were disliked in England during the Second World War, when they willingly paid the high rents for houses and flats the English could not afford. The GI's got all the girls; Englishwomen were not used to men who spent money carelessly. The English Tommy, who was paid much less, resented his American ally.

But there is another reason why English girls prefer Americans. They are as kind in their sexual adventures as they are with money. With the Englishman, like the Frenchman, it is like going to the loo—necessary, but something to forget as soon as it is over. The American is better in bed because he is healthy, vigorous, and considerate.

On the average, the American man is taller than the Englishman. He generally eats better food, which makes him stronger and a better lover. The American is not segregated from girls like the English boy who is shipped off early to boarding school and college. In this unnatural all-male environment he has no contact with girls when his interest in sex begins. While the Englishwoman, in revolt against the Englishman, is free with her favors and like an open urn, the American woman holds out for marriage and sells her sex more dearly.

The American man is less complicated than the European. The American woman is something else. She is trickier. She is more cruel. She makes the man pay every inch of the way. She calculates every step. She looks him up in Dun and Bradstreet and analyzes him like a computer. The American woman has the best-equipped kitchen in the world and is the worst cook. The Frenchwoman is the best cook and has the worst kitchen.

But while the American man is a good lover, and more simple, he too is playing the Game. The important man usually marries a woman who is a reflection of his success, a mirror of his importance.

The American women who pick off the best men are careful to maintain an impeccable reputation. They lure him at the beginning, and when he is thinking "I can have this woman," she is hard to find. And if found, is encased in ice. Perhaps this is why the American man has become such a good lover. He has to consider the woman all the time, or he cannot get to first base. It is also undoubtedly a throwback to the pioneering days, when women were in short supply and men learned to please a woman who could pick the mate she wanted. American women are in control of the social life, and the men prefer it that way. In England a man can invite a former girl friend to dine with his wife, and she does not object. American women have divorced their husbands for much less.

What I have enjoyed most about the American as a lover is his lack of inhibition. He takes sex as a natural thing, and if you sleep with him before marriage, it makes no difference as to whether or not he wants to marry you. If he wants to marry you, what you have done before is immaterial as long as you say you love *him*. "I love you and

I want to marry you, and if you love me you will want to marry me," is the never-fail good line of the American female. Use it; you'd be surprised how often it works.

The American man feels inferior to the woman. When she condescends to allow him to love her, he is eternally grateful. I would always hear from Charles and Mike and Joe and Tom and Bart and Jimmy and Arnold and David. They would never quite lose sight of me and would always have a warm feeling for me. Years later, when I was on the *Today Show* to promote a book I had written, I received an unexpected call from Tom, who had heard me in Corpus Christi, where he lives with his wife and children. He thought I sounded great, he told me enthusiastically. Dear Tom.

The earl was the only one of my English lovers who attempted to keep in touch with me, even after I had refused him. When I married for the second time, during the Second World War, he sent me a cable wishing me luck and asking me to bring him five hundred American cigarettes on my next visit. After the war ended, we were out of touch because I was usually traveling in search of stories. When I was in London about four years ago, after he had separated from a wife he detested, and I had divorced my second husband, I called him. He was out. I left a message with his answering service, from whom later in the evening I received a message spoken to me by the operator over the phone. "My darling. I am longing to see you again. I have to go out now. I have called and you are out. Please phone me tonight, no matter how late you get in."

I was touched. We met the next day. He had been now in love for several years with someone else, but he would always love me, he said. He invited me to visit them in Switzerland, where he was living at the time. I promised, but never did. The earl had come to America twice to persuade me to marry him, but I was not quite comfortable with him, and when he drank, he was difficult, although he apologized when he was sober. I could not take a bad drinker twice.

No, he was not for me. If I married again, it would be

an American. They do not encourage their wives to play golf or other sports with them, but they are respectful and friendly, and uncomplicated lovers. "I don't like depravity," I said once, and then, laughing, added, "although I have probably done every form of it." Well, at least in my imagination.

The American millionaire socialite who wanted to set me up in great style had once suggested that he would like to have another woman make love to me while he watched. I indignantly declined. He was the only American I ever knew who was even slightly decadent. I am sure there were lots of them around, and more sure later when I read some of the modern, realistic books, but I was never interested in them. There is nothing wrong in what a man and a woman say and do together, and perhaps I am being old-fashioned, but I could never be part of an actual orgy or group lovemaking.

An American woman I knew in California who now lives in London gave me explicit details of an orgy she had attended in Belgrave Square. When asked, "Why not come to the next one?" I laughed. I was no longer a girl, and the idea of rolling around on the floor and making love to a series of strangers did not appeal to me. Would it have interested me when I was younger? I don't think so. I have had many affairs, but I have usually been discreet. Mike never knew about Bart, and Charles had never heard of Joe, or Peter about Jimmy. Or . . . I could fill a book.

Another reason why I prefer the American man as a lover is that, unlike the European male, he usually does not boast of his conquests. Of course, there are men— and women—in all countries who find the affair incomplete unless they inform a hundred intimate friends. But the American man is least likely to spread the good news. Except for the homos, he is secure in his manhood and therefore a better lover. The American men I have loved have been discreet, especially if they were married and having an affair.

CHAPTER 6

The Other Woman

A lady should never be the "other woman" if she can avoid it. As the third part of the triangle, her position is unfair and unpleasant. She is anathema to the Wives' Union. Her family is disgusted with her. Her friends are unhappy and disapproving. Her life is a series of brief encounters with someone else's husband. She is often very lonely. Sometimes she is a better woman than the wife in possession, but she is always regarded as a thief, a fox among the innocent chickens. She lives in a constant state of expectation—and depression. "I love you, I hate my wife, I'll get a divorce" is the chain that binds her. She usually accepts the situation at the beginning, but as the years go by without a change in the status quo, she often becomes as nagging and destructive as the wife he wanted to leave at the beginning of the liaison. In our present society, the "other woman" is a fool.

And yet, why should a few mumbled words in the ceremony of marriage give the wife a stranglehold for life on the man who loved her enough to undertake the burden of supporting her, which he is expected to continue after there is mutual loathing? I think the marriage contract should be reviewed every two years, and if it is in the red, there should be a divorce, leaving the woman free to marry a more suitable mate and the man able to legitimize his union with the "other woman."

I have been the "other woman" twice in my life. Consciously, that is. Automatically when meeting a man for the first time, before you know his failings, you think of wooing him from the woman in his life—his wife, his girl, or his mother. You feel sure you could if you tried.

But in both cases that I was conscious of my secondary position, it happened without planning. This is what I find so interesting about love and life. The major events creep up on you. They are in full bloom before you realize what has happened.

I would never have chosen to be the "other woman" in the marriage of Sean X. As Swann said ruefully about Odette, he was not my type. Short, roly-poly, with grizzled hair—a former Irish Rugby player who played a dirty game.

Also, Sean was a Catholic, or maybe it was his wife who was the Catholic. There was no chance of his getting a divorce to marry me. And in any case, that was the last thing I wanted. Besides, I was already married.

I acquainted him with this fact as soon as I saw he was smitten, which was as soon as I met him. I was introduced to Sean by Mr. Cochran. Some of the other girls, all better dancers than I, earned extra money in the excellent after-theater cabaret at the Criterion Hotel, across the road from the Pavilion. I needed the money but did not dare audition for the show. You had to be a really good dancer for the Criterion, and I could only kick to a point nearer my waist than my shoulder. As for doing splits, there was always a huge inverted V visible.

"Don't forget to smile," my husband warned. And now I was smiling at Sean, who had come to the Criterion with his friend and business partner. They were in the construction business and were very rich and important, or so I gathered from Mr. Cochran's respectful attitude as he introduced them.

"I think you are beautiful," Sean said, sitting down in the seat vacated by Mr. Cochran, who took his cue and departed to a ringside table. "I have been at the Pavilion every night for the past week just to watch you."

I was cool but automatically charming to this fat, bewitched man. "I would like to buy you a present," he said almost at once, and I sat up and took notice. My chorus-girl dream was for rich men to shower me with money and jewels, although when it came to the point of going to bed with them, the presents lost their luster. Besides, I never knew whether you should go to bed first and expect the presents to follow, or get the present first and then refuse to go to bed. It was a problem, like accepting dinner in an expensive restaurant and then fighting for your honor in the taxi afterward, feeling you had cheated him, although you could be more righteous on a full stomach.

And now this man was offering me a present at the very first meeting. How lovely. "What would you like?" he asked, looking like a fairy godfather who could bestow fantastic gifts. What I wanted was money to pay the landlord; the telephone, gas, and electric companies; the grocer; the butcher; and the candlestick maker. But you couldn't come right out and say that.

"Oh, anything," I answered airily, hoping it would be something expensive that I could pawn right away.

"It will be in your dressing room tomorrow night," Sean announced benevolently. He sat with me during the show and then returned me to Mr. Cochran, who had been giving me encouraging smiles when I looked in his direction.

Sean's partner was in love with a famous musical-comedy actress who was starring at the Threatre Royal in Drury Lane. Later they were to marry. Sean was married, Mr. Cochran told me: "I thought you should know. He's mad about you. He's very rich," he added.

I promptly indulged in wonderful fantasies about never having to worry about money. I would pay off all my husband's debts. I would take care of a poor relative whose husband had died, leaving her with four small children. I would help some of the girls in the show. I would be very popular. Everyone would love me.

The present from Asprey's in Bond Street was beautiful —a big leather case containing an exquisite dressing-table set in shining blue enamel encased in solid silver. Two hairbrushes, two clothes brushes, and several toilet bottles in crystal, topped in silver and blue enamel.

"It must have cost two hundred pounds at least," Clare exclaimed, more admiring than envious. Two hundred pounds could pay a lot of debts. My initials were not yet on the merchandise. I could pawn them and probably get a hundred pounds. But they were too beautiful to sell. Our creditors would have to wait for their money.

Somewhere in my travels I lost the leather case, but I still have the brushes and bottles. On today's market I could probably get five hundred pounds for them. I will leave them to my daughter, who will probably sell them, especially since she knows how I got them.

Sean was at the stage door that night to take me home in his big Daimler. I allowed him to kiss me on the cheek. He was nice enough, but I had no intention of "paying the price."

What a dance I led this poor man. The less I gave, the more he wanted me and the more he gave me. "Miss Speedicity" he dubbed me affectionately, as I collected various presents and cash for this and that. He thought I was the gold digger of all time, and with him I was, but this did not diminish his yearning for me. I did not tell him that at eighteen I had refused a millionaire to marry Johnny, who I knew, was going into bankruptcy. Extracting presents from Sean was a game. How far could I go? How much would he spend? I had made a discovery; it was more rewarding to say, "Yes, thank you," than the bleak, "No, thank you."

"I don't know if I can ever get a divorce," Sean told me candidly. "My wife would never agree to it. But I want to marry you. Perhaps," he said hopefully, "my wife will die; then we can marry."

I told Sean nearly everything about my husband and his problems—that he was impotent and out of a job. Sean found him work as a salesman of bricks. A car went with the job, and I learned to drive. On weekends, with

Sean safely at home with his wife, my husband and I drove to the country or to Brighton. I had no idea how to back a car, neither did he, and one time when Johnny was trying to guide me backward into a road, I ran into him. Luckily I was barely moving.

Johnny put up with a lot from me, as I did from him. I did not tell him that Sean was praying for his wife to die so that he could marry me. Or that I was praying for her to live so that he could not. I had an impotent husband who could not support me without help from other men. And yet I loved him—as a father I had never known, as a mother loves a son, as a sister loves a brother. I loved him in every way except as a wife loves a husband. But it didn't seem to matter. As long as I was working and money was coming in, I felt safe under the blanket of marriage.

As Johnny was often around, I had to explain him, and we decided that I would introduce him as my Uncle Johnny, which in a way he was. I told him all about the men I went around with, except when and if I had a serious flirtation or affair. We closed our eyes to that situation. Looking back, I realize that we should have divorced. It was a dreadful marriage.

After I left the stage, I insisted on being known under my proper name, and, in truth, being a married woman made no difference to the chase. In fact, it made me more popular with men like Randolph Churchill and Tom Mitford, the only son—with seven sisters—of Lord and Lady Redesdale. Tom and Randolph were cousins and great friends. They often visited me, but when Randolph suggested we should all go to bed—it was afternoon—I threw them out. I was safe. Men could pursue me without the possibility that I might expect them to marry me. Only Sean cared that I was married, but felt sure that once his wife died, in answer to his prayers, my marriage would prove no obstacle. I decided to leave the stage after undergoing an operation. The operation was not necessary. I was suffering from indigestion caused by the precarious life I was leading—dancing and singing lessons every day, the show every night, suppers with the different men, warding them off, not warding them off, and the ceaseless money troubles.

Sir Robert sent me to the Queen's doctor, who called in another specialist, who, finding nothing wrong with me, ordered an operation at ten the next morning. Sir Robert informed the doctors he would pay for everything, their fees, the exclusive nursing home, special nurses around the clock.

When I told Sean about the operation, he too insisted on paying for "everything." It would upset him if I told him about Sir Robert, so I kept quiet. Sir Robert learned about the double payments in one of those rare accidents of a crossed telephone wire. He listened in while I was thanking Sean for giving me the cash to pay the bills for the operation.

Sir Robert told me sorrowfully that under the circumstances, he could not continue his friendship with me. I was glad to see the last of him. He had once raped a girl of twelve, he had told me in a confessional mood. He too was Catholic, and I wish he had told this to a priest, not me. I had wanted to drop him before the operation, but he had begged to take care of me.

My husband knew that both men were paying the bills, and he accepted this as a tribute to my beauty. There were no reproaches. If it was all right with him, it was all right with me, and I handed him over the money from Sean. I should have kept the money and left Johnny, but I needed him even more than he needed money. Being married gave me an aura of respectability in my desperate search for sex and love. Of course, it was wrong. If only I had valued myself then as I do now. Some of our behavior seems incredible now. Once when Johnny was visiting me in the nursing home—he came every afternoon and evening—Sir Robert's name was announced by the nurse, and my husband leaped hastily into a wardrobe in the room and stayed there suffocating until Sir Robert left.

Because the surgeons had to remove something, they took out my appendix. But I still had indigestion. After the operation, Sean begged me to leave the stage. I was in no hurry to return to it. It had been a tremendous strain

—a nightmare of being nice to people I did not like and was afraid of. I had joyfully accepted the operation as an escape from the tensions of my life. Problems swirled outside my room in the fashionable clinic. Inside I lay quietly listening to music on my radio while Johnny sat in an armchair reading. A month's recuperation in the south of France with Johnny—all expenses paid by Sean —was a happy time for me. Also, for the first time since my marriage, I had time to think.

I wanted to stay married to Johnny, but how was this possible with Sean paying the bills? I was frightened of the future. What if Sean became tired of waiting for Miss Speedicity to pay up? How would Johnny and I live? The time had to come to pay the debt. I did not tell Johnny. I did not have to. He was twenty-five years older than I, and he must have believed that I had slept with Sean a long time ago.

It would have to be lunch, I told the delighted, patient, longing-to-be lover. He arranged a suite at the London Waldorf Hotel in Kingsway.

I took my time with lunch. Starting with Scotch smoked salmon with thin slices of buttered brown bread. Grouse on toast soaked with the liver of the bird, bread sauce and bread crumbs, crisp chip potatoes, string beans. A fresh peach for dessert. I copied Sean as he pressed the skin all around the peach, then peeled it slickly with a fruit knife. Petits fours. Coffee with cream. Sean kept looking nervously at his watch. He had a business meeting at three, and it was nearly two-thirty. He beckoned to the waiting water to take away the table.

He rushed me into the bedroom, neither of us undressed completely, and he had me in a hurry. I managed an orgasm because I was not tense—how could I have been after that enormous meal. And because I was not trying to impress him. He had waited a long time for this, and the delay could have made him impotent, but thank God it did not.

After this we lunched together once a week, in the same suite at the Waldorf. He waited patiently while I gorged myself. He could not eat much himself, as he had an ulcer. Then we rushed through sex, jumped into the car, which dropped him off at his office and continued to my home in Chelsea—a home furnished courtesy of Sean.

He was more in love with me than ever, and he was praying harder, he told me, for his wife to die so we would never have to be apart. I prayed even harder for her to live so that I would not be asked to divorce Johnny to marry Sean.

Somerset Maugham wrote a novel, *The Painted Veil,* in which the husband prays for his unfaithful wife to die. On his own deathbed the husband said, "The dog it was who died."

In the case of the praying Sean, it was he who died. He had already had two operations for ulcers. The night before his third, his nurse mailed his penciled note to me: "You are the last one in my thoughts. Don't phone the nursing home. I will find a way of letting you know. Don't worry." He died on the operating table. Cancer, all over his stomach.

There was another woman in Sean's life before he met me. He had supported her in great style for about five years. The relationship came to light after his death, as did the presents he had given me and the money he had "lent" to Johnny, to supplement his salary. He was not as rich as I had thought, and had been spending capital. There was not a great deal of money left in his estate.

"We must live more modestly," I insisted to Johnny. "We must live on what you earn as a salesman until I get a job. We can't afford this house; let's find a small flat in Battersea." It would mean giving up the fancy society friends I had been able to keep up with because of Sean's generosity, but I wanted to make a new start in circumstances we could afford.

Johnny had what he called a brilliant plan. After leaving the stage, I had been fairly successful as a free-lance journalist. I had not planned a writing career. Rather, I had stumbled into it when I wrote two articles about my life on the stage. The *Daily Express* had accepted my first article, "The Stage Door Johnny by a Chorus Girl." And the second, "My Screen Test by a Film-Struck Girl," landed in the *Daily Mail.* The *Sunday Pictorial* had bought some stories from me, and paid the huge sum of eight guineas.

I was off and away in my new career until I met A. P. Herbert at a Cochran Charity Matinee and he gave me some pointers on how to write. Until I forgot them I could not sell anything.

Fired with ambition because of the acceptance of my articles about the stage, I had written a long piece titled "Lords of Literature," about the four Fleet Street Lords —Beaverbrook, Riddell, Kemsley, and Rothermere. After an agonizing wait, it had been bought by *Nash's Magazine,* a slick periodical, and I was paid the vast sum of twenty-five guineas. Putting words on paper has always come easily to me. At the orphanage my essays had often been read to the assembled school.

I had been told so often that I was beautiful that I believed I could sell my articles more easily if I delivered them in person. Editors were men, and it was hard for them to resist my eager expectations. It would be like hitting a child to say no. I sold almost everything I wrote, and was earning about fifteen pounds a week in England as a free lancer. The editors usually took me to lunch and were amused and touched by my happy prattle, and rather startled by the saucy stories I told quite deliberately to create an aura of sexiness. I was something new and fresh for the blasé bosses of the literary pages, and my articles were usually startling enough to merit publication.

Viscount Castlerosse, Lord Beaverbrook's highly paid page-two *Sunday Express* columnist, explained to me about syndication in America. The same article could appear in hundreds of newspapers, and each paper paid for it. Instead of eight guineas, I could make eighty guineas on the one article. "How amazing," said Johnny, his mind racing with the possibilities.

Before we could move to Battersea, he suggested with his usual enthusiasm, "Why don't you go to New York and sell your articles for syndication?" He never doubted that I would succeed at whatever I put my mind to. America. Syndication. It was worth a try.

He was sad when he saw me off on the *Aquitania* at Southampton. He had made me pack a big trunk, for I was to stay as long as was necessary. He had a premonition that this would be the end for us. I loved him, but it was not a marriage. I would always love him, and help him financially until the bleak day in January, 1965, when his sister sent me a cable telling me of his death.

Walking around the deck before the last blast for visitors to leave, I did not guess that I was going into the arms of another married man. That for the second time in my life I would be the "other woman."

Charles was big, brown-eyed, dark-haired, in his late forties, with a protectiveness that enchanted me. Here was a man who would look after his woman. I was in love with him almost immediately.

He was married, but his wife was at the seashore with their two children. It was early June when I met him. Every summer, New York, before home air-conditioning, was a city without wives. They were in the country or by the sea, and saw their husbands only on weekends. The city was a lovely place for a single girl. Attractive, successful men tumbled over themselves to have a lady companion for the evening. They were all cheating on their wives, who did not seem to care, or accepted the fact as long as the liaison was not broadcast, and as long as the husband supported them and did not ask for a divorce. But few did.

Before leaving England I had written a novel, a murder mystery titled *Gentleman Crook*. My husband thought I might find a publisher in America, and he obtained a letter of introduction for me to the head man in the biggest publishing firm in New York. The publishing tycoon read the letter as I sat in his plush office trying to seem at ease. Charles, the head of a large printing conglomerate, was in his office, glanced at me from time to time and seemed to like what he saw. His approval made me very confident, and I flashed my most winning smile.

"Perhaps," he said tentatively as I turned to leave, "perhaps we could discuss your book over a drink? How about this evening? I'll meet you at the Stork Club," shaking my hand warmly at the door. I barely touched the sidewalk as I walked back to the Elysée, a small good hotel between Madison and Park Avenues in the mid-Fifties. I had made a conquest. He was powerful and he would help me. The worries of the months since Sean's death vanished. I would get a job. I'd send for Johnny, and we would live happily ever after in this fantastic city.

I had a letter to the brother of Valentine Williams, the successful writer of detective stories. Douglas was the New York representative of the London *Daily Telegraph.* He knew everyone. I called on him and casually asked about Charles. Yes, he was very important, and very much married. His wife was about ten years younger, and he had married in his late thirties.

Douglas took me to lunch at a steak house near the *Daily Mirror* on Third Avenue. There was sawdust on the floor, and red-and-white tablecloths, and the steak was superb. There was a freshness and expectation about New York that I loved. This was my city. I was sure I would do well here.

Charles and I arrived at the Stork Club at the same instant. "Good," he said when we were sitting on high stools at the long bar. "I like women who are punctual." He offered me a cigarette, and was pleased when I said I didn't smoke. "I don't drink much either," I added. "In that case"—he grinned—"you'd better have an old-fashioned."

I had two, leaving most of the liquid and eating the fruit that was skewered on a thin stick, the slice of orange, the cube of pineapple, and the cherry. "Come on, drink up, don't waste a good drink," Charles urged. I shook my head and laughed. "I'm not a drinker, I only like sweet things." The old-fashioned became my favorite drink because of the fruit. Years later when a man told Charles he had seen me drunk at a party, Charles called him a liar. He knew I did not drink.

So I cannot blame my capitulation to Charles on alcohol. I was drunk on something else. I believed that for the first time in my life I had found a man who was strong and who would look after me. It was such a welcome change from looking after Johnny.

In my times of enjoyable sex I have found that you either go to bed with the man on the first date or you do not go to bed with him at all. If you are over twenty-one, in right possession of your faculties, and if you fancy a man, what is there to stop you? Why wait?

It was the most natural thing in the world to go to bed with Charles on that first evening. I wondered whether I should let him come to my apartment—the first step in making love. If you don't let him inside the door, he cannot have you. But if you like him and don't let him in, where is the feeling of victory as you listen to his retreating footsteps? Sometimes it is more exciting to wait before you go to bed with him, but if you hesitate too long, you might get to be only friends instead of lovers. Whereas a good lover always becomes a good friend.

I had my period, and I thought, oh, well, I can let Charles in, because nothing will happen. Most men won't touch you then, but it made no difference to Charles. Once he started kissing me, he knew he had me. There was no asking "May I?"

Whenever a man asks me, I always say no. I want them to take me. I am the original woman in the cave, dragged around by the hair and loving my masterful man. How Women's Lib will hate me for this! But I was born with a built-in longing to be conquered. Charles was masterful, and I was his happy slave.

I had a lovely time with him that summer. I met interesting men in all spheres of New York life—bankers, publishers, newspaper owners, writers, politicians, painters, sportsmen, millionaire real estate owners. All were married, of course.

Jack, good-looking, in his late fifties, had been the president of a New York bank, but he had lost his job in the crash. He still had some money coming in, and lived in a quietly furnished town house. He was married and had a girl who bloomed by his side in the summer. Janet became my best friend in America.

We met in the Ritz Garden—that lovely Ritz Hotel on Park Avenue, which was pulled down to make a high tower of glass for thousands of office workers. She lived across the road at 277 Park Avenue. It was an enormous conglomerate of apartments, where, it was rumored, many married men kept their girls.

Janet paid her own way. She worked and had her own boutique at the Madison Hotel on 56th Street, to which I moved later to save the bother of keeping house. We were often a foursome, or a sixsome, the men relaxing without the eagle eyes of their wives to make them self-conscious.

I went on a weekend trip with Charles to Pennsylvania. He was trying to net a famous publisher for his conglomerate. We stayed with the businessman and his wife. They put us in the same room, which made me only slightly uncomfortable. I was in love with Charles. It would have been hypocritical for him to creep into my room when the others were asleep.

He held me close in his arms all night, and although it was somewhat uncomfortable at first, I was soon used to sleeping in a smothered embrace. I went with him to Chicago for the World's Fair; we had a drawing room in the train, and we both slept in the lower narrow berth. That *was* difficult, and I was exhausted when we reached Chicago in the morning. I slept all morning, while Charles kept his appointments.

He had business in Detroit, and I went with him. Afterward we visited the fantastic lakeside home of one of his married friends quite a long drive from Detroit. The rooms were enormous, with huge windows, a large terrace, and exotic flowers and shrubs. There was a wide, sandy beach and enormous, beautifully colored butterflies. Everything was on a large scale, including the steaks which our host barbecued for us. The next morning Charles took me on the lake in a rowboat, and when we were far enough out, we slipped out of our swimsuits and swam nude in the warm water. It was heavenly.

I was so brazen about loving this man that I went in the evenings to his apartment on Park Avenue, wearing my riding clothes, so that I could ride with him at seven in the morning in Central Park. After dinner we read awhile—he was always reading magazines and business reports—and then went to bed. There were two single beds, and we slept in his. I sometimes wondered, what will we do if his wife walks in, but she was a long way away, so there wasn't much chance, and besides, I didn't really care. It was a long summer, and he was mine.

Charles helped me with money, although I did not need it. Soon after arriving in New York I landed jobs on the *Daily Mirror* and the *New York Journal.* I was paid forty-five dollars a week on the *Mirror* and seventy-five by the *Journal.* It was two months before the newspapers learned of my double job. I had not known that you couldn't work for two newspapers at the same time. Both papers were owned by William Randolph Hearst, and I thought it was all in the family—until my byline appeared on the same day in each paper.

I enjoyed the commotion, but had to make a decision. I chose The *Journal* because of the higher pay. I was happy, and feeling secure, took chances as a journalist that I might have been afraid to take had I been lonely and unhappy. I not only had a column on the women's page—my first article was entitled "Who Cheats the Most in Marriage"!—but very often my byline appeared in big black letters over the lead story on the front page. I was sent as a special feature writer with Dorothy Kilgallen in charge of the news on many of the big out-of-town stories. Whenever I was in doubt about anything, I called my lover and he told me what to do.

Then, alas, and inevitably, the summer came to an end. After Labor Day, the wives returned en masse to the city. No more dinners at his apartment. It was now a hurried drink at one of the popular bars, then perhaps a hasty half-hour in bed in my apartment, and he had to go home. We met almost every day for lunch, but it was not the same. Sometimes he would chance an evening, and we dined with Jack and Janet. His wife became suspicious. Once when I was walking with Charles on Fifth Avenue he spun around in answer to a firm hand on his back. "Where are you going?" his wife demanded. "None of your business," he said, and walked away with me. He was furious.

I was sorry for his wife, but I did not dare look back. For all his anger, I knew that the encounter had shaken him. It was nice to have a pretty girl on the side, but he did not want to break up his marriage, that is, not until I went to England to cover a royal wedding. On my return I could have had Charles for the asking. And it was he who was doing the asking.

I have learned from experience that when a woman is too easy to get, she sometimes loses her value for the man who has taken her. It is like the old Groucho Marx story. When he was accepted by a golf club in Los Angeles, he scoffed, "If they take *me,* they can't be much good."

This theory applies mainly to men who are not entirely sure of their charm. The confident man expects the girl to be bowled over right away, but even he puts a higher premium on merchandise that is valued highly by its owner. Let him think he can't have it, or is losing what he had, and he wants it more than ever. Men are like children—take away the toy they thought belonged to them, and they scream for it.

I had not intended to play this calculating game with Charles. It was merely that I had lied about my age by two years! I was in my twenties, and he was approaching fifty, and after I reached twenty-four I remained stationary at that age for two years. So when I was returning from England by ship in the mid-1930's—no one except the intrepid solo adventurers flew the Atlantic in those days—I was a bit upset when I received a cable on the boat stating that Charles would meet me at quarantine.

The reporters and photographers always came aboard with the quarantine officials on one of the tugs that chug the great liners into the harbor. I was afraid he would take my passport from me in order to help me through quarantine—you sometimes had to line up for an hour for the passport and medical people. He would see my real age and wonder why I lied. To this day I cannot come right out and say how old I am—except to my children when they demand too much of me.

I sent Charles a cable telling him not to bother, that I would phone him after the ship docked. "Do you think she has a lover aboard?" he asked Jack anxiously. Jack was rather cynical and said it was possible. Charles went into deep depression. His slave must not be freed. He would take the big step. He would ask his wife for a divorce, goddamnit, and he would marry me. And would meet me at quarantine.

There he was on the small boat climbing up the steps into the side of the ship, knocking at my cabin door. I kissed him hurriedly and said, "Wait here. I'll get my passport stamped and I'll be back." This man who was so used to ordering me around waited meekly for my return. He helped get my baggage to his car, took me to the Madison Hotel, and very humbly begged me to marry him.

At the beginning I would have liked to marry him, but I too had grown used to the status quo. While I am anti-Women's Lib, I have always been independent. Charles was very selfish and very bossy. You had to do everything his way. But this was not why I said no. It was his children. He loved them very much. He was the kind of man who blamed you when things went wrong. One day he would accuse me of taking him from his children. I told him this, and he gave me his word, but I knew he would eventually blame me.

I was still married; Charles had met my husband but did not think highly of a man who could not provide for his wife. I could get a divorce. Whenever Johnny borrowed money from me, he wrote that he did not mind taking it because he would set me free whenever I asked.

When I asked Johnny for a divorce, there was no problem. The earl was on the wagon, and I thought, then, that perhaps I would marry him. But by that time the decree nisi was absolute. In the winter of 1937, I had met Scott Fitzgerald, who was married, with a wife who was mentally ill and confined to a sanatorium. I chose my position as the other woman in Scott's life, rather than be married to anyone else, even a belted earl. In actual fact I was much more than the other woman in the life of Scott Fitzgerlad. As Edmund Wilson reassured me, "You were his second wife." I was, in all but name.

CHAPTER 7

Some Other "Other" Women

Some of my best friends have been the "other woman."
Patsy. . . . She is now happily married. But she gave some
of her most important years to a bastard of a man who
was married with children and who gave her the usual
malarkey that he was unhappy in his marriage, that he
would get a divorce, that he would then marry Patsy.

She was twenty-three when she met him. At twenty-
three a girl starts to get a bit worried in the competition
of finding a husband. Girls a few years younger have
usually grabbed the best men. Patsy had graduated from
college, content with her B.A. She had no ambition to be
an intellectual. All she wanted was to have a good time,
get married, and raise a family. She was and still is very
pretty and very sweet, although rather critical of men.
She expected them to be as perfect as they seemed to be
at their first meeting.

Sometimes Patsy was blissfully happy with her married
man, whom she met at a cocktail party he attended without his wife. Patsy liked him right away. He took her
home to her apartment, and while Patsy was not the
promiscuous kind, they might have made love then and
there, but her roommate was home.

I was not surprised to learn that the man had fallen
in love with my pretty friend. I *was* upset when she told

me that she was just as much in love with him. Patsy has always been popular with the boys. She has a soft, gentle personality that is rather deceptive.

Before meeting her married lover she had asked me, "How can I get to know the kind of man I would want to marry?" I thought awhile and suggested, "Why don't you give a party? Invite all your girl friends and tell them to bring a man—not that you are going to steal them, but when *they* give parties they will invite you back, and there will be new men for you to meet, and you might find the right one."

Cocktail parties and buffet suppers are good breeding grounds for the single girl to find the single—and married —man. Patsy was a good cook, and the table was spread with the most gorgeous delicacies. Everyone had a good time, and they were all attentive to Patsy, but the only man who paid her close attention, a professor from Yale, became very drunk and had literally to be ejected at two in the morning when most of the other guests had long since departed.

"Don't give up," I counseled the disappointed Patsy. "You'll see, you'll have lots of invitations." She had some, and at one of the parties she met the married man.

It looked hopeful for her when he left his wife. They were together every evening, and she was happy, although she avoided her friends because she felt awkward about her situation. After two weeks he went back to his wife and saw Patsy for only an hour before dinner every day.

She was unhappy. To have a man for an hour when she thought she had him completely was depressing. I stepped in where no one can tread with success. "Give him up," I begged her. "You are too attractive to waste yourself like this."

"Oh, but he went back to his wife only to explain that he wants a divorce," she assured me. I looked at her in amazement. How could she be so stupid? He left his wife again, but she had become pregnant, and he went home. Even this did not cure Patsy. She loved him, she wanted him, and for her there could be no other man.

Five precious years. Her mother was in despair. Her pretty daughter would always be attending the weddings of her friends and remaining single herself because of this awful married man.

I had a house in the country and was delighted when Patsy came down for lunch and tennis one Sunday with a good-looking man she had been dating for two weeks. He was not married, and he admired Patsy. He was a lawyer with a good firm. Patsy took him home to meet her mother. But she still had the image of the married man in her heart. As long as he was there, she could not want another man. But she had made a beginning.

In six months she met another man. She was almost thirty. I am not sure how much she was in love with him, but she was cured finally of her lover. The new man was rich, with a nice apartment in Greenwich Village and a house in the country. The wedding and the reception were at the Plaza. Patsy's mother beamed with happiness. I see the couple now and then, and they are still adjusting, but the marriage looks okay and the expected baby is drawing them closer every day.

Thank God my own daughter never fell in love with a married man. Having done it myself, I know what misery, what a "thin" life it gives you. My daughter married a few years ago, and I am very happy with her choice. More important, she is.

The news item merely stated that Mr. X, an Australian multimillionaire, was suing Mrs. Y, a well-known American society divorcée, for the return of his presents, which, he said in the complaint, were given because of her promise to marry him. The presents included a house in the South of France, a bushel of jewels, and a yacht.

He was married when he met the lady. I knew his wife and children, and he had seemed devoted to them. They had a beautiful house at Ascot, with an indoor swimming pool that with one press of a button opened to the sun. There were guards day and night to protect the family.

Another house in Biarritz was a showplace and had been featured in *House Beautiful*. You felt you were living in a pleasure dome, with the enormous swimming pool as a further oasis. If the wife had not gone to New York with the children they might still have been happily married.

He met the American society girl at a rather wild party he had thrown for some business associates. He had not paid her any particular attention at the time. Three months elapsed. It was May, and he had chartered a yacht for a three-month cruise in the South Pacific. He had a girl—rich, middle-aged men always have a girl on the side —but after a week on the yacht she left him to marry a young, but not rich, man. Three months on a boat without a woman was not to be tolerated. He wondered if he should invite his wife and children. No, they were better off in Long Island, where he owned another home. Desperate, he went ashore to telephone his good friend, a famous actor—double-gaited in terms of sex—who was in London.

"That American girl who lives in London. She was brought to my house by ——. Do you know her name?" He did not, but he called a friend, who not only supplied her name but her telephone number. The summer would not be wasted after all.

He phoned the lady and said he was sending his private airplane to bring her to him. She listened coldly while he pleaded. She was well off herself—she was born rich, and the husband she had divorced was rich; but he was much richer, by about a hundred million dollars.

"No," she replied crisply. "I can't do that. But some friends of mine have invited me to their home in Hawaii. You can call me there in a few days. Then I'll be delighted to visit you on your yacht." There was nothing said about staying on the yacht.

He sent a car for her, and she did not return to her friends. She is a very attractive blond, and he fell in love with her. "I will divorce my wife if you will marry me," he told her, breathing passionately into her hazel eyes.

She remained cool—a common trait with women who marry rich men.

This is one man who actually meant what he said. He would give his wife a ten-million-dollar settlement, and how could she refuse that? She didn't. While openly affectionate, she knew of his affairs and had been bored with him for a long time.

With the divorce under way, he took the American woman to Cartier's in Paris and chose a solitaire diamond engagement ring that would have made Elizabeth Taylor envious. He tossed in an expensive diamond-and-emerald bracelet and brooch, plus a few other glittering knickknacks—a million dollars' worth of jewels for his future bride. The house in the South of France cost two hundred thousand pounds. He was not being extravagant, he reasoned. She had promised to marry him, and it was a good investment. It *was* a good investment, but not for him. For her.

While they were in Paris the millionaire had to attend a sudden business conference. He and his fiancée checked into the Ritz for a few days, and placed the jewels in the hotel safe. His fiancée put her own small collection of jewels in the safe, and persuaded the millionaire to give her authorization to withdraw her jewels. "I might need them while you are away," she said. He agreed reluctantly.

Barely waiting for him to leave the hotel, she hurried down to the lobby, requested that the safe be opened for her, swept all the jewels—his and hers—into her handbag, ordered a car to Orly Airport, and flew to Switzerland, where she deposited the gems in a bank vault.

He will have a difficult time getting them back. He had divorced his wife to marry this woman, and she had made a grade-A fool of him. He was so upset that he began to lose his concentration on his many business ventures. When I last heard from him, he was in bankruptcy, although he still had assets of several million dollars—but not nearly enough to pay his debts. I can hear a smug married woman growl, "Serves him right. He left his wife, didn't he, for this other woman? He got what he gave." Then why do I feel indignant with the woman and sorry for him?

She is a divorcée in her late thirties, a shoe buyer for a top store; she is known as one of the toughest and most successful women in the Fifth Avenue merchandising world.

They met through mutual friends in New York. He had a reputation as a woman chaser. She ignored him. Piqued, he concentrated on her until she finally yielded.

He is an Austrian, married to an American woman. They own a shoe factory in the north of Italy, but they live in Austria in a large rambling hunting lodge with beautiful grounds and stables full of hunting thoroughbreds. Their boar hunts are a magnet for the celebrities of Europe.

He has been married three times and has several children. He was very much in love with the divorcée. While still loving her, his commercial instincts took over. She could help his business, which had been failing.

He invited her to view his shoe factory in Italy. She met his wife, and for a few days they were a chummy threesome. "I love you," the shoe baron managed to whisper to the divorcée when his wife was out of hearing. Perhaps she did hear. Her manner toward the important shoe buyer from New York changed. She was suspicious, and her suspicion grew when her husband made many excuses to visit New York without her.

"Look at these orders for shoes," he boasted, hoping to placate his wife, who didn't quite know what to do. Was it really business, or was it hanky-panky? There was one good way to clip any budding romance—keep him short of money. The wife invented all sorts of excuses for extracting money from her philandering husband, who had been rich when they married and now had to ask his wife for spending money.

When he went to New York, he had no money and borrowed from the shoe buyer, who did not object to accepting his I.O.U.'s as long as he kept saying "I love you. I am going to marry you." He informed all his and her friends in New York, including me, "This is the woman I am going to marry."

On each anniversary of their meeting—there have been five—he brought her a trinket in gold inscribed "I Love You," with his name. The presents, the visits, the pro-testations, were enough for the divorcée, but not for me.

After four years, I said carefully—you have to be careful when pointing out the obvious to a woman in love, or they can end up hating you: "Don't you think he is using you?" I retracted the words immediately when a cloud darkened her face: "No, of course not. I'm sure he loves you." Then she admitted, "Sometimes I think he is using me. But why would he not only tell *me* he loves me, but he tells his brother, who lives in America, that he loves me and wants to marry me."

"When you are not there?" I asked skeptically. Well, she didn't know about that, but he certainly said this when she was present. She was sure he wanted to be free of his wife. "She's bad for him, she takes away his confidence. I'm good for him. If he gives me a chance, I can prove it. If he would stay with me, even for a month, he would realize that I'm good for him and she's bad for him."

In the past two years their meetings have always ended in quarrels. When he comes to New York—his visits have been getting less and less frequent—the divorcée is happy and absolutely sure he will leave his wife and they can marry. She has a house in the country, and they go there and are happy until he suddenly develops an ulcer and has to return at once to his wife and doctor in Austria. He usually stays in her New York apart-ment, but pretends he is staying with his brother, "Be-cause my wife is calling me from Austria every morning, and she will be suspicious if I gave your number."

Suspicious! The wife is aware of everything that is going on—I sometimes think she is the mastermind—ex-cept for the one fact that her husband has promised to marry the divorcée. That little piece of information has not been passed on. She could hardly be in the dark about her husband and the other woman's interest in what she regards as her property. Certainly not after the husband invited the divorcée to spend the New Year with him in Austria. She went to Austria and received humiliating treatment from the wife that should have cured her permanently and would have shattered a less determined woman.

The "other woman" is not usually so brash. She usually stays in the shadows, the back street of Fannie Hurst's novel. But he loved her, didn't he? He concluded every letter and cable with "I love you"; why should he not spend New Year's Eve with her when he was planning to spend the rest of his life with her?

Every time she told me this, I said to myself, "But he isn't. He has no intention of ever divorcing his wife; why can't you see this?" I could not say what I thought, that as soon as she had given him enough orders for shoes to make him a rich man, he would drop her completely, or at most call her casually when he happened to be in town. How can you say this to a woman who is in love and who has never given up on anything she has wanted?

A few months later the divorcée flew to Vienna and telephoned her lover. His wife answered. "He is not here," she said sternly. "He is at the factory in Italy." "On Sunday?" the other woman said incredulously. "Please put him on the phone; it is an urgent matter of business." "On Sunday?" the wife mocked. "Look," she added, "my husband is not here; he does not wish to see you, and stop writing to him and phoning him. I'm his wife. We don't want you bothering us. You're—you're, you know what you are? Paranoiac!" And she hung up.

The divorcée flew back to New York utterly depressed but not ready to give him up. "I know he hates his wife, and he knows he would be happy with me," she persisted. This is true. The wife is cold and very calculating. The other woman is bursting with love and warmth, which she wants to lay at the feet of her shoe king.

"After five years, don't you think the time has come to give him an ultimatum?" I said. How could she go on like this? "I'll have to think about it," she replied. "Give him up, and you will find someone else," I assured her. "You're attractive and intelligent, except about this man. There must be another man for you."

"Where?" she demanded. "Look around," I suggested. "I've looked around," she replied. We were lunching in a popular restaurant. "*You* look around," she added. "Is there any man here you would want to marry?" I looked and had to admit not. "But," I reminded her, "you said you did not like him when you first met him. You grew to like him." "He suits me," she explained. "I'd rather have him this way than not have him at all, and perhaps if I gave him an ultimatum, I might never see him again."

I could not accept a situation like this. I have to be sure the man wants me, or I vanish. But *she* can, and it is a good thing we are all different. I have met the man. He did not appeal to me at all. I often wonder what women see in certain men, but this woman can see all his faults. "He's a womanizer, he's a liar, he's unreliable, he's weak, and sometimes I think he hates me. But he suits me, and I'll get him in the end."

She will. If you want a man badly enough, you usually get him. But when you get him you sometimes wonder, was it worth the struggle?

We all know about the famous governor who left his wife of thirty years, the mother of his grown-up children, for a much younger woman. While his marriage had not been ecstatic, it was serviceable and workable. When the younger woman became pregnant, he bestirred himself. His wife politely stood aside and gave him the divorce— for a price. She could have hung on, but she is a nice lady and she was as bored with his ambitious politics as he was with her sedate way of life.

Wives should watch out when the man is reaching fifty. Men like to preen themselves like the peacock. It would be ridiculous to put on a young-man act with their long-time wives. They must have a new young mirror to reflect the virility that will soon pass into old age. The clever wife looks the other way while this is going on and keeps her fingers, but not her legs, crossed.

Clare Boothe Luce wrote in her play *The Women*: "It is being together at the end that counts." Perhaps, but not if your life together is unhappy.

Women who jump hastily into divorce can find themselves alone when they are too old to hunt for, or want, another husband or companion. Children have a good habit of growing up, and they are soon gone, sometimes to live in other states or countries. And the wife who divorced too impetuously is left alone. Barbara Stanwyck always regretted her divorce from Robert Taylor, rushed into because he had an affair with an actress in his Italian film. The wise wife hangs on until the storm passes. Usually her husband is glad that she did. It is cheaper to stay married to the first woman, and when you are old you share a solid wedge of the past. Besides, the older man who leaves his wife for a younger woman is likely to die earlier than if he had remained with his wife, since a young woman expects sex all the time.

The rich printer and his wife are alone now except for servants in their big apartment in town and estate in the country. Their children are married and gone away. He still nags her, and she still nags him, but they would die without each other. In recent years I have become friendly with the wife. I like her. I often wonder how she can stand the bullying of her husband, but I have come to the conclusion that she loves it. It makes her feel that her husband is still strong and powerful and she is his dutiful slave. The scenes give her life some meaning. Actually, I am sure she does as she pleases, perhaps seeing plays and films in the afternoons because her husband will not go out at night. She looks after him, rubs his back, cares for his arm when the arthritis makes it painful. She sees that he has the right food, and not too much to drink. Dinner guests must leave early, because he wants to go to bed. And when he is ill, she employs the prettiest nurse available. She encourages all of his former girl friends, including me, to come to the apartment and to stay with them in the country. "It keeps him young," she told me in a burst of confidence.

He was late coming home for dinner one evening, and his wife was in the nearby streets looking for him, fearful that something had happened. In her anguish she called on me, just in case our liaison had been resumed and he would be there. After thirty-three years? She apologized humbly when he was not. I advised her to go home, he would surely be there soon. "Don't tell him I was here," the wife pleaded. I promised, thinking, "How times have changed."

Sometimes I wonder, if I were the wife, how would I deal with the "other woman." No woman has ever tried to take any of my men from me. When I am in love there is no chance of another woman poaching. At least I don't think so. Having been the "other woman" myself, I believe I would know how to deal with her.

A rich New York husband married to his wife for sixteen years began playing around. He met a girl with whom he fell in love. She insisted he get a divorce. When he told his wife he wanted a divorce, she laughed. "Oh, come on, you're having a nervous breakdown." And, still laughing, walked away. They are still married. He does not see the girl.

It is up to the wife who wishes to fight the other woman to refrain from making scenes about her. If she keeps talking about her, she makes her too important. The husband will think more about the other woman than he does about his wife. Of course, the wife must make herself as attractive as she can. But it isn't always because she has her hair in curlers or uses cold cream that he has gone off with another woman. Men are naturally polygamous. They want other women, usually for a one-time go. But they are creatures of habit, and unless the wife has made them utterly wretched, they do not want a divorce.

The smart wife will not admit the existence of another woman, even if he parades her before their mutual friends. Not to know is the first line of defense for the wife. If she does not know, her husband cannot ask for a divorce. They will not quarrel about her. The quarrels sometimes get out of hand, and before the wife knows it, she is screaming "I'll divorce you!" and the "other woman" has won.

CHAPTER 8

How To Get a Rich Man by Really Trying

I have learned by experience that it is not difficult to get a man for one night. Almost any man will want almost any woman for one night. The trick is to make him want you for life, or until another man, woman, alimony, or death do you part.

You can get what you want, but only what you want. If you think small, you will get small. Think of a cottage, and that is what you will get. See yourself in a palace, and you might get a palace. Think of a poor man, and you will find a poor man. Set your sights on a rich man, and that is what you will have. Go after whichever man you want, and in most cases you will win him.

It might be instructive to learn how certain women landed their rich, important men. What were their methods?

The famous blond ethereal beauty. . . . When she was eighteen she married a well-known businessman. He died a few years later, leaving her with a small son but no money. He had been a gambler. She made no attempt to pay his bills, but declared his estate bankrupt and looked for a job.

She was not a girl to moan about bad luck. She has always taken action when things went wrong. She had been poor. Her father died early and her mother had married a bookkeeper. The mother was greedy, and the child grew up believing that having money was the most important thing in life. She still believes that money and power are essential for happiness.

She vaguely remembered her father naked, doing his setting-up exercises in the morning. Her childish fingers had once grabbed his penis, and he had pushed her away angrily. Was this why this beautiful, earnest, and intellectual woman is frigid? She was a challenge for the rich, powerful men. To warm her up would be a triumph. The man who could capture her and make her melt just for him would be envied by his friends. This was how she had landed her first husband. But now he was dead, and she determined to make men work for her.

She became a model. But she was too stiff ever to become a really good one. Besides, this was not her goal. She was too clever to be content wearing someone else's clothes. She knew the medium well, and she decided to become a designer. There was no problem about getting an angel to back her. A short and homely but tricky and very successful financier told me she had gone to bed with him when he promised to back her in business. He did not quite put it this way, but you knew, looking at them huddling together —she slim and ascetic-looking, he greasy and gross.

Her business was a flop, but the publicity established her as something more than a beautiful face. She immediately opened another office—designed for the people she knew, used lavish fabrics, and charged enormous prices. This time she was very successful.

There was no problem now about money. But she wanted something more satisfying, a husband. In America a woman without a husband is not invited too often to the rich apartments and elegant country houses. Particularly if she is beautiful and brainy. The members of the Wives' Union are not crazy. With a husband, you can go everywhere, and if you are dissatisfied with your own, you are able to snatch someone else's.

When I lived in England reading the American magazines and newspapers, it had always intrigued me; everyone was always married. It was always Mrs. So-and-So, no matter how young the woman was. The wives ran the country, unlike in England, where the men do. Every American debutante was a failure until she could proudly write "Mrs." in front of her name.

The pretty designer was determined to carry off a rich and powerful man. The first rule in a campaign of this nature is to be noticed, to be talked about, not as a loose woman, but as an unusual woman. She would outwit the wives, make herself conspicuous, so that not only the husbands in her age plateau but the wives would also be aware of her existence.

In those days, most women wore dark colors in the daytime—the little black, navy, or brown dress. White was a color for virgins, which she had not been for a long time. In white she would get attention.

She dressed in white, from the little hat crowning her pale golden hair to her small feet encased in white shoes and stockings. Her dresses, coats, gloves, and handbags were all white. One lunchtime I saw the white vision enter 21 carrying a long-stemmed white rose. It was as though an apparition had descended from heaven. Everyone at the bar and the tables stopped talking to stare. She looked like a bride, and that was the idea.

She attracted the attention of a famous Wall Street stockbroker, who sent her a dozen white roses every day and escorted her to restaurants and the theater. He was between marriages, and all the divorcées and single women were trying to land him, but he had eyes only for the lady in white, and she might have settled for him —he was fairly well-off, and much liked—but she was confronted with bigger game and dropped the stockbroker. It might have been an accident, but I think it was suicide when he drove the white car he had bought for her into a wall and was killed instantly.

She attended his funeral, dressed in her favorite color.

One of the mourners, one of the richest men in the world, with interests in every type of business—oil, steel, coal, hotels, shipping, horses—took her home in his chauffeured Lincoln Continental. She marked him well, and was thinking up ways of meeting him again, without seeming too obvious, when she learned he would be a guest at a party given by Elsa Maxwell, as she herself was.

He was happily married, with three daughters, and was an Orthodox Jew. He always made a point of thanking God for the many favors he had received from Him. All this was known to the blond beauty, but she was determined to have him, and let God try to interfere!

To start her campaign, she moved into a lavish suite at the Pierre Hotel. She had the suite redecorated in white, with white curtains and draperies, white carpet, and white furniture, including a white baby-grand piano. She was the fragile white centerpiece. It was rather like the inside of a white-lined coffin, with an angel in residence.

The tycoon, happy in his marriage, had never strayed from the marital bed. But he had never met anyone like the lady in white—so beautiful, so intelligent, and so genuinely interested in him. He was dazzled and delighted when she asked him to tea at her suite in the Pierre. He was hanging onto his cup and listening to her good analysis of what was right and wrong with everything when she suddenly buried her face in her delicate hands.

"Are you ill?" he asked in some consternation. He was a married man, and there must be no scandal. If something were the matter with her, he must get out as gracefully as he could. She removed her hands from her face and looked at him with a radiant smile that also managed to be wistful.

"I shouldn't be saying this," she said in the most dulcet tones, "but I have fallen in love with you. It happened when I saw you at Elsa's." She did not tell him that she had known he was to be there and had gotten several hours of beauty sleep before going to the party to concentrate all her ensnaring charms on him.

Now she drew him close to her on the white settee,

looked deeply into his eyes—he felt he was drowning in a green sea—and intimated that she could not go on living unless he made love to her immediately. He was delighted. No one had ever found him sexually attractive before, not even his wife, a good religious person like himself.

As soon as his sperm was awash in her vagina, she burst into tears and wailed, "It was wrong. I can never see you again. After all"—dabbing her eyes with a white lace handkerchief—"you are a married man." "I thought you had taken that into account," he said miserably. He was deeply distressed about his effect on this fragile, beautiful, defenseless woman. He tried to comfort her. "Don't be unhappy," he coaxed. "We can meet occasionally like this, and I will always be your friend." She pushed him gently from her. "I want to be your wife," she said. He was truly amazed.

He had no intention of getting a divorce; he loved his wife, and he told her this. Of course, it was true that she did not appreciate him as much as this lovely passionate creature. He had never enjoyed sex so much. But to divorce his wife. He hardly knew this woman. "Let's be friends," he said hopefully, cupping her face in his hands.

Looking into her big woebegone eyes, he felt like a brute. "Why can't we be good friends?" he reiterated. She smiled bravely but said nothing, while tears rolled down her cheeks from each green lake. He wiped them away with his handkerchief, kissed her warmly and left. "Good," he thought; "that is settled. She will be my mistress. I'm rich; why can't I have everything in this world that I want?" God would understand.

The next day she left for Switzerland. Not a word for him. Just a message from the hotel to inform callers that she had gone to Switzerland for an indefinite time. Yes, she had left the name of the hotel where she was staying in Zurich, the Dolder-Grand.

He sent his trusted personal aide to entreat her to return to New York. But the man returned alone, with a sealed letter. She loved him, she wrote. She admired him more than any other man she had met in her life, but she simply could not have a liaison with a married man. There was also her son to consider. There must be nothing in her life that could hurt her precious boy. "I will come back to you," she wrote, "when you start proceedings for a divorce."

A divorce. She loved him that much. He had not thought of going too far with her, but now he was sure he was in love with this ethical lady. He had been a virgin, aged thirty-three, at the time of his marriage some twenty years previously. He was a smart business-man, but he knew nothing of the wiles of women. He did not want to lose this passionate good woman. The messenger returned to Switzerland. If she really wanted to marry him, he would get a divorce.

Her reply was full of happy longing and happy, happy love and hopes that soon they would be together forever. Until then she would stay in Switzerland and dream of their future together.

It has always been a wonder to me that the smartest, the most intelligent men are so damn simple. It almost makes me scream. Any dumb blond, let alone any moder-ately intelligent woman, can fool the cleverest man. She can grind him into little bits, spit him out, and go on her way without a backward glance. Why women are shouting for liberation when they have always been top dog with a man who is in love beats me.

Out of the blue, the tycoon informed his wife that he wanted a divorce. She was a gentle soul, and she loved her husband. She had taken his love for granted. They had never had a serious quarrel, and he had always treated her with respect. Where had she gone wrong, she asked her husband piteously. It was not her fault at all, he assured her. He had fallen in love with another woman and wished to marry her.

She promised to think about it, and he could be sure she would do what was best for them both. The next afternoon she jumped out of the window of their twelfth-floor apartment overlooking Central Park. The horror of his wife's death was on his conscience all his life.

He married the lady in white and realized almost im-

mediately that he had never been in love with her, or
she with him. She was an iceberg in bed, although she
had been so exciting that first and only time before their
marriage. She ate little and became even more delicate.
He acquiesced at once when she suggested separate bed-
rooms.

He longed for passionate sex again and took a mistress who worked as a TV producer. She was pretty, knew
her way around in bed, and he was comforted. As long
as he had her, he could put up with his wife. He promised he would take good care of his mistress in his will,
but like so many rich men with good intentions toward
their mistresses, he never got around to including her in
his will; he probably never intended to.

During his lifetime, he bought his mistress a townhouse, which she sold before the property explosion sent
prices sky high. She invested the hundred and fifty
thousand dollars she received for the house in a television series and lost it all. If she had waited, she could
have made half a million dollars and been comfortable
for the rest of her life. She has been ill, but she is too
kind ever to become bitter. "I just wish that I had pushed
him into a divorce when he wanted to marry me," she
told me. "But I never insisted, because his wife threatened she would commit suicide as his first wife had done,
and he could not have taken that."

It sounded familiar. I had not insisted on a divorce
when I was in love with Scott Fitzgerald. Zelda had not
known of my existence. We were very careful to keep it
from her. We did not want her to feel abandoned. If I
had insisted, he would have divorced her, because he
needed me very much.

If you love the man and you know you can make him
happier, insist on the divorce. But I guess if I had to
do it all over again, I would not push Scott. When you
love, that is all that matters—at the time, anyway.

"We all make mistakes," I told my friend, which was
meager comfort. It is a mistake to rely on the promise of
a married man. Women who give themselves in return
for a promissory note are fools.

The lady in white switched to black soon after the marriage. Black went better with her blond hair. She became interested in women's liberation and made speeches all over the country for the cause. Her husband was a male chauvinist, and he grew to detest the woman who had upset his personal life so drastically.

They lived apart in the last years of their marriage; she bought a large house in California, a place her husband never visited. She saw him again only when he died and was in an open coffin at Campbell's on Madison Avenue.

As the lovely widow in voluminous black veils, she was the chief attraction at the funeral. He provided well for her, knowing that in New York a widow was entitled to half of her husband's estate. The rest went to his daughters. There were millions for them all, except for the mistress who had given him happiness in his last years.

After his death the widow bought a chateau in the Loire country to which she retires in the summer. In the spring and fall she occupies her husband's magnificent apartment on Central Park South, from which his first wife fell to her death. She is respected by all who don't know her well, and every now and then I see her name heading a glamorous charity. Her opinion is always being sought. She is considered an authority on everything and is still a loud champion of women's liberation.

I wonder whether I could have maneuvered such a man into marriage. I would have to be more calculating than I am, and to love sex and the man less. When you are carried away by love and your physical desires, you don't think of money or position. You just want the man, and you want sex with him. You want loving arms around you. You forget everything else, including the future. The widow has money and respect, but is she happy? With all that money, respect, and attention, I suppose she is as happy as she can ever be.

Well, that is one way of getting what you want from life—to be cold and calculating. Nor does it hurt to be original and make the most of your looks. It helps to dress with confident originality—it makes the man feel that he has found a treasure. *You must not be fat.* Men say they like a woman they can get hold of, but this is not true. The rich men mostly marry thin women who look like models.

With some men you must give all at the beginning, as the lady in white did, then be tantalizingly unavailable. You must rouse him at the start, or there will be no chase. Men who are used to getting what they want in business are intrigued when a woman they could knock down with a light push holds them off at will.

There are men who are flattered when a woman finds them so irresistible that they lie down for them the first time they are alone together. It's a gamble. You cast your sex on the bed and hope that you land a big prize.

In matters of the heart, women are more adventurous than men. They take on situations that would daunt a man who is not afraid of risking millions on a fast decision.

That poor little girl from St. Louis, Missouri—her father was a carpenter, she was a reporter. At the age of twenty-one, red-haired and sexy, she decided to emerge from her Midwestern environment and try her luck in New York. At a party in Greenwich, Connecticut, she met a sharp young press agent from whom I learned the details of her remarkable career with men.

"She was a swinger, a lovable screwball," he told me. "I drove her back to New York, and we went to bed. She'd as soon go to bed with you as kiss you. . . . Sooner.

"She went to bed with every man who took her out. They'd compare notes. She was a good lay, although she didn't look it. She had one of those aristocratic faces, a tall, stately figure, a sort of don't-touch-me look that disappeared as soon as she was alone with a man.

"She had lost weight by the time I met her, and was working as a model. She didn't earn much. Hardly able to get by on what she made, she lived in a walk-up in Greenwich Village, between Sixth and Seventh avenues— one room in a dingy building. She was a girl on the town, out every night with a different man; she was everybody's girl, you know, the whore with a heart of gold, except that she did it for nothing. She liked sex, and there were never any strings or demands."

His nasal twang softened. "I decided to help her. I tagged her the 'St. Louis Heiress,' although she did not have a dime to her name, not even a cent. Columnists are very gullible; they have to be, to fill up all that white space. I introduced her to all the society columnists, who described her to their readers as the 'St. Louis Heiress.'

"She—Sally Ann—married the son of an important Broadway producer. Mama disapproved; she did not come across, as expected, with the money for their support, and they divorced, all very friendly.

"We had to do something about her, had to fix her up with someone who could take care of her. There was this rich man in New York. He was fat and good-natured. Everyone was always saying, 'Gee we've got to fix up Stinky with a girl.' We decided the girl was Sally Ann.

"They went to bed on the first date and married a week later. (If you are good in the hay, as we used to say, the man will hate to let you go.) He was not used to working, but he took over a real estate agency in Westport. They lived in a twenty-eight-room house, had five children in ten years, and then moved to San Francisco and were reasonably happy.

"They were quite social, and Sally Ann, who was gay and outgoing, became friendly with the woman who ran the experimental theater in San Francisco.

"One day she casually told Sally, 'A producer in Hollywood is looking for a girl with your physical proportions—tall and beautiful—for a picture he is making. I think you'd be right for the part. It means going to Hollywood for a test.' "

Sally Ann was hesitant. She had a good life, she was confortably well-off, and she had never acted in her life. She discussed it with her husband, who thought it would be fun for her to go to Hollywood and take the test.

"I'll be back in a few days," she promised, kissing him and the children good-bye. The producer of the film, one of the leading oilmen in America, who was making films as a hobby, flipped at first sight of this tall, healthy beauty. His marriage to a leading film actress had been going awry for some time.

Naturally Sally Ann went to bed with him the first time he took her to dinner. Afterward, holding her tightly in his arms, he asked her to marry him. Sally Ann almost passed out with surprise and pleasure. He was not only a multimillionaire, but he possessed one of the proudest names in America. He was a ——. (Can you guess?) It cost him three million dollars to get his divorce. But having sex with this woman who knew so much about making love—cunnilingus, fellatio, everything—he reckoned it was worth it.

Sally Ann returned to San Francisco to inform her shocked husband that she wanted a divorce. No one knows whether money changed hands, but his resistance soon melted, and Sally Ann promised they would always be good friends.

A few minutes after the multimillionaire was granted his divorce, he married the former reporter from St. Louis. After marriage, Sally Ann, who had been every man's girl, behaved with the utmost propriety. Her behavior was impeccable. In the twelve years of their marriage there has never been a word of gossip. She handles herself with dignity, she is gracious, almost royal. Without any previous training, Sally Ann plays her role in society with the expertise of a Queen Elizabeth.

After marrying well, some former trollops mess things up by allowing their promiscuity to get the better of them. They have careless assignations with other men and are usually caught in the act. But Sally Ann, who, if she were to coast without sex for the rest of her life, would still be ahead of the game, has been completely faithful.

She is satisfied with her position in society; she enjoys the clothes, the jewels, the limousines, the travel, the stately mansions, and her unassailable position in the most exclusive society in the United States and the world. It would be comforting to less successful women if I could report that her husband is a bore. But he is not. He is attractive, amusing, intelligent, and very happy with his wife, who makes him a king because she looks and behaves like a queen.

The real queens and princesses sometimes look like washerwomen, while the women who started life in poor circumstances and married giants of industry or society look like royalty. To reach the goals they set for themselves early in life, they must have energy, ambition, and cleverness.

A once-famous film actress possessed all three, and still does. She was born in Hawaii in poor circumstances. Her mother was Oriental, her father an underpaid American—"chi-chis," the British in Asia call the children of mixed parentage. She worked as a salesgirl.

An ex-officer in the Indian army met her in Malaya when she was eighteen years old. "She was very beautiful, exotic-looking, with her high forehead, slanting eyes, and exquisite face," Terence told me. She had a different name then, a less exotic one. He liked her very much, he confessed, but it was rare for a British officer to get entangled with a local product, and if you did, you certainly never married her. Nonetheless, he had a proprietary interest in her subsequent success. He has followed her career in the newspapers and is proud of having known her at the very beginning, when she was just a pretty girl who was sometimes invited to the officers' mess. He was the only person who saw her off when she left for Paris. "You're a fool to leave," he told her. "You'll never be successful there." "Wait and see," she said with a confident toss of her dark head.

It was impossible then to foresee her present position as a glamorous international hostess. British royalty are frequent guests at her home in Monte Carlo, where she reigns over a beautiful palace of marble.

Once arrived in Paris, she obtained a job in the Folies Bergere which was very popular with Americans in Paris and the well-known people of films and the theater. A famous European producer was a guest one evening. He was captivated by the camellialike face and signed her for a small role in a period picture he was planning with a top male star.

After sleeping with the girl, he decided that she could play a leading role. When the film was released, she was hailed as a star. A famed Hollywood producer signed her to a long-term contract.

I met her shortly before the release of the picture. I would guess she was then in her early twenties. It was on the tennis court of a mutual friend. While the rest of us were running around, sweating, and looking disheveled, Miss Chi-chi sat daintily in the shade of a large striped umbrella, cool and attractive.

The European producer was divorced by his wife, and it was a foregone conclusion that one day she would marry him. But first she would fall in love with a famed star in Hollywood, and become engaged to a powerful film executive there. After receiving some expensive presents she broke the engagement with the excuse that marriage would interfere with her career, a statement I never believed. Certainly Norma Shearer's career reached new heights after she became Mrs. Irving Thalberg when he was head of production at MGM.

The reason the girl broke her engagement to the producer was not that he was homely and thirty odd years older than she, but that she had fallen in love with a debonair French nobody who wanted to be an actor and was making a living as a wine taster. He reminded her of the smart British officer she met in Malaya.

As a columnist, I was important to the career of the girl from Honolulu. She invited me to Sunday lunch at her house on the beach in San Clemente. The wine taster was acting as host, and the girl's adoring eyes followed him wherever he went. Other guests included the Fredric Marches and their children, and Douglas Fairbanks junior and senior, both unmarried at that time.

Through the actress, the wine taster met important producers and directors. One of them put him under contract, and he became a star in his own right. It was obvious to me from some of his remarks that he had no intention of marrying the girl who had helped him so much. When I questioned him, he replied, "What, risk being father to a group of yellow children?" For a wife he chose a society girl with an aristocratic French pedigree. The actress went back to Paris and married the European producer.

Her supreme confidence under the gentle exterior always amazed me. There was steel and ruthless calculation under the soft smile. She lived with her knight in Paris, a charming hostess for their beautiful house in the Bois de Boulogne. I visited them, and she showed me around, proudly pointing out the masterpieces on the walls and the exquisite antique furniture.

The can-can dancer had grown with the job. You could not see any differences between her and the duchesses she invited to her elegant dinner parties. But I noticed the lines of boredom around her pretty mouth. Soon after, she and the producer were divorced. He gave her a munificent financial settlement. After his death she kept the expensive *objets d'art,* the jewels, and the antiques, all of which she had removed at the time of the divorce.

I sometimes wondered whether she was as passionate as she looked. Could anyone as clear-headed as she was be truly dedicated to sex? Passion is a full-time career and can lead you astray, as I know. It was more the promise of sexual eroticism on her half-American, half-Oriental face. She looked like a piece of delicate porcelain, with sympathy flowing from her almond-shaped eyes. When her acting career was over, she married one of the richest men in America. He is nothing to look at —squat and plump—but he allows her complete freedom. She became a nymphomaniac. I put it in the past tense, because she is now in her sixties, and while she is slender and unlined—thanks to face lifts and daily massage—and could pass for forty-three, the bones of a woman in her sixties are inclined to creak a bit. There was a succession of one-night stands, and a lengthier affair with a young, virile Hollywood dancer. She bought him a house, which he refused to return when he left her. She has everything, even children, which she did not want and could not have until it was too late, and she plays her role of mother to her adopted sons and daughter as efficiently as she worked at being a movie star, and is as proud of them as she is of her social reputation. Her success is not an accident. It happened because of single-mindedness of purpose. It was not an easy road from her poor beginnings in Hawaii, but the chi-chi, laughing gaily all the way to the top echelons of society, made it seem easy.

Last year there was a fashionable wedding on the East Coast that no one thought could happen. Both parties were already married when they met at the Bel Air home of a film tycoon. The woman is in her mid-forties, strong, capable, but feminine and helpless-looking. The man is sixty-two. He is fabulously wealthy, worth at least sixty million dollars. Sitting next to him at dinner, the lady turned on her fascination at top heat. He did not have a chance to escape. Nor did he want to.

The woman has had a remarkable life. During the Second World War she was in a concentration camp in Poland. She always wears heavy necklaces to hide the scar on her throat. After the war she went to Italy, where she was supported in great style by a succession of rich men. They say she married one of them. She was wealthy in her own right when she arrived in Hollywood, and soon after married a well-known film producer.

She invited me for a drink at her charming house in the best section of Beverly Hills. I found several other important columnists there. She enjoyed good publicity and was always pleasant to the writers, who presented her in glowing terms to their readers.

Most of the money accumulated by the producer from his good films was dissipated in the lavish parties given by his gregarious wife. She sometimes took over the fashionable Bistro restaurant in Beverly Hills to entertain the important people who visited Hollywood. The producer lost his golden touch at the box office, and what with taking care of his ailing ex-wife and their child, he found himself in financial difficulties. The wife paid the mortgage on their expensive home, on condition that it was transferred to her name.

They had seemed happy, but with his money gone and his virility a question mark in the Beverly Hills boudoirs, his wife was ready for a change. She planned to ditch her husband and to live with the millionaire, playing the role of a woman who needed protection, but with the understanding that both she and the millionaire would obtain divorces, then marry. The lady from Poland had expected her husband to divorce her, but he was stubborn. After much weeping, arguing, and pleading, he agreed to free her, on one condition—that she would deed back the house to him. She fought like a lioness defending her cub. She was a woman who got; the only things she ever gave were parties and presents to useful people. She was amazed that her kind, gentle husband could be so obstinate, but she had to give him the house, which today is worth a quarter of a million dollars, perhaps more.

The wedding was attended by two hundred recognizable names in society and the arts, and, of course, members of the press. Everyone remarked how sweet and demure she looked. I knew her too well to be fooled. She reminds me of Jackie Onassis, who has always wanted to be among the richest, most beautiful people. The former inmate of a concentration camp can now afford everything her calculating heart desires.

As for Jackie, with her lisping, babyish voice and a permanent "Please help me" expression on her face, *she* wanted the money, and *Ari* wanted the cachet of capturing the most-publicized woman in the world. They had known each other before John Kennedy became President. He, too, had been a guest on Ari's yacht. The gossips said that Onassis was after Jackie's sister, Princess Lee Radziwill. The rumors were right. But after the assassination of President Kennedy he wanted Jackie, who wanted the money. Underneath that woebegone, wide smile, Mrs. Onassis is made of steel, a necessary ingredient for a lady to get the man and money she wants.

John Lennon's wife Yoko Ono, masterminds every move John makes; this, more than anything else, broke up the Beatles. Outwardly, Yoko is meek, mild, and fluttery. Did you see her on that *Dick Cavett Show?* She behaved as though a million yen could melt in her humble mouth. Her seeming humility captured Mr. Lennon, who still doesn't realize that under her kimono, his wife is wearing the pants.

For some light relief, how did Zsa Zsa Gabor hook Conrad Hilton, who, as you know, has all those lovely hotels? Zsa Zsa, who was younger then, but just as sharp as she is today, refused to go to bed with Connie unless and until he married her! He had never met such a virtuous lady as Zsa Zsa. This was a long time ago, when men prized virtue. Zsa Zsa is a bad actress, but in real life her performances merit a triple A. Since their divorce two decades ago, Hilton has not had the nerve to marry again. He is still good-looking, although now in his eighties, and is still pursued by adoring, not-so-clever women.

If you wish to marry a billionaire, you must often settle for an old man. Recently, a famed film actress of the 1940's and 1950's married a multimillionaire almost old enough to be her father. The secret marriage took place in Nevada, but just to be sure of him, she insisted on a second ceremony in California, where they have that lovely fifty-fifty property settlement when you divorce.

She had been married twice before, the first time to a cameraman whom she soon left to marry a powerful film promoter. Unfortunately, her second husband lost most of the money earned by his early excellent films, so that his widow was in poor financial shape when he died. This is one of the pitfalls of marrying a rich man when you are not in love with him. He might lose his money.

With new stars coming up, the delicate-looking, seemingly vague actress was no longer in demand for films.

Luckily the current husband has not seen a movie for twenty years. To him she is still a glamorous star. What a break for her that he was still star-struck!

How had she nabbed him? Proximity—a valuable catalyst in getting a man. They each had a home in Santa Monica—the house was the one possession left from her previous marriage. Now they share a magnificent beach home in California and a beautiful town house in New York City. Her money troubles are over. She has always seemed timid, but never sexy, even when she was younger. It is my guess that she and her rich new husband are cuddling more than copulating. That is what she wanted, and that is what she got. It could not have happened if she had revealed her true powerful, determined self.

I am reminded of the elderly man who recently married an attractive widow who had been married twice previously. Her first husband was the son of a powerful statesman. Her second was rich and famous. It is not an accident that her husbands have all been important men. She has always been a cool customer who, beneath her helpless, charming facade, pursues what she wants relentlessly; and what she has always wanted are power and money.

Her present husband is richer and more important than her previous spouses put together. The marriage seemed sudden, but they have known each other for a long time. During the Second World War he was in London on an important mission. They met at that time. He was married then and would not consider divorcing his wife, who died recently. It was the go signal for the iron lady, who was then a widow.

She called on him, ostensibly to sympathize over his sad loss. A few visits later, he asked her to marry him. Timing, like proximity, is an important key in the marriage door. Or the moral in this instance could be: "Never give up."

My own chief problem has been that I am not disciplined enough to wait for what I want. I want it *now.*

Impatience can lose you a good contract or a good husband.

Another of my problems has been that I prefer to spend my own money. I am uncomfortable when I ask for money even when the man is my husband. Ever since I have earned a good income I have found it delightful to be extravagant. It is my own money, I have worked hard for it, and I can spend it how I like. No asking a man, even my husband, for money to buy this or that. No explaining how I spent the money. When I gave up my column for a while after my second marriage, I had to ask my husband for money. "But I gave you five pounds yesterday," he sighed. "What did you do with it?" "Oh, taxis, Elizabeth Arden," I replied with growing irritation. I had two children with him, for which I will be eternally grateful, but I yearned to be independent again, and maneuvered my column back so I was able to pay all the bills for their support and did not ask anything from my husband. I acceded at once to his demand for a divorce when he wanted to marry another woman.

But when I was on the open market again, like every single woman, I was looking for another husband. I met a trim millionaire of sixty on the Super Chief to California. I had recently returned from England after the divorce—my husband had provided the evidence when a detective he had hired to shadow me had produced nothing incriminating, which was a miracle, or else he was a bad detective.

I was on my way back to California in 1944 to rejoin my baby daughter. The millionaire was in the Super Chief with his very plump European wife, whom he had married when he was eighteen and she in her early twenties. She was a despotic Russian and had nagged him into success. Her personality was overpowering, and he was scared of her. When she heard that I had returned from England to be with my child, she liked me. She was a mother of eight herself, and money and maternity were her ruling passions. As for her husband, she passionately masterminded every move he made, in business and in private life.

Martin owned several prosperous breweries. I knew him slightly, having said hello to him at some cocktail parties. We all dined together on the train, and afterward in Beverly Hills. Whenever I was in Washington, they usually gave a dinner party for me in their twenty-two-room townhouse in Georgetown.

I did not care for the wife too much; she was too domineering. It was a man's place to rule; I have always believed this, in spite of my experience with my first husband. A woman can get whatever she wants by her God-given trickery, but the man should have the cachet of king.

I liked Martin except for his fear of his wife. He was powerful in his own world, and I usually reacted favorably to a powerful man. We met by accident one day on Fifth Avenue; he was openly delighted, and asked me to lunch with him the next day. I suggested 21. I realized he was careful with his money when he chided me for leaving most of the spinach on my plate. I always leave vegetables to the end, and if I am not hungry, they remain on the plate. How could such a rich man be concerned whether I ate my spinach? Rich men were all the same, and I wondered why I bothered with them. But I did. The idea of getting my hands on all that money has always fascinated me—as long as it is out of reach. When it is mine for the taking, the salt loses its savor.

I met another rich man, Vernon, at about the same time—he was in oil in Texas and held a large number of shares in the Rexall Drug Company. On the same day, I received a package from each millionaire. Two small boxes. Jewelry? No. The Washington millionaire had been passing his favorite cake shop and could not resist, he wrote, sending me a slice of his favorite cake. The Texas millionaire's box contained a new type of pill for losing weight—they were being put out by Rexall. I ate the cake and took the pills, hoping one would counteract the other.

On another journey to California, Martin was on the same train. There were mutual exclamations of joy as he passed the open door of my bedroom. We dined together, and afterward he returned with me to my bedroom, where the bed had been made up during my absence.

Motion of any kind, especially in a train or boat, always makes me feel sexy. We went to bed, and for such a skinny miser, he was a wonderful lover—considerate and strong. He could have kept on for days. His wife had trained him to wait for her half-dozen orgasms before allowing him to come.

I enjoyed the long train ride. I was so relaxed and happy that I believed I was in love with him. After this, Martin found many excuses to come to California. "I love you," he told me. "I want to marry you." What about his wife? Would he dare to ask for a divorce? I did not mention it, as I was sure he would not.

But he wanted to do something for me. "Can I be a godfather to your son? I have fourteen godchildren already; one more won't make any difference." And because he liked to boast, he added, "I send them all one hundred dollars every Christmas. Fourteen hundred dollars. Now it will be fifteen hundred." Martin was sorry for me, he said, bringing up two children without a husband to help me.

On Christmas my son received a check for one hundred dollars. After three years, my daughter, who was three years older and very bright—she was an incipient tricky woman—said to me, "Mommy, I'd like Martin to be my godfather too." She did not have to explain that she too wanted the hundred dollars. "Well," I said, "you'd better ask him; I don't think *I* should, he'll think we are after his money." I did not quite wink at my daughter.

Martin was leaving for New York, and I gently nudged my daughter under the table and whispered, "Ask him." Hesitantly the child said, under her breath, "Will you be my godfather too?" He was flattered by the request. "If your mother tells me at Christmas that you have been a good girl," he said, "then I will be your godfather too."

A few days before Christmas, two envelopes arrived, one addressed to my son, the other to my daughter. They could barely sit still while I opened them. There was a check in each one—for fifty dollars! She had the grace to give it to her brother.

One day I received a telephone call from Florida. Martin's wife had suffered a serious stroke. She was always losing her temper, and with her high blood pressure and weight, she was lucky not to die right away.

"I hope we can be married soon," said Martin, trying to sound glad and sad at the same time. He somehow managed it. The wife lingered for another year, during which time I realized I could never marry him. When I told him I was going to Zurich to write about the struggle for women's suffrage, he asked if he could meet me there. He wants a free ride, I thought, and vowed I would make him buy me a present.

"You can come if you buy me a watch," I said airily. I was somewhat embarrassed asking for a present, but he was so eager to see me in Europe that he agreed at once. "Sure, I'll buy you a watch." Zurich. After unpacking, I said, "All right, let's get the watch." Instinct warned me it might be a struggle. "Well"—he hesitated—"I'm not sure I am going to buy you a watch." "You are the stingiest man I have ever known," I exploded. "I'll tell you something; I don't *want* you to buy me a watch. I already have a watch. I wouldn't take a watch from you if it was the last watch in the world. You are a miser. Go away." "I was only kidding," he said weakly. "Come on, let's go to the shop." He had to persuade me. As a digger for diamonds at this stage in my life, I was a flop.

The agreeable Swiss salesman brought out a tray of watches. The one I chose was the smallest, but it was the most expensive they had. "I'll get this man to spend some of his millions," I vowed silently. I almost threw the watch in his face when he started bargaining with the salesman.

I have never bargained, except when I buy a house. But to bargain for a watch that was worth every cent of the thousand-dollar price! I took the salesman aside and whispered, "Don't yield."

It has been my experience that men who are not rich

are the most generous. The first fur coat I ever had was a birthday present from Scott Fitzgerald, who was broke. My second husband gave me the minks for my first mink coat. I bought my subsequent fur coats myself and was happy to be able to afford them. When I bought my daughter a mink coat, this gave me even more pleasure. Who needs to be liberated? It is because I am a woman that I have been able to earn as much as I have.

Miserliness is the least attractive vice, and while outwardly Martin made a great show of his philanthropies, he usually spent money only when it could be deducted from his income tax. And he rarely paid taxes at all. His accountant had so contrived his income that he lived on an expense account and received no visible taxable income.

After his wife's death, he invited me and my children to stay with him in the big town house in Georgetown. He met us at the airport in the cheap car he had borrowed from his daughter—he had several grown-up children and a dozen grandchildren, and he wore them like a badge of virility. I looked around for a porter to carry the bags. "We don't need one," he said vigorously, picking up a suitcase in each hand and giving the smaller ones to the children and me. He was critical of my children, telling me, "When I am their father, I will make them behave." "You will never be their father," I said under my breath.

During our brief visit to the stingy millionaire's home my children slept in a room adorned with prints featuring several naked, maternal women. They were amused, and my son raised an imaginary glass to the ladies and said, "Bottoms up!" We roared with laughter, and Martin came to see what was the joke. We told him, and he managed a vinegary smile.

The next day I gathered up my children and left the town house, following a fierce quarrel with Martin whom I now thoroughly disliked. My children detested him, and I could never marry a man unless my children approved.

Martin was now fair game for every unmarried woman in Washington. He redid his home in sparse Scandinavian style, always looking over his shoulder to be sure his wife would not appear and strike him dead at such wanton waste of money.

I continued to see him when I came to Washington. He had a marvelous cook, and the food was reason enough to visit him. I was still trying to convince myself that I could love him and enjoy the comfortable life I would have as his wife. Actually, I lived better than he did. I had a good cook in California, a big house, a garden with lemon, orange, and fig trees, a good bed to sleep in, and I was free to go where I pleased. As the millionaire's wife, I would have suffocated.

He gave me a cocktail party on September 15, 1964, ostensibly for my birthday and for a woman friend of mine who was also a Virgo. The friend invited a recently widowed Canadian-born beauty winner. She was blond with a fair complexion, tall, slender, and elegantly dressed. Her late husband had been planning to make a film in the chateau country in France. She brought a French duke and his duchess to the party.

I could see that Martin was impressed with the importance of the French couple and the looks of the blond woman. He called her the next day and asked if he could take her to dinner. She was living with her old mother and her old dog in a tiny apartment in an unfashionable neighborhood. When he took her home, he asked if he could come in for a nightcap. She was safe because her mother was there, although asleep in the bedroom they shared. "No," she said gently but firmly. "I never allow men to come into my home at night." He was very impressed with her virtue. When I was safely back in California, he assiduously courted the beautiful widow.

There were two obstacles to marrying her. Her old mother, who bored him, and her old dog, whom he detested. She was furious when she caught him kicking the dog, and with a less impoverished lady the romance would have terminated there and then. But she was determined to capture this eligible bachelor.

He was thirty years older than she was, wizened, and

obnoxiously boastful about his money. He sometimes startled dinner guests by declaring, "I want to give away some money," and everyone became tense, wondering how they could get it. Marriage with Martin would solve all her problems. But she knew that to get him, her mother and her dog would have to go. She put her mother in an old ladies' home; and her dog—she adored her dog— was placed in a kennel nearby so she could visit him without her rich admirer's knowledge.

Soon afterward I received a cable from the miserly millionaire to say he had married the poor widow. Within a month of the marriage, the mother was extracted from the old ladies home to live with them in the town house—with so many rooms, surely one could be spared for her old mother—and the dog was reinstated. Her husband yielded, but once I saw him kicking the dog when his wife was not looking. His new bride is just as domineering as the first had been, although much younger and prettier. She is a hypochondriac, but when she is up and about he is proud to be seen with her and tells his acquaintances that he makes love to her three times a week. "Not bad for a man who will be seventy-five next birthday," he boasts.

If his wife knows about this, she takes no notice. She is clever and glad to be the wife of one of the richest men in Washington. From the looks of her—although you never know with pale, thin women—she does not seem too passionate. At last report they were still happy, and, miraculously, the former miser was spending some of his millions on her, as though money would soon be out of style. He bought her a house with an indoor swimming pool in New York State—grandchildren are not invited, lest they pee in the pool—and another house in California, a sable coat, and jewels by the bushel. The woman had set a high price on herself, and her husband still believes she had condescended to marry him.

That is another way to get a rich husband by really trying very hard—remove the obstacles, act regally, have important friends, and don't give in to him on the first date. But it would never be my way. If I like the man very much, the relationship is not complete unless we go to bed. There was always a man in my life, and I could never play games with him, except games in bed. The White Lady used the other method of capturing her prey—dazzling him, then withholding herself until and unless he would marry her. Which is the best method? They all work. Study the man, and you will know which method is best.

When Elizabeth Taylor is after a man, she pursues him relentlessly. I have known her since she was twelve, when Mickey Rooney was making sheep's eyes at her on the set of *National Velvet*. Mickey was a big star then, and Elizabeth was aware of his potential, but she was an innocent little thing, and besides, Mama was always around.

Her interest in sex started early, even by today's precocious standards. At fifteen her figure was exquisite, and I can still see Orson Welles' drool of approval as she entered the commissary at MGM wearing a red sweater and a short navy skirt that showed every curve of her rounded young body. Elizabeth was a little princess adored by everyone who knew her. The delicious figure and beautiful violet eyes were irresistible.

Although closely guarded by her mother, she managed at the age of seventeen to get engaged to young Ed Pauley, whose family was extremely rich. She stayed with them on their yacht off the Florida coast, and the gossip columns were abuzz. Walter Winchell mentioned her every day in his column and titled her "The Most Beautiful Girl in America," which she was. When she married Pauley, she would give up her career, it was announced. But Elizabeth had second thoughts. She kept the career and gave up Pauley. Soon she was wearing a tiny gold football, signifying that she was almost engaged to Glenn Davis, the famed West Point football player. She introduced him shyly to me at Ciro's one evening. He was stopping in Hollywood for a few days on the way to Korea. He would return in two years to marry her, they told me.

But Elizabeth was impatient, for freedom from her mother, for sexual experience, and when Nicky Hilton, son of millionaire Conrad Hilton, visited her on the set of *A Place in the Sun* at Paramount, he was as good as married to her.

The glamorous wedding at the Church of the Good Shepherd in Beverly Hills was abloom with every kind of white flower—for purity, I thought, an unexpected tear in my eye. Elizabeth was taking instruction in the Catholic Church—she always joins the faith of the man she loves. She became Jewish when she married Eddie Fisher, or was it Mike Todd? When Elizabeth is in love with a man, she gives everything she has—her devotion, her body, her mind, and her soul. She wants to be exactly like the man she marries, including drinking, swearing, and religion. As Richard Burton is not Jewish, I doubt whether Elizabeth still is. Elizabeth is totally feminine. But when she wants a man, she uses every trick in the book. Nothing can stop her from getting him. Who would have thought she could ever disentangle Eddie Fisher from the bosom of her best friend and twice bridesmaid, Debbie Reynolds, and their two children, whom Eddie adored. He was completely dazzled by Elizabeth. He was thrilled that such a beautiful girl should want him so desperately that she was prepared to risk her career by taking him from dear little Girl Scout Debbie.

It was brazen theft, and while there were some harsh words hurled about, there was also admiration for a girl who could pull off such a difficult coup without batting a repentant eyelash.

Her career bloomed, but Elizabeth became ill. When she was starring in *Suddenly, Last Summer* in London, she burst into tears and told the director, Joseph Mankiewicz, that she had made a dreadful blunder, meaning her marriage to Eddie.

Except for the partial hysterectomy of two years ago, Elizabeth has not had one day of illness since her marriage with Richard Burton. And who could have prophesied that she could pry Richard loose from his Sybil?

"What, divorce my wife to marry Elizabeth?" he said in reply to my question at the height of the furor in Rome. "Never!" he roared.

Richard had not reckoned with Elizabeth's singleness of purpose. She wanted him, and would admit of no obstacles. In one of her stories about their relationship Elizabeth stated that she and Richard decided he could not break up his marriage, and they parted. She went to her home in Switzerland, and he went to his home in Switzerland. Well, Switzerland is a small country, and leaving a man after you have roused him to a mad passion for you is sometimes the best way to get him. Richard stated recently, "Elizabeth is sometimes obstinate, but in the end she always yields and does it my way. She knows I am her master." This is the way to hold him.

Mia Farrow did not have a chance with Frank Sinatra until she left him, saying it was the best way, that because of his family—Mia was younger than his oldest daughter—they could never marry. She stayed with her good friends Mr. and Mrs. Richard Burton in Rome, where they were co-starring in *The Taming of the Shrew*.

"Stay here," Elizabeth advised her. "You see, he will come to you." Nothing happened, and Mia returned disconsolately to Hollywood, where Sinatra immediately called her and proposed.

Elizabeth does not usually play a waiting game. She chased Michael Wilding all over Europe when he was on the verge of asking Marlene Dietrich to divorce Rudolf Seiber to marry him. But what could the poor man do when Elizabeth was on his doorstep, announcing to the press that she had come to marry him?

You can see there are no absolute rules on how to capture an elusive man. Rita Hayworth played it silent and cool, and Aly Khan could not rest until he made her his wife.

He had been in love with Gene Tierney before Rita. "Gene is the only woman who has never bored me," he told me. Gene believed they would marry, or she would never have gone to Mexico when he cabled her to come. If she had remained in Hollywood, he would have gone there to meet her, and they might have married. Gene was a contained lady, and when it was all over she suffered a breakdown.

Rita's face promised Aly a wild sexuality, so he married her, and when the wildness became commonplace, he realized that she bored him. The thought communicated itself to Rita, and she left. She is not rich, but she will never starve. She had her cake but did not digest it. She made the mistake of giving up her career to be a tongue-tied wife. Her fame had attracted this connoisseur of women—her fame, her silent glamour, and the sexuality that millions of people all over the world found so exciting. When she became an ordinary woman, he lost interest.

So, the tongue-tied Rita did nothing to get Aly. Elizabeth did everything to get her men. Mia ran away. They were all successful. But the most successful method, in my opinion, is just to want the man. Send that thought into the atmosphere, and you will get him. Men are like children, as I have said before. I can't say it too often. Once you realize this, you can lead them by the nose—anywhere.

Any woman can get a proposal from a man if she wants him enough. The dear simpletons are so flattered. But you must want him, and never doubt the eventual outcome. I've seen this happen over and over again. Want him, put your blinders on so that you cannot be distracted, pursue him relentlessly in your own way, and he is all yours. Men the stronger sex indeed! The strongest, most intelligent man is like clay in the hands of the weakest, most stupid woman.

A pretty starlet proved this with a well-known British film producer in London. When I first met him he was happily married with four children. At that time he was an agent and should have stayed one, because as a producer he gave a role to a sexy, inexperienced actress, with whom he fell madly in love.

The next thing I knew, she was starring in his new production and he had left his four children and his wife, who agreed to divorce him so that he could marry his pretty discovery. I would see them in the smart places in London, holding hands, looking passionately into each other's eyes.

The last time I lunched with him in London he dropped me off in his car at my home. Suddenly he pulled up his shirt and showed me two enormous scars across his stomach. "Ulcers," he said bitterly. "I left my family for that bitch, and she left me for that black actor. That silly blond ruined my life."

I was discussing this sad story with a member of the Wives' Union in England, and when I commented that I felt sorry for the man, she snorted indignantly, "He got what he gave. He left his wife, and then the girl left him. Serves him right." The famous black star has not yet married the silly little actress. Perhaps he does not want a brood of white children. Or perhaps she has not tried hard enough.

Say what you like, marriage is still a girl's best friend—no matter what the girls who are living with men without a wedding ring will tell you.

There are so many ways to lead a man to the altar. Just choose the method to fit the man, and *think positive.*

CHAPTER 9

Six of One...

In early June 1941, I suddenly realized that no one had
wanted to marry me lately. Was I slipping? I was lonely
and I deliberately set out to make men want to marry me.
Within a year, six men were begging to buy me a wedding ring. How did I do it? Simple. I *wanted* men to
want to marry me. I put out all my sex antennae and
caught not only proposals of marriage, but propositions
from men who did not ordinarily fancy me.

When I had arrived in New York several years previously, in 1933, I believed I was experienced in the art
of love. My naïveté was an asset, especially in America,
where men retained the myth of protecting their women.

I settled into an apartment in the East Fifties. Within
a week I landed the two jobs on New York newspapers.
My total capital had been one hundred pounds. The fare
money took fifty-five pounds, and with only forty-five
in hand I had to earn money quickly. I was lucky with
my assignments; scoops fell into my lap—I forced my
way into situations where more experienced reporters
feared to tread. I had the energy of desperation.

At first I was lonely in America. I missed the friends
I had made in London after leaving the stage. The men
who had been to Eton and Oxford, the girls to smart
finishing schools in Paris and Lausanne. I had ice-skated

with them at the International Sportsmen's Club and rid-
den with them in Rotten Row and Richmond Park and
in the country. I had played tennis and squash with
them. There were Tom and Randolph and Dennis and
Jock and Ian and his wife; the Honorable Jack; the
Honorable Bill; Buster; and David, who was a viscount;
and Edward, who was an earl; Christopher, who was
married to the daughter of a Scottish duke; and Paddy,
who had captained the cricket team at Eton; and some
high-born journalists who wrote society columns.

When an acquaintance went with her family to Grindelwald for two weeks, I went with them and persuaded
the parents to allow her to accompany me to St. Moritz,
where the Honorable Jack and his nephew, the Honorable
Tom, were waiting to give us a good time. The Honorable
Jack was asexual. He was charming to all the ladies and
friendly with the men, but he had never had a girl
friend, to anyone's recent knowledge. He had been married to a German princess before the First World War,
but she had divorced him before the Armistice. He was
in his fifties and an excellent skater. He taught me my
threes and eights and how to waltz if I held on very
tightly to his arm.

The Honorable Jack had introduced me to his nephew,
the Honorable Tom, who had introduced me to Randolph Churchill, as good-looking as Tom. With blond
hair, blue eyes, and regular features, Tom was like a
Saxon lord. I danced at the Palace Hotel with the Honorable William—his mother was a famous American-born
peeress. He was a good dancer but otherwise rather limp.
He took me back to Suvretta House in a closed sleigh
and was silent all the way. The high altitude had given
me an excruciating toothache, and I longed to be alone
to use the remedy I had bought earlier from the chemist.

I undressed and wrapped my head tightly in a
big handkerchief with a lump of claylike substance cling-
ing to my jaw, according to the chemist's instructions. I
was beginning to doze when the Honorable William
stormed into my bedroom and tried to rape me. In the
struggle I managed to wrench off the handkerchief and

the clay. It was bad enough that he thought he could burst into my bedroom, but to see me with my head tied up after I had looked so glamorous at the dance. I managed to hiss, "If you don't go, I'll scream at the top of my voice." He fled.

I felt pleasantly virtuous at having repulsed the Honorable William, and told the story of his attempted rape with a great show of indignation to my friends, who did not like William. Very few people did.

When I liked a man but did not want an affair with him, I had the old problem which all women have—how to keep him interested without having to go to bed with him. I often used the excuse of my period. "What a pity, I'd love to but I can't." Or, after my marriage was in the open, I stalled, "I'd love to, but my husband is suspicious; we'd better wait until he calms down." I enjoyed teasing a man until he could stand it no longer. But I resented his assumption—after I had driven him up the wall—that because he wanted me he could have me. The excitement was in making him want me. I can see myself, cheeks aflame, eyes promising everything, always, it seems in retrospect, in a state of heat. There was a name for a girl like me—cockteaser. I was on fire for sex most of my waking hours, and men knew it. I exuded an odor of sex more compelling than a mating call. I could have gone to bed with a different man every night had I wished. My life after I left the stage was a round of cocktail parties, lunches, dinners, movies, theaters, nightclubs. But I was careful of my reputation.

Through Bunny Tooth, who sold old masters in a Bond Street gallery, I met some of the fashionable writers and artists of the day. I liked to be with them, but they did not excite me sexually. They, however, would have liked to make love to me. I had become a perfectionist at small talk, although I became tongue-tied if the conversation took a serious turn. I was very pretty, and I didn't walk, I flew. They liked to have me around; I was decorative and very sweet, according to the general opinion. Older people always smiled at me while I danced or skated. I was so obviously enjoying myself.

And now I was in America with a whole new set of friends. Except for Janet, I did not care for the society of women. They were always talking about books I had never read, servants, recipes, children, or who was in love with whom, names I did not recognize.

My first meeting with Janet had not been auspicious. When we met at the Ritz, she was astonished to find five old-fashioned cocktails in front of me when she arrived with Jack. She was convinced I was an alcoholic. I can still see her amazement when she saw me take the cherry from each glass and send the drink away.

I was no longer lonely. I could relax with Janet; I did not have to be fascinating all the time. And it was fun talking about our men. I was more candid with Janet than I had ever been with a man. I could tell her about my longings for sex without ever shocking her. And I listened to Janet's outpourings of her own desires. Unlike most American women I was to meet, she gave her love freely. She was disappointed and unhappy when her lover went off with another woman, but that did not deter her eternal optimism that the next man would stay permanently. A decade later, one man did, and she married him.

I met exciting new male friends. Quentin Reynolds was back from Germany, where he had been on assignment for *Collier's* magazine. He had been smitten with an English writer, Margaret Lane, who had returned to London after working for the King Features Syndicate in New York. He was told that another English girl—Sheilah Graham—was on the scene, and he made a point of meeting me. He took me to the fights and hockey matches and introduced me to the top sports writers in New York. We went for a weekend to the home of the Gene Tunneys near Stamford, Connecticut. I met Deems Taylor, the composer, and Heywood Broun, Westbrook Pegler, and other writers who had homes nearby. I liked Quentin and his close friend John McClain, but neither appealed to me physically. Quentin frequently chided me for being in love with a married man, Charles, but at that time I was bewitched.

At the Brouns' swimming pool you could not swim unless you were naked. I had never stripped in daylight; I refused now, and was called a sissy by Quentin. Years later when Quentin was suing Pegler for calling him a coward in England during the war, Pegler tried to find me to prove that Quentin cavorted at the Brouns in the nude. I detested Pegler for his vitriolic attacks on Mrs. Eleanor Roosevelt, and stayed out of sight until the case was over. Quentin won, but it was a Pyrrhic victory. It ruined his health and broke up his marriage. The last time I saw him was at a first night in New York, shortly before his death. He was bloated and looked very ill.

In 1934 and 1935, I was enjoying life very much. I was again a part of a group, and popular with men. It was exciting dining out every night, going to the theater, and to the Stork Club, where Walter Winchell had his own room upstairs and where the debs came to dance, slouching around the small dance floor with their young men.

I missed Johnny, and when he wrote that he was lonely, I sent him a ticket to come for Christmas and the New Year. He slept in the single bed I bought especially for him. I was now used to sleeping alone, as I was restless in bed, especially after a late evening. I loved having Johnny with me. He met Janet and all my new friends. We rode in Central Park. Quentin took us to a hockey match at the Garden. Johnny loved New York, and he told me he would come back, but now I wanted to be free. I wanted a chance for a normal life with a man who would love, cherish, and support me. I was sorry when Johnny left for London to see some powerful steel men, he claimed. What a pity it was only a dream. But I knew that even if he could support me I could not live again with an impotent man.

But while the men I knew wanted to have affairs with me, not one of them asked me to divorce my husband in order to marry him. Was this because I had lazily accepted my position as a married woman and had not

tried to get a husband because I already had one? I was
out of the competition.

I took stock of my credits and liabilities. I was pretty
—beautiful, the men always said. My smile would melt
an iceberg, my husband believed. They all raved about
my complexion, my English advantage over American
women. The soft rain of my native land was like damp
cotton for preserving the skin. My constant state of
always expecting something wonderful to happen made
me fun to be with. I was the child you wanted to give
presents to, to see the instant smile of gratitude. Each
man felt that ultimately he would have me, and I fostered
that belief. At first I used the four-letter words so freely
uttered in very high—and very low—English circles. But
the American men were shocked, albeit excited, when I
said, "Fuck it!"

My debits—I must lose some weight. Baby fat, they
called it, but I was not a baby anymore. I must give
up the cakes and chocolate. I must do something about
my hair, thin it out, cut it short. I would have regular
facials at Elizabeth Arden and have my thick eyebrows
plucked.

I asked an admirer, Alex Perlberg, a millionaire realtor
whom I had met at an elegant beach club on Long Island,
for the name of a good dressmaker. He sent me to a small
company which made dresses, suits, and coats for Bergdorf Goodman. He did not offer to pay for them, and I
would have been embarrassed if he had. I was earning a
good salary; with my magazine articles, it came to five
or six hundred dollars a week.

I had been very careful with my money; now I bought
only the best. My bill at Elizabeth Arden's was several
hundred dollars a month. I bought dresses from Saks
Fifth Avenue, Bergdorf's, and Bonwit Teller, shoes from
Delman's, hats from Lilly Daché, and evening gowns
from Nina. I was like a woman who had been starving
and now could not eat enough of all the goodies spread
before me. I was putting a higher value on myself, and
men who were discriminating took me at my own valua-
tion.

There was always someone who said he was in love with me. I was free to do as I pleased, but some of my mother's warnings were hard to forget. The men who appealed to me were virile without too much talk. I liked a rugged professional football player who was also a good dancer. I could feel his penis harden as we danced at the Stork Club and El Morocco. He never mentioned marriage, although he was quite unencumbered. Was it because I was now self-sufficient and made no demands? The affair was sometimes the most important part of a relationship; I was on fire until the affair was consummated. But it did not mean I would want to see him again.

Lady Rose D. in London had sworn to have a hundred lovers before she married, and she had them and then married a very rich marquess. Availability sometimes led to marriage—if you wanted marriage. The shy, insecure men were pleased if you took the initiative in sex. They were grateful, especially if you helped them to relax to the point where they could function strongly. If I liked such a man, I was patient. The most respectable men were often the most violent, biting, slapping, and screaming. I did not care for this. When Mr. Perlberg came uninvited into my bedroom at his country house in Connecticut, he behaved like a madman, screaming and whinnying like a horse. It was easy to push him out. The next day he asked me to marry him. I refused. I imagined he was too excitable to be good as a lover and/ or a husband.

You can make things happen just by wanting them and believing they will. Now I thought only of marriage, and within a year six men asked me to marry them, and dozens wanted to have an affair. Proposals and propositions. It was a busy year. The earl, far away in England, absorbing my new attitude by osmosis, decided that with Scott Fitzgerald dead he would make me marry him. I was amazed that he should suddenly want to marry me, when we had had a fairly long affair, and been apart for several years. He had been unhappy when I told him I was leaving for America, but reconciled; he said he was sure I would soon return. And now years had passed, during which he had sent me impassioned cables, "longing, darling, to be in your arms."

I discussed the earl's new proposal with Janet, who said, "You'd be mad not to marry him. Besides, I want to visit you in your castle." But I did not want to marry the earl. There would be too much to tell him about my past life, and to be a countess would be a strain.

Another reason for refusing the earl a second time was that I believed I could not have children. I was afraid he would divorce me if I could not give him an heir. He was sweet and gentle but could be difficult when he was drinking.

I'd had some female trouble in New York, and visited a gynecologist on Park Avenue. When he left the room, I turned around the card on which he had been writing, and saw the words "Primary Sterility." I thought this meant I was sterile. I took no further precautions, beyond douching, and I did not become pregnant until after my second marriage, which proves that heaven looks after foolish women as well as drunks and children.

Perhaps my pseudo-sterility was because I felt most passionate just before my period and during it. But why did I feel excited and longing for sex at this time, if it was not the right time to make love? Dogs and cats make love when they are in heat, as do other animals, as far as I know. So why not humans? In biblical times, a woman has been considered unclean and segregated during her periods, but this was superstition, or why would I have this overwhelming desire at this time, this burning state of heat?

Years later I learned that a woman was more inclined to become pregnant in the middle of the month, or about ten days after the onset of the period. I also learned that childlike women found it difficult to conceive. They are babies themselves, immature, wanting pleasure and gratification without responsibility.

Mr. Perlberg, who had previously been in love with a beautiful blond lady "on the coast," continued in hot pursuit, proposing frequently. I enjoyed dining at his town house in New York's East Seventies. The food and wine were good, and beautifully served. His estate in Connecticut had acres of lawns and lovely flowers, with a swimming pool and a tennis court. At one time I went there every weekend, driving up with him in his chauffeured limousine. He was in his sixties, and thin, his very tanned skin wrinkled and leathery.

I remember him today mainly because one Saturday evening in his paneled dining room I ate corn on the cob for the first time. There were two little forks stuck in each end of the corn, and I watched as the other guests splashed large gobs of butter on the corn and bit lustily into the kernels. Some of them had six helpings. I had one. I was not sure I liked this dish. It smacked of Indians. The energy with which the others attacked the delicacy rather nauseated me.

Like most things in my life, I was to like corn on the cob the more I ate it, until it became an obsession. I sometimes put food on a par with sex. The more you have it, the more you want it. As a child I had been disciplined so severely that now, free to do as I pleased, there were no boundaries to my desires. When I liked something, I had it. If you said yes, you had more fun than if you said no. Your telephone was always ringing. You were invited to the best restaurants; there was always someone who wanted to give you a good time.

New York was fun for a girl on the town. There was so much to do, so many cocktail parties, so many dinners in elegant apartments with the East River for a front yard, or high up in a penthouse on Fifth Avenue with the lights twinkling in Central Park. It was a fairyland in winter, with the snow. There was skating at Rockefeller Center and tennis at the exclusive River Club and the Piping Rock Club on Long Island; lunches at the Yale Club, Harvard Club, or Princeton Club; the World Series and the championship boxing matches and the college football games. I loved being part of the happy groups of men and their girls, who liked me and mistook my precise English accent for a sign of a good background.

After six weeks in England covering the British war effort—the U.S. was not yet in the war—Janet and I rented a house in Locust Valley on Long Island, a cottage on the estate of a rich family whose names often appeared in the society columns. Tim Durant, whom I had met when I first arrived in New York (he was a member of the Stock Exchanges), visited us in the cottage and brought a friend who had a stately home nearby. His wife and children were away, and the horses needed exercising—would we ride with him? I jumped at the chance. Johnny had had me taught at the fashionable Cadogan Riding School in Belgravia, and while I was always a bit apprehensive, I sat a horse very well and had learned to jump small fences.

We rode over the bridle paths of the Glen Cove estate owned by Otto Kahn, the financial wizard. He had been in love with Grace Moore and helped so much with her career. To be the mistress of Otto Kahn was considered something very special, and no one despised Miss Moore. I thought it would be marvelous if we came across him and he fell in love with me. But he was now very old and undoubtedly past passion—and it was only a thought, anyway.

The owners of the big house arranged for us to use the facilities of the nearby exclusive Piping Rock Club. We played tennis there on weekends, and while we felt like interlopers and did not know anyone, we liked the club and enjoyed the enormous buffet lunch on Sundays.

One Sunday there was a dog show at the club, with dogs of all sizes yapping and prancing around. Janet and I decided to watch the judging. Janet loved dogs, but I had never had one except Meg, an enormous wolfhound given to us by an acquaintance of Johnny's who was going abroad. As a child I had been chased and bitten by a fox terrier, and I had never lost my fear of dogs. The huge wolfhound with her sad eyes terrified me. She followed me around the apartment. I sneakingly led her into the bedroom, then locked the door on her. When my husband came home, I wept, begging him to take

Meg away. Fortunately, the owner had not yet left England and gave the dog to another friend.

Standing near us at the dog show was a tall, good-looking, extremely well-dressed man with a card in his hand taking notes on the form of the dogs. He looked admiringly at me—something I did not find extraordinary. Most men did. But this man made me look back. His smile was open and friendly. I was enchanted with his little porkpie hat with its bird feather, and I was pleased when he started a casual conversation with us. He talked mostly to Janet, but he looked at me all the time.

We introduced ourselves. He had accompanied the lady over there—he pointed to a chic and slender woman. He was spending the weekend with her, her husband, and children. She was busy talking to friends. We stopped looking at the dogs, and he brought us tea and cake. When Janet had to make her usual visit to the powder room, he asked for my telephone number, which I gave —too eagerly, I feared afterwards.

He called me the next day, and this time, because I wanted him to fall in love with me, I played a more cautious game. Dinner? No, I had an engagement, but I was free for a drink. He called for me, his porkpie hat at a rakish angle, and was visibly delighted to be with me. He wanted to know everything about me. How often I have poured my life story into masculine ears! I told Todd of my journalistic work and my experiences on the stage. He was the nephew of a famous political newspaper columnist, he had been to Yale, but his father had died just before graduation. There were debts, but he had this job in a brokerage house and was doing well, and wasn't life glorious? He kissed me lightly on the cheek when he dropped me at my apartment. I did not ask him to come in. He begged to see me the next evening. I thought for a few seconds and said yes.

Todd knew all kinds of delightful small restaurants that served excellent food. He was the confident, sophisticated New Yorker, and I enjoyed being with him. He was careful not to press for more than I gave, but I knew when we kissed and danced, his arm around my waist, that he was falling in love with me.

A few weeks before Thanksgiving, a young couple invited us to visit at the home of the man's parents, twenty miles from New Haven. The parents would be away, and we were a foursome. We would attend the football game and spend the weekend in the country. Todd guided me around the university and showed me the rooms he had occupied when he was a student. I loved his enthusiasm and being a part of the crowd cheering for Yale. We had small flags and rosettes with the Yale colors and were disappointed when Yale lost. We hurried back in the car to the house, singing Yale songs all the way.

The men made a hot drink laced with brandy, and we were all a bit drunk when we sat down to the roast and all the trimmings. We had wine with the meal, and liqueurs afterward, and when we could drink no more and there was some wine left in the bottle, I tipsily suggested that I would spend the night in the icebox using one of my nipples for a bottle stopper. "Not on your life," said Todd as he scooped me up in his arms. I squirmed slightly, still a few pounds overweight, until he desposited me on the bed in the pretty bedroom with its maple furniture, dainty white muslin curtains, and gay wallpaper. He stood over me, hesitating, and I reached toward him and pulled him down beside me.

It was the most natural thing in the world that we would make love. He was very gentle, careful to rest his weight on his elbows—if only more men did this! We made love many times in the night, and I was content, living for the moment only—which is the happiest way to live. I had no worry about what could happen tomorrow, no thought of my work. I was in love with him, or so I thought.

Back in New York we slept together in my apartment almost every night, and Todd was happy and falling more deeply in love with me. One evening after the lovemaking in my comfortable double bed he asked me to marry him. It had not been difficult to get the proposal, and now I was not sure that I wanted to marry again. Todd was too nice to keep on a string, and I said, "No, but can't we go on as we are?" He was hurt by my hesitation and insisted on marriage.

Was it because he was not rich that I did not want to marry him, I wondered. I stalled for several weeks until Todd gave me an ultimatum: "We get married or we stop seeing each other." The more he pressed, the less I wanted to marry him. It would be the end of adventure; it would be the finale to the unknown, which so fascinated me.

I missed Todd and called him. We had dinner together, but we were both strained. "Why won't you marry me?" he demanded angrily. I could not tell him that our affair had started as a game to see how many men would want to marry me. And while I thought I was almost in love with him, he was too immature for me, as I learned when I knew him well. Underneath the gaiety was a resentment that his father's death had made him poor. His charm was superficial. There was little underneath to assure me that my life with him would be interesting.

We parted. He was unhappy, and wanting to talk about me, started to visit Janet, swearing her to secrecy. Janet had a seventeen-year-old daughter who fell in love with Todd and asked him to marry her. He became engaged to her, perhaps to make me change my mind. I was amazed when Janet told me of the visits and the engagement.

When his stratagem did not work, Todd vanished. Her daughter was distraught, and Janet was worried. Soon afterward the girl eloped with a man she had known for only a few days. Janet had been divorced for ten years from her daughter's father, who had died when the girl was fifteen and left his money in trust for her until she was twenty-one or married. The apartment on Park Avenue was large, and Janet could not afford it without her daughter's income. Unasked, I gave her a check for five hundred dollars to see her through until she got rid of the apartment, with a note: "This is a gift, a thank you to America, which has been so good to me."

Some of the confidence I had acquired in America vanished when I was back in London for six weeks in the summer of 1941. It was difficult to renew my friendships with the men I had known. Most of them were in the service or away from London.

Johnny was pleased to see me again, though we had divorced in 1937. It had been arranged by the lawyers. My husband had to pretend to commit adultery; a detective burst into the room to find him with a woman; both were undressed, but not in bed together. Johnny had balked at that; he gave the co-respondent the bed while he tossed on the couch.

The divorce had made no difference to our relationship. He still asked me for money, which I always gave, sometimes grumbling at the amount, and he wrote to me in America at least once a week. He kept clippings of my stories, which were syndicated in the *Evening Standard*, and pasted them into a scrapbook. He was as proud of me as a journalist as he had been when I had "jumped to fame" on the London stage.

I was tired and wanted a change of scenery. I had visited Florida in the winter of the second year of my stay in America with my business magnate. I had stayed ten days with Janet and Jack, who was renting a villa, living in an illusion that he was still rich. We had a marvelous time, swimming, gambling, going to the races at Hialeah Park, the greyhound races, and the jai-alai matches.

This time I would go to Florida alone. The season had not yet begun. The weather was sunny and warm, with a soft breeze that raised my spirits sky high. I cannot live anywhere unless there is sun. I swam every day.

I met Joe and Al almost at the same time. They were both in the Air Force branch of the Navy. College men, with war in the air, were enlisting for training as pilots.

One day I was in the water when the strap of my swimsuit broke. I came out holding the top of my suit, and lay down on the sand to dry off. "Compliments of the United States Navy," said a pleasant masculine voice, and a towel landed on my middle. I sat up, smiled, and thanked the owner of the voice, who came over and sat with me. He was young and fresh-looking, with curly dark hair. After some talk, he asked if he could take me to dinner.

After dinner we walked on the beach, the warm wind ruffling my hair. I was happy. Joe was in his white uniform with the Navy shoulder boards and brass buttons and the peaked cap that makes every man a hero. He looked glamorous and brave. He put his arm around my waist and leaned over to kiss me. His mouth was sensuous, and I was a million miles away from reality. The kissing excited us, and when I said I had to go in, he came with me without asking, and I did not stop him.

The lovemaking—orgasm not too quick, not too slow —was accompanied by the waves splashing rhythmically on the sand. Afterward we were both ravenously hungry and walked to a coffee shop on Collins Avenue for hot roast-beef sandwiches. He could not get enough of my face, looking at me constantly and marveling at his good fortune.

I saw Joe every night for five nights. And every night we made simple love in my room, his rhythm coinciding, it seemed, with the sea. It was like hearing another language, listening to his talk of his life in Pennsylvania before he had joined the Navy. He had worked for the Bethlehem Steel Company. Every man in his family worked for Bethlehem Steel. He had attended Penn State University in University Park, and with the war coming he got in early to get his wings as an officer. He interrupted his remarks to tell me how attractive I was, and how glad he was that I had broken the strap of my swimsuit, or he would not have dared to talk to me.

Joe told me he could be transferred any day to Texas, but we hoped it would not be until my vacation was over. When he told me he had to leave the next day, he promised, "I'm coming to New York on my first leave to marry you."

This was my fourth proposal of marriage in six months, What had I done to bring it about? I analyzed my behavior with Joe. I had not held him off when he came to my room on the night of our first date. I had made no demands on him. I had not been coy or difficult. I had given myself freely. I had been completely natural, with no future designs on him whatsoever. Did I want to marry him? He had a degree in engineering and could give me a good home in a nice Pennsylvania suburb. I liked him, but I was not in love with him.

"You'll meet other girls in Texas," I told him. "None like you," he insisted. The reason I was so attractive to him was the other men I had known. It had made me uncomplicated in sex. I was easier for a man to be with. I was no longer uptight about sex, and this, in turn, made him comfortable. I tucked Joe away at the back of my mind. I did not think I would ever marry him, but who knew? Anyway, it was nice to know that he wanted to marry me.

I found Al in Miami the day after Joe left. It was as though he had been waiting in the wings. I was quite relaxed, not looking for adventure, although the tennis pro at the hotel had asked me to have a drink with him after the late-afternoon game, and it was obvious from his wooing words that he wanted to go further than a drink. Perhaps I would. Nothing was urgent, nothing was important, although exercise always made me feel well, and the warm sunshine of Miami made me drowsy and in a mood for sex.

I had known Al in California, where he had worked for *Time* magazine. Except for attending the same Navy Air Force officers' training school, he was nothing like Joe. Al had been to Yale; he moved in Whitney, Vanderbilt, and Astor social circles. His sister was married to one of the richest upper-crust members. He had barely given me the time of day in California, when he had been in love with a beautiful starlet. But this was Miami, and he was lonely and delighted to find a girl he knew. He telephoned me at the hotel after seeing my photograph in a local paper. As a journalist recently covering wartime England, I had been interviewed. It was the slack season, and a pretty girl was always good copy.

Al, whom I had imagined to be sophisticated, proved to be very shy. He stuttered when he paid me compliments, and could barely look at me. I regarded him as a boy, although he was only a few years younger than I. He was nice and very careful. He called for me every evening at seven o'clock in the old Ford he had rented, and we had an early dinner because he had to return to his post by ten o'clock.

He talked shyly of our mutual friends in California and New York and was stumblingly enthusiastic about the stories he had covered for his magazine and the scoops I had written for my syndicate.

When he said good-bye on our first evening he fumbled with his cap and did not even touch my hand. He looked away while making a date for the following evening. On the second night he shook my hand formally when he said, "Good night; may I see you tomorrow?" I wondered when he would be bold enough to kiss me. I liked him, but I wasn't going to help him. Each night that he did not kiss me made a kiss more awkward. After the fourth dinner, Al leaned forward stiffly and brushed a kiss that landed on my nose.

The evening before I returned to New York, Al, desperate but determined, kissed my lips. I had become attached to him, and perhaps it was just as well I was leaving. He had shown me around the naval base and introduced me proudly to his fellow officer trainees. He had overcome his conversational shyness and was now talking almost fluently.

Well, that was that, I thought. It had been pleasant having Al take me to dinner each night. I was refreshed from the vacation. I had played tennis every day—the conceited pro could not understand why I refused to see him in the evening—I was tanned from the sunbathing on the beach, and I had enjoyed the swimming.

I had been back in New York for a week when Al telephoned me at six in the morning. He was driving in from Florida and had reached Philadelphia. He was coming to see me. "You haven't deserted or anything like that?" I asked sleepily. "No," he laughed shyly. "I have a few days' leave and I want to see you. I've missed you."

He was almost asleep when he arrived at eight-thirty. I had a breakfast interview at nine-thirty and said he could use my bed. He was gone when I returned. There was a note: "I'm staying with the [John] O'Haras. Let's have dinner tonight." His courtship was slow. He was in New York for several days, and I knew he was gradually getting to the point. On Sunday we would dine with the O'Haras; then he had something important to ask me. Obviously he was planning to ask me to marry him. I was pleased. Al was attractive, intelligent, nice, and as a civilian he had an interesting job. This time I might say yes.

It was Sunday, and I went to a concert at Carnegie Hall. Halfway through the program, the concert was halted with an announcement: "Ladies and gentlemen, the Japanese have attacked Pearl Harbor. The United States is at war with Japan." I was shocked. Then I thought, what will this do to my date with Al?

We had a brief meal with the O'Haras, then took Al to the airport, from where he was to fly to California and the war in the Pacific. Soon after, when I married Trevor Westbrook, I had a letter from Al, asking, "Why didn't you wait for me? I wanted to marry you."

Six proposals in a year, and I married the last one. We had met in London on my recent visit, and with America now involved in all the theaters of war, Trevor Westbrook, an authority on aviation, came to Washington with Churchill, Beaverbrook, and all the experts. I was sent to the capital to cover the meetings. Trevor was at the same hotel, and before he returned to England we were married across the bridge in Virginia.

CHAPTER 10

... and a Baker's Half-dozen of the Other

Propositions—before my second marriage I was combing them out of my hair. The aura of sex I had triggered off was so powerful that it trapped most of the men who came close enough to feel it.

A multimillionaire with a well-known name, his own airplane, and a fleet of racing cars, asked me to be his official mistress. I had tantalized him with promises until he could stand it no longer. One night he gave a party for Marlene Dietrich. The wife from whom he had been separated for some time was to be present, but I had not been invited. I was "press," and while he liked me and wanted an affair with me, he did not want to read about his party in my column. I was annoyed and let him know. I started by pretending to have a tantrum, and became so worked up that by the time I yelled, "If I'm not good enough to be invited to your silly party, you're not good enough for me," I was in a rage. Of course, I would write about the party, and I told him that. It was the only reason I wanted to go. I am not comfortable with many strangers. I can take a big party only if I go there with a notebook as a working reporter. On these occasions I usually make several trips to the john to write down what is being said. I find it hard to remember what I don't like.

130

All the star actresses and the wives of the producers, the directors, and race car drivers wore full-length evening gowns and every jewel they possessed. This was an occasion. Marlene looked wistful and nodded absently when she saw me. The men swarmed around her. I wondered if she had affairs. Surely she did. At the beginning of her career in Hollywood she was Trilby to Joseph von Sternberg's Svengali. Did they go to bed? He had done a lot for her. Only a lover would do as much. She was discreet, because, apart from von Sternberg, she was never linked with anyone—except Michael Wilding.

My host whispered in my ear that he would call me at home when the party was over. I resented this. Because he was rich, did he think he could call me in the middle of the night and I would come running? He must think I was easy. He was attractive enough, and rich, but he had never sent me so much as a flower. If there is one thing that I dislike, it is a stingy millionaire. What is the use of money if you don't spend it? I have paid for meals with millionaires who miraculously did not have cash or cards on them when the bill was presented.

I took the phone off the hook before I went to sleep. I was tired. I did not wish to be disturbed. Let him call. He could not get through. I awakened at six in the morning, saw the unhooked phone, and without thinking put it back on. It rang immediately, and I answered. "You bitch," my frustrated suitor shrieked. "I've been calling you all night. You deliberately put your phone off the hook." "I did not," I shouted back. "It must have been out of order." And hung up. He called me later in the day. He was still angry, but apologetic, and I relented. I went back with him to his home. As I expected, expensive paintings, beautiful furniture, servants, and the feeling of being drenched in luxury. I remembered the fun I'd had with him—going flying with him in his plush private plane, watching the Indianapolis 500 with him by my side. He had sometimes placed a small, usually unsuccessful bet for me. It was soothing to be in such close proximity to so much glamour and money, about two hundred million dollars. It made him more attractive, and I wanted to be in love with him.

He took me upstairs to his enormous bedroom. We undressed and slipped into the big bed, touching each other, he kissing my nipples, I jerking his average-size penis, hard and ready. The lovemaking was adequate. I had expected something more—a golden penis?— and felt let down. He did not hold me in his arms afterward; there was no break in his reserve. I have always wanted more than just an affair; I have wanted to be loved. This man loved only himself.

I soon learned that ours was not an exclusive relationship. I was having my hair done at Elizabeth Arden's when I heard his voice. I retreated into a cubicle because I was in curlers and I did not want him to see me like that. He was with a famous, beautiful blond film actress, and he was buying her all the Elizabeth Arden products, laughing as they chose some flimsy and expensive nightgowns. I guess she wasn't good in bed, because the next day he asked me to be his official mistress.

The wires of my sex antennae had become crossed. I had wanted him to marry me. I did not want to be a kept woman. I would not be comfortable in such a situation. He was adequate as a lover, but was it because of his money that I had gone to bed with him? Without the atmosphere of his wealth, would I have wanted him? I refused to be his mistress. I felt virtuous and rather flat. I had refused to be kept by a billionaire. If he had asked me to marry him, I would have said yes. Why did the others want to marry me, and why, with all my sex antennae at full blast, did he want me only as his mistress?

Had I been too obviously impressed with his social and financial position? The richer and more important the man, the less impressed the girls he wants should be. But this was not my nature. I had liked this man. For whatever reason—probably his wealth—he had excited me. But after we had made love, I lost interest in him; in fact, I rather disliked him. What I was looking for was

sex with love. It was better afterward when I liked the
man, although I could enjoy sex for its own sake while
the state of heat lasted.

Mack. . . . He fell in love with me when he saw me
tap-dancing in the hall of a mutual friend while I was
waiting for my coat. I was whirling around and almost
fell into his arms. We laughed, and he asked me to wait
while he got his car, and he would see me home. He
forced me into my bedroom and tried to have sex with
me. I did not want him—he was blind in one eye, it
seemed to glare at me, and he was married. I struggled
madly as he tried to take off my dress and panties.
After several minutes, while he tried to separate my
legs and could not, he became angry and unexpectedly
slapped my face. I stopped struggling. In his anger he
was behaving like a masterful man, and being a feminine
woman, I usually react to a man who can master me.
I now desired him as much as he wanted me. I kissed
him passionately, and he had me, with my clothes on,
his pants at half-mast. He couldn't get over it. "You
wouldn't yield until I smacked you. Why?" He then
apologized for hitting me, and vowed he never would
again. It was a one-time affair, although we became
good friends. He puzzled over why I would never again
have sex with him. He was always asking meekly if he
could. He was a gentle soul, and after the one time he
never tried to force me. Perhaps that was his mistake.
But he was really not my choice for a lover.

Monroe was in his late twenties, and already a famous
author and playwright. He looked like a bull and behaved
like one. I met him at a party given by Salka Viertal—
Garbo's friend and the writer of many of her films. He
sat next to me one evening. His eyes seemed to suck me
into him. He didn't have to tell me what he wanted when
he asked me for a date. We dined at Romanoff's, and he
could barely eat for wanting me. He was the egotist of all
time, dismissing as second rate most of the contemporary
authors. But I could not resist his enormous virility, and
was as eager to get home and into bed as he was. He
turned me over and had sex like a bull. The affair

lasted for several months, until his job in a major studio was completed. He married soon afterward and lived with his wife in Switzerland. I sometimes bump into him at Sardi's or 21 when he comes to New York to promote a new book. He has become a heavy drinker, and it saddens me to see him so drunk. He still writes books that land somewhere in the middle of the best-seller list, but only because of his reputation; his writing is mediocre. The bull has become a sodden steer. The balls are gone.

Gerry made love like a sexy puppy, in and out, in and out, huffing and puffing in quick gasps. He was a young New York actor brought to Hollywood to play a small role for a major studio. He stole the picture and became a star overnight. I interviewed him and liked him. He was as shy as Monroe was boastful, but just as sexy. He was married, but his wife lived at their apartment in New York. He asked me along with some others to make a recording of a scene in a Shakespeare play. It was great fun, and afterward we all went to dinner at Musso Frank's in Hollywood. Gerry sat next to me and made whispered love, took me home, where he had me face to face, as I imagined a puppy would if he could.

Gerry was one of two actors whom I allowed to make love to me. I took a chance because they were both so attractive and because they seemed to love me. The other actor was tall, wide, and a great lover. After an orgasm his penis was still hard. He could go on until I was exhausted. He never was. There was no talk of marriage from either, and that was fine. I would never want to have married an actor—except Gary Cooper. The rest are too insecure.

Mike. . . . I liked the secure way he put his arm around my waist when he walked me home from a huge sit-down dinner at the Pierre Hotel. He stayed the night, and he was warm and deeply satisfying. I never saw him again, and did not want to, although I am sure we would be friendly if we met again.

Art was in his mid-thirties, and a vice-president of a large advertising company. He thought I was very clever, and was proud of my career. I was appearing on radio—

my soft English voice was my credit card—and getting to be well-known. Art was a wonderful lover, healthy, kind, amusing, and he adored me. We have always been friends. I bumped into him at the airport a year ago —we were both going from New York to Los Angeles— and he was the same Art, warm and full of pleasure at seeing me.

Dick was a gentleman from Georgia. He was a publishing executive, and we met when I was interviewed by Cecil B. De Mille on his Lux radio show. Dick took me to a party in Beverly Hills, where a drunk insulted me. I cannot bear to be humiliated in public, and fearful that I would burst into tears, I asked him to take me home. Comforting me, he became passionate, and it was a natural thing for us to undress and get into bed, where we whirled into the universe with hot, sticky sex. After I was quite comforted, I suggested, "Let's go back to the party." Good girl," he said approvingly. The party had been given for an important client, and he would be missed.

We saw each other whenever he was in town. His work frequently took him to Los Angeles. He had tried to be a writer in Paris, and knew Henry Miller, whom he introduced to me when Miller was in California. Afterward Miller said to Dick, "This girl is obsessed with her cunt." How did he know? I had not mentioned sex once, finding Miller boring, and disliking him for having left his wife and children to go to Paris and starve until he was accepted as a writer of what I then believed were pornographic books. The four-letter words were startling to read. If anyone was obsessed with sexuality, he was. I met him years later in Paris during the filming of his *Tropic of Cancer* and reversed my opinion. He was kind, humble, and I liked him very much.

When Dick was divorced by his wife, he asked me to marry him. I thought I might be in love with him, but when I discussed this with my magnate, he warned me against marriage with Dick. "It will be like your first marriage, insecure. He has only his job. What if he lost it?" I was alarmed, and I did not marry him. Six months later he married someone else. She became an alcoholic, but he was faithful to her. I obviously had not wanted to marry him, or I would not have asked advice from the one man who was selfish enough to want to keep me in bondage to himself.

I was tired of being odd woman out, receiving propositions by the bushel and proposals from men I did not wish to marry. I did not realize then that fate was saving me for an association with a man that would transcend every previous experience in sex and love.

CHAPTER 11

The Real Thing

I had believed I was in love with Johnny. My heart had beat fast when I heard his footsteps coming to the room where I worked as his saleswoman. Before our marriage, when he had kissed me I almost rocketed through the ceiling, but the intense heat had become tepid with his impotency.

I was sure I was in love with Charles, even after I refused to marry him. At the end I knew I had been in love with what I believed was a masterful man. He had seemed strong, able to manipulate events, always there to help me if I got into trouble. But the first time I needed help, he had remained silent.

I was doing very well on the *New York Journal,* at the same time writing articles for top magazines—*Vogue, Woman's Home Companion, Ladies' Home Journal, McCall's.* I even wrote some articles for *The New York Times* under a pseudonym. The day came when the women's editor of the *Journal* realized I was earning more money than she was. Or maybe the novelty of the brash English reporter had worn off.

I was having a drink with Charles in the Madison Bar when a letter was delivered to me. As of Monday, it stated, my services would not be required by the *Journal.* I was stunned. I had thought I was indispensable. I passed it to Charles. In the awkward silence, I waited for him to say, "Don't worry, I know most of the newspaper publishers, I will help you get another job." He had often assured me of this while I was securely entrenched in my job.

He said nothing. He merely looked uncomfortable. The next day I called on Joe Connolly, head of King Features, who praised my work and for whom I wrote occasional articles for the Hearst Sunday pages. He took me on right away, at double the salary.

When I called Charles to tell him, he said, "Well, you didn't have to worry, you know I would have helped you." Perhaps he would have, but I had needed to know at once, not when I no longer needed his help. This was all I needed to cure me of my infatuation. It was as though someone had wiped my glasses and I was seeing clearly again.

I had been in New York for two and a half years. It was time for a change. I learned that the Hollywood columnist for the North American Newspaper Alliance was quitting. I applied for the job, and taking a cut in salary, I got it, based on my column in the *Journal* and my scoops.

Charles was sorry that I was leaving New York and tried to dissuade me from going. But he realized I was determined, as much to break the liaison with him as to do something completely different in a city I had heard so much about when I had lived in London. Once at the Ritz I had seen Joan Crawford with her husband, Douglas Fairbanks junior. Her face was covered with chalk-white makeup. Everyone was staring at them, and they were trying elaborately to be casual. Were they all like that in Hollywood, I had wondered.

I had interviewed several of the film stars in New York—Carole Lombard, who was very friendly and told me to look her up if I ever came to Hollywood; Claudette Colbert, who was charming; Merle Oberon, who told me she was in love with Leslie Howard, who was planning to "get a divorce to marry me"—how often in my life I was to hear this from the "other women."

I had met Charlie Chaplin in London through Randolph Churchill and his sister Diana, who later committed suicide. Charlie was very much in awe of the Churchill name and openly showed his admiration. I was very much in awe of Randolph, but as I knew he admired me, I was at ease with him, or pretended to be. After dinner Chaplin, at Randolph's request, did his famous tramp walk, and everyone at Quaglino's applauded. He too told me to look him up if I ever came to Hollywood. With all these famous people liking me, I was sure I would do well there.

When I arrived, on Christmas Day, 1935, I looked them all up in the telephone directory. None of them were listed. No one in the movie world, except perhaps the extras, has his or her name in the book. Even I, after bothersome calls, was unlisted. It is probably different now, when so many are out of work and longing to be called.

I had expected to like Hollywood, with its emphasis on the outdoor life. The tennis was good, and I loved the swimming, the ocean, the mountains, and the desert, but I always felt chilly when I moved out of the sun. Southern California has a strange climate, and you have to get used to it. I didn't care for the people too much—the agents and the actors, and the lecherous producers.

There was the intermittent affair with Dick, who was headquartered in New York. But there were long gaps between visits. Then I met Scott Fitzgerald in Robert Benchley's living room at the Garden of Allah. He was sitting alone, half-smiling, a Coke in his hand, looking at the rest of us as though he were a million miles away. I did not know who he was, and when I looked again he was gone.

I asked Benchley, "Who was the man under the lamp over there?" "Oh, that was Scott Fitzgerald," he replied. I had heard of him, of course, in connection with the Roaring Twenties. I had not read anything he had written except for accounts of his juvenile escapades with his wife, Zelda, which I did not particularly admire. Yet he had seemed interesting, and I was vaguely sorry that he had left. Bob told me that Scott had been on the wagon for several months and did not like large groups when he was not drinking. He had invited him because he believed he was lonely in Hollywood, and because he thought he would be news for my column.

I saw Mr. Fitzgerald again at a benefit at the Biltmore Hotel in Los Angeles to raise money for the Anti-Nazi League. I was a guest of Marc Connolly at his long table, parallel with the table hostessed by Dorothy Parker and her husband, Alan Campbell. The guests at both tables were all dancing, except for Scott and me. He was facing me and smiled. I recognized him and smiled back. I was on fire that evening because that very day I had promised to marry the earl, who had left immediately for London to inform his mother.

Scott studied me with his head tilted to one side and said, "I like you." I laughed and replied, "I like *you*." I loved the way he was regarding me—a mixture of admiration, tenderness, and desire to know me intimately. "How about the next dance?" I said brazenly. Suddenly I wanted this attractive stranger to hold me in his arms. He had promised the next dance to Dorothy, "But after that?" I nodded. It was as though we were the only people there. The others were murals on the wall. But the party was breaking up, and we did not dance that night.

We met again after Scott asked Eddie Mayer, a writer brought to Hollywood after the Broadway success of *The Firebrand*, his play about Cellini, "Do you know a girl here I might like, nothing serious, of course." Eddie thought I might be the girl. "She's engaged to an earl, he's in London, and I'm sure she doesn't want anything serious either." With his amazing intuition, Scott said, "I wonder if she's the girl I saw at Benchley's and at the Biltmore." He proceeded to describe me in detail— "Blond hair, green eyes, a complexion like smooth peach notepaper, a marvelous mouth, a great smile, and a great flirt."

He begged Eddie to call me. I had another date for dinner, but when Eddie insisted that Scott Fitzgerald would be disappointed if I didn't come, I brought my date with me, and the four of us went to the Clover Club on Sunset

Strip. I danced with Scott all evening, ignoring the two others completely.

I must have fallen in love with him that night, although I used to think it began after we were lovers, when I was taking a bath in his apartment and he carefully placed a small pillow under my head. The tender gesture bound me to him forever.

There is never a complete answer to why people fall in love with each other, but I will try to explain why I loved Scott. He was very handsome with his ash-blond hair, broad forehead, and well-set wide-apart blue-green eyes. He had a habit of looking at me, with his head at an angle, absorbing my face and body, so that I felt I was part of him; I once said to him, "If only I could walk into your eyes and shut the lids behind me." He listened intently to what I had to say, treating me as an intelligent woman whose opinions merited respect, at the same time regarding me as the most beautiful woman he had ever met. When he danced with me he was like a college boy protecting his girl from hordes of men who would try to take her away from him. I loved his gentleness, his great sense of fun, and above all, his deep love for me.

It is harder to explain why he loved me. I was pretty, but Hollywood was full of beautiful women. It was perhaps because I had and still have an eagerness and expectation that whoever was running the world had a special interest in me and would always give me what I wanted when I wanted it. My poverty as a child had made me appreciative of the material possessions I had been able to earn. I was a worker, unlike his wife, Zelda, who was more brilliant than I, but a dilettante—I thought. Her letters—with their fantastic imagery—which Scott usually read to me, were marvelous. "But," he cautioned, "they are the letters of an insane woman, they don't add up, they are splashes of beautiful colors, like her paintings, but like them, they have no logical meaning."

Perhaps he loved me because although he was in the lowest depths of his career when I knew him, I respected him enormously. To me he was never a failure, he was always a success—except when he was drinking. I might not have fallen in love with him if he had been drinking when we met. I have always been scared of drunks and the insane. To me they are almost the same. While he was terrifying when he was on a bat, in actual fact it was the least part of our relationship—a total of about six months in our three and a half years together.

There have been stories that he died in my arms, insinuating that we were in bed together. Actually he was reading the Princeton alumni magazine in the green armchair in my living room on a sunny afternoon four days before Christmas, 1940, when he jerked to his feet, clutched the mantelpiece, fell down, and died.

In the past two decades there have been at least a dozen books written about Scott, but none of them, including my own accounts, told the whole story. In 1958, when *Beloved Infidel* was published, it was the custom to gloss over the truth when it was unpleasant or would reveal too much of the deceased and the author. Among the biographers of Scott's personal life, with the exception of Andrew Turnbull, who knew him as a small boy when Scott and his family were living in the Turnbull mansion in Maryland, I am the only biographer who knew him intimately and completely as a mature man. He was forty when I met him, forty-four when he died. During those years Scott confided his hopes, frustrations, his childhood, his relationships with his parents, Zelda, and his daughter, Scottie. He adored his father, despised his mother, loved Scottie, and never said anything derogatory about Zelda, although he was sometimes bitter about their marriage. He was no longer in love with her, but spoke of her with immense compassion. He wept while reading some of her letters, and I wept when she wrote to her "Do Do" the line from Rupert Brooke's *Grantchester*.. "And is there honey still for tea?" I doubted whether he could ever love me as he had loved Zelda, but he loved me with all the part of him that was left from his wrecked life, and I was content with what he gave me.

I won't go into a long account about Scott in this book, but among other published misconceptions about Scott, I must comment on Ernest Hemingway's posthumously published book, *A Movable Feast*, which predictably slapped those who had helped him. He made a monster of Gertrude Stein and a sissy of Fitzgerald. The scene in France where Scott complains that Zelda has found his penis too small and he wonders whether it is, and Hemingway suggests they go to the men's room to find out, does not sound like Scott. He could say and do outrageous things when he was drunk, but never about his own person.

He was very drunk when he told Arnold Gingrich, the editor of *Esquire,* that I was a great lay, and other remarks he would never say when he was sober. His quaint, old-fashioned confession to Nunnally Johnson that he was living with his paramour was because he was embarrassed about being in love with a girl he could not marry. He was puritanical and would rather have married me than live in what was quaintly called sin.

In a recent book Helen Hayes is quoted as saying that she thought Scott treated me badly. I never thought so. I was over twenty-one, I could have left him at any time. But I would rather have been Scott's girl than be married to anyone else, even an earl.

At the beginning of our years together he talked of getting a divorce from Zelda, and because I was deeply in love with him, I wanted to be able to marry him. He could have divorced Zelda on the grounds of her insanity, but how could he hurt his daughter's future with this charge, or abandon a helpless woman whom he had loved dearly and to whom he was bound for all time by their past?

He told me her family had made him feel responsible for her illness, that her sister accused him of keeping her in the sanatorium to get her out of the way. I wept when he read me the letter. He said he wanted Zelda to get better to end his responsibility toward her, but I doubt whether even then he would have considered himself free.

I never asked him to get a divorce. I did not want to add to the problems that had made him turn to liquor for relief. And when he drank, I was glad that I was not his wife. I had not traveled the long route from an orphanage in England to be shackled to a man who found it hard to stop drinking once he started. But I should have asked him to get the divorce. We were good for each other, helped each other, and loved each other. We had great times visiting different places almost every weekend—San Francisco, Carmel, La Jolla, Santa Barbara, Monterey, Philadelphia for the Army-Navy game, New York, Connecticut. He was shy, rather timid, and very fastidious in the long intervals between the drinking bouts. Then Scott, who winced if you said "damn" when he was sober, was careless of his language and of his clothes. I can see him now, his face flushed, a filthy handkerchief in his breast pocket, smiling devilishly, organizing everyone, and being completely compelling, until he fell flat on his face or started a fight. He still wore suits from Brooks Brothers and had a fancy taste in bow ties and pink shirts, but drunk, he looked like a tramp.

Taking everything into consideration, my years with Scott were the best of my life. I learned for the first time how wonderful it is to be completely devoted to another person. Before Scott, I had been selfish. Now for the first time I loved another being more than I loved myself. I gave Scott every part of my body, mind, and soul. Real love is *not* never having to say you are sorry. It is giving without any thought of receiving— to your man, to your child. Because of Scott I was a better mother for my children. I wanted a child with him, but he would not take on any new responsibility. One of my charms for him was that I had a life that did not depend on his. He knew I could go on living if and when he died, which he realized could happen soon.

Scott had second sight. He knew what I was thinking before I said it. Sometimes when he began drinking I looked away from him so he would not know what I was thinking. In spite of illness, little money, and numerous worries about his work, he was generous in all areas. He helped young writers, he gave me his dwindling years to help me in my work, my education, and my life. He showered me with flowers and bought me my first fur jacket, which he then stole when he was on a bender, because he knew how much I loved it and wanted to punish me for refusing to see him. I was so angry at the moment of discovering the loss, I believe I would have sent him to prison. I could take almost anything from him, but not the theft of the fur he had given me for my birthday. Of course, I cooled off, and when the lawyer suggested sending a policeman to his home at five in the morning, I protested, "Oh, no, you can't wake him up, he sleeps so badly."

When I first met Scott on July 14, 1937, there was nothing of the Roaring Twenties about this fairly short, very pale, rather slender man. His daughter, Scottie, has her father's eyes and wide attractive forehead. The rest of her face is her mother's. When I met her four children, I was disappointed because none of them looked like Scott. They took after their handsome, dark-haired father, except for one girl, who looked like her mother.

Scottie was with us the first time Scott took me out on his own. After dropping her off at the Beverly Hills Hotel, where she was staying with Helen Hayes, he drove me to my hillside house at 1530 North King's Road, and because I thought I might never see him again—he had been the disapproving father all evening—I asked him to come in.

Scott's version of this in *The Last Tycoon:*

A wedge of light came out the opening door and as a girl's voice inquired, "Who is it?", Stahr looked up. There she was—face and form and smile against the light from inside. It was Minna's [Zelda's] face, the skin with its peculiar radiance as if phosphorus had touched it, the mouth with its warm line that never counted costs. . . . With a leap his heart went out of him . . . and stayed out there with a vast benefi-cence . . . Stahr's eyes and Kathleen's met and tangled. For an instant they made love as no one ever dares to do after. Their glance was slower than an embrace, more urgent than a call.

I was in his arms, we kissed passionately, and holding him close, I led him upstairs to my bedroom. The love-making was urgent and yet considerate and tender. After-ward we remained in each other's arms for a long time:

She leaned her head to the left then to the right, trying to catch his face against the twilight. She leaned too far and too long and it was natural when his arm touched the back of her upper arm and shoulder and pressed her forward into the darkness of his throat . . .

Was Hemingway or Zelda right in sneering at Scott's masculinity? He was very satisfactory for me, and I had been around. I have seen all shapes and sizes—big ones, little ones, thin ones, fat ones, and it isn't the shape or the size, it is how you love the man that counts. Unless you are an animal or a nymphomaniac, lovemaking starts in the head. The measure of your enjoyment of sex depends on how much you love the man. If you love him, you can tell him how to please you. With any man I have loved I have never thought whether he is big or little.

Just how important is the size of a penis? Personally, given the choice between a donkey or a chipmunk, I might choose the latter. A huge penis can be painful. While sex is self-lubricating, if a big object is trying to enter a space too small for it, the experience is not pleasurable. After one encounter with a large penis, I was sore for days. Walking straight was painful. The man had been so proud of his large cock he could not understand why I refused to try it again. Seven inches is enormous. For me, six inches is too big. Five is a better size, four is all right, and three is too small.

According to Dr. David Reuben, men look overtly at the penis of the man urinating next to them and are envious if it is bigger than their own. If this is true, they are wrong to be jealous. *Chacun à son* penis. It is how it is manipulated that counts, and the man who is in love will make it count.

I have always thought that sex was a normal thing. No one gives, no one takes. You partake. It was an equal experience with Scott and me. We were comfortable with each other, in sex, in everything. One day he showed me a book about Bali. "Did you know they have a special way of making love?" Scott asked me. He turned to the page illustrating the Balinese method of making love.

Many years later I had fun teasing Bob Hope and Bing Crosby when they were making *The Road to Bali*. They followed me all around the set begging me to demonstrate how they make love in Bali.

It's quite simple—as most good things are. Instead of the woman's legs around the man's, his legs are around hers, which means that hers are close together, and his penis is held in a tight clutch. If a woman has had several children, this is a good way of tightly surrounding all sides of the penis, which gives greater pleasure to both partners.

Early on, Scott asked me how many lovers I had had, and was visibly shocked when I answered, "Oh, about eight." He had been completely faithful to Zelda, he told me, until her affair with a French aviator, and even then he had been unfaithful only after she was confined in a sanatorium. There was room in his life for only one woman, and I was glad then, and still am, that he chose me to be the woman in the last years of his life.

He soon accepted my past sex life as part of the woman I had become and part of my fascination for him. He expressed his attitude in his poem, "For Shielah: A Beloved Infidel." (He always spelled my name wrong.)

> That sudden smile across a room,
> Was certainly not learned from me
> That first faint quiver of a bloom
> The eyes initial ecstasy
> Whoever taught you how to page
> Your loves so sweetly—now as then
> I thank him for my heritage
> The eyes made bright by other men.
>
> No slumbrous pearl is valued less
> For years spent in a rajah's crown
> And I should rather rise and bless
> Your earliest love than cry him down
> Whoever wound your heart up knew
> His job. How can I hate him when

He did his share to fashion you
A heart made warm by other men.

Some kisses nature doesn't plan
She works in such a sketchy way
The child, tho father to the man
Must be instructed how to play.
What traffic your lips had with mine
Don't lie in any virgin's ken
I found the oldest, richest wine
On lips made soft by other men.

The lies you tell are epic things
No amateur would every try,
Soft little parables with wings,
I know not even God would cry,
Let every lover be the last
And whisper, "This is *now*—not then"
The sweet denial of the past
The tale you told to other men.

I'm even glad someone and you
Found it was joyous to rehearse,
Made it an art to fade into
The passion of the universe.
The world all crowded in an hour,
Textbooks in minutes—that has been
Your fate, your wealth, your curious dower,
The things you learned from other men.

The little time you opened up
A window, let me look inside,
Gave me the plate, the spoon, the cup,
The very coat of love that died
Or seemed to die—for as your hand
Held mine it was alive again
And we were in a lovely land
The world you had from other men.

But when I join the other ghosts
Who lay beside your flashing fire
I must believe I'll drink their toasts

To one who was a sweet desire.
And sweet fulfillment—all they found
Was worth remembering. And then
He'll hear us as the wine goes around
A greeting from us other men.
—S.

In recent years there have been innuendos that Scott Fitzgerald was a homosexual or had homosexual tendencies. In Elliott Gould's film *Getting Straight* the professor is insisting that Fitzgerald was a homosexual and trying to prove it with the illustration of Nick Carraway and Jordan Baker in *The Great Gatsby*. When Elliott, whose Ph.D. depends on agreement, shouts desperately, "Well, if he was, Sheilah Graham will be very surprised," the audience laughed as one man. I thought, wouldn't they be surprised if they knew that Sheilah Graham is in the audience and laughing with them.

Scott Fitzgerald a homosexual? Absurd. He was sensitive. There was nothing of the beefy bull about him. He was a finely tuned instrument. He was at his best with women because he understood them. He loved women, as most of his stories prove. He put them on a pedestal. He put me on a pedestal. He made me feel better than I was, more intelligent, more valuable, and I became better and more valuable. I loved him for treating me as an intelligent woman whose opinions were worth listening to.

He discussed the chapters of *The Last Tycoon* with me after he wrote them. He listened attentively to what I had to say. He rewrote the scene where Stahr is trembling and unable to function with Kathleen in the unfinished house at Malibu. I knew too well how to help the anxious man. I was proud that he took advice from me in his own field.

. . . . She discovered that he was trembling. . . . He discovered it at the same time and his arms relaxed. Immediately, she spoke to him coarsely and provocatively and pulled his face down to hers. Then, with

her knees, she struggled out of something, still standing up and holding him with one arm, and kicked it
off beside the coat. He was not trembling now and
he held her again, as they knelt down together and
slid to the raincoat on the floor.

Scott originally had Stahr say something intense, which
would have left him impotent. By taking control and
being coarse, Kathleen brought the blood from Stahr's
head to where it belonged at that moment, his penis,
which became hard, and he was able to function to their
mutual satisfaction. It was only when Scott was very
drunk that he was unable to make love, and usually
he did not try. He might tremble with a small amount
of liquor, but I—and Kathleen—knew how to cure that.

Scott discussed with me the problems he was having
in the studios. He would be on a film for a few weeks
or a few months, then be replaced. He agonized over it,
but he always hoped the next script would prove his
ability to work for motion pictures. He wished he could
direct the films from his scripts, but they wouldn't trust
him; in any case, he was not physically strong enough.

Scott enjoyed films, and we went to all the previews,
he making notes on what was good and what went wrong.
I think it was unfair for the author of *Crazy Sundays*
to pick the unimportant bits of dialogue from Scott's
scripts to prove the sort of thing he was writing.

In the course of my work I read many scripts, and I
thought his scenario for *Cosmopolitan*, based on his fine
short story "Babylon Revisited," was very, very good. It
was so good that Lester Cowan, who bought the story and
Scott's ten weeks of scriptwork for $5,000, kept the orig-
inal for himself. He sold a later script by the Epstein
brothers to MGM for $100,000. How Scott could have
used the money. Lester says he will make the Fitzgerald
script one day. He expects to make another fortune from
it.

Cowan bought *The Last Tycoon* from the Fitzgerald
estate for $75,000. I have a letter from Scott in which
he bequeathed me what he had written of the book and

the plan. There wasn't much money in the estate when he died, and I made no mention of the letter. He would not have wanted me to. When you love someone and he dies, you do everything he would have wanted you to do, as though he were still there.

It was his dearest wish that Scottie should graduate from Vassar. She was in her second year when Scott died. She told me she would leave college to get a job. I protested, and informed the Gerald Murphys and Judge John Biggs, who was executor of the estate, that Scott would have been unhappy if she left Vassar.

In the day of success, and when money flowed in, Scott had taken out a life-insurance policy for $250,000. He had borrowed against it, so that with the unpaid premiums of the last years, there was only $30,000 due. "And," said Judge Biggs rightly, "we must use this for Zelda." Scott's friends saw that his daughter could finish her education.

I was angry with Scott for dying. He had no right to take every part of me, leaving me totally desolate with nothing for anyone else. I did not even have the dead body, I remembered sadly, like Marion Davies, who awoke from her sleep to find they had taken away the body of Mr. Hearst from their home. She had loved and lived with him for thirty years.

Once the man is dead, the "other woman" in his life, the woman he loved when he died, has no rights. The wife, whom he no longer loved, is usually promptly on the scene, receiving all the respect due to the widow. The woman who looked after the man, loved and was loved by him, is described contemptuously as his mistress.

After Scott's sudden death I was completely dazed and in shock. I had to bury Scott in my own way, using the bodies of other men to obliterate all trace of him— James, John, Richard, Peter, Lewis, Irwin. I went to bed with sympathetic acquaintances until one day I called Scott's doctor and begged, "Please help me." He told me sternly, "You know Scott would not like this." "I know," I sobbed. "I will stop, Scott would hate me like this."

I was angry when a man who had known Scott well

asked me to dinner at his home, and when I wept—I was always weeping then—he put his arm around me, for comfort, I thought. It was a hard struggle to push him away when he tried to get on top of me.

A young director lured me into his home in Bel Air on the pretext of showing me a newspaper clipping that had been complimentary to Scott; some had not been —there was a horrible piece by Westbrook Pegler, and I wanted to kill him. The seduction had been carefully planned—champagne on ice, the best caviar, and all the trimmings. I had barely finished reading the article when the director clumsily attacked me, almost knocking me over in the process. I dashed around a table, and he ran after me. It was like a Groucho Marx comedy. But I did not laugh. I was indignant. I looked back from the safety of the door. The director was sitting on the couch, his head buried in his hands.

I left Hollywood and went to New York to finalize arrangements to go to England to write about the war for my syndicate. On the train I met S. J. Perelman and his wife, Laura, who were going east with the bodies of Nat West and his wife, Eileen, who had died in a car crash the day after Scott. We sat up far into the night talking about Scott and Nat.

I had first heard of Mr. West from Scott, who gave me *Miss Lonelyhearts* to read. He would have written more excellent books had he lived longer. As would Scott. Edmund Wilson and other top literary critics believed the half-finished book, *The Last Tycoon,* would have been Scott's best work. Mr. Wilson was kind enough to write in *The New Yorker* that but for me Scott might not have had the courage or stamina to start it. "She gave him a base from which to work." If I did, it was slight repayment for the great experience received from Scott—that of loving completely, and knowing the real thing. I never knew it before—or after Scott's death.

CHAPTER 12

Substitutes for Sex

Overheard, a boy of fourteen, asking a girl of fifteen, "Do you masturbate?" A slight pause; then, "Doesn't everyone?" It would seem so, but I have been sure of this only in recent years. Masturbation was a vice you practiced with the utmost secrecy. Boys did it in bed, or when they took a shower. Girls did it under the sheets, or in the bathroom, or as I did, by just thinking of exciting sex. If I stood quite still or sat still, the feeling for which there has been no adequate description mounted to explosion point. Once I was in the Potsdam Palace with my first husband and a saucy thought popped into my head and before I knew it I had an orgasm while I stared at Kaiser Wilhelm's heavy furniture.

They say that babies masturbate as soon as they can put their little hands near the right place. Monkeys masturbate in full view. So do dogs, by rubbing and rubbing until a slight froth appears. And men, women, and children have apparently been doing it since the dawn of time.

"You'll go blind," fathers used to warn their sons. It was too delicate a subject to be mentioned to girls. The guilt of the masturbators could have filled a hundred oceans.

Now it is almost a virtue to masturbate. It is certainly nothing to be ashamed of or even conceal. It is considered normal, a healthy release from tension, a substitute for sex. They do it in all the X-rated films right before your eyes.

I still think masturbation is a private business, and I was embarrassed when I saw *The Fox,* with Anne Heywood in the bathroom, her hand between her legs, breathing hard into the steamy mirror. It was my first experience of masturbation on the screen, and it made me feel uncomfortable, not sexy. Perhaps because it was too theatrical, too unreal.

It was more exciting in *The End of the Road.* To watch a schoolmaster jerking himself off while Stacy Keach, the star, saw everything through the classroom window. As another voyeur, I had a quiet orgasm in my seat.

But I am tired of seeing films full of pornography. When you have seen one person masturbating, or on his or her knees for cunnilingus or fellatio, you have seen them all. I have never thought masturbation was wrong; I have thought it a necessity. But I have always kept it to myself. Until now.

I don't really recommend it. Solo sex is a lonely pasttime. It has no future. Nature intended the sex act to prolong the race. When you use the pill as the men did a rubber sheath when I was a hot little number, you are really masturbating, although someone else is doing it for you.

While masturbation is not a bad substitute for sex, and it does relieve you and help you to sleep when you are keyed-up and nervous, there is none of the comfort and satisfaction you receive from lying in bed with a man and having good sex with him. It is not the act itself that is so important to a woman. It is the before and after. The long heating up. The fast explosion. The relaxing. This is what a woman remembers. You cannot re-create the actual orgasm in your mind unless you are masturbating, the substitute for real sex.

If you have gone without sex for a long time—I used

to think a week was eternity—an orgasm will come almost by itself. When I went up in the mountain train to St. Moritz after staying with my friends in Grindelwald, when there was no question of sex—the two males were a grandfather of seventy and his grandson aged ten—I was on fire thinking of the possibilities of finding an attractive man at Suvretta House. Just thinking of it, concentrating on the area, gave me an orgasm, and I felt much better. I was twenty-three.

I have read that you start to grow old after twenty-one. In my experience, the peak of a woman's longing for sex is from twenty-five to forty-five. I have heard of women who are sexually active until they are eighty; Ninon de Lenclos is the usual example cited, but I hope this is rare. One of the joys of getting older is that the insistent trumpet of desire diminishes, and you can get on with other things, like reading, traveling, or writing a book.

I do not know whether men masturbate more than women, but I would think so. It is easier for them, and men have told me that even when they are getting regular sex they still masturbate. Personally, I have never felt the desire to masturbate when my sex life has been adequate.

Warming up by hand or finger has always been used in sex. Virtuous women who are still virgins when they marry—are there any left now?—believe it is all right to have a male finger in the vagina, as long as it does not go too far, and provided the finger titillates until there is an orgasm. Some men who come too quickly use the finger afterward to bring the woman down from her nervous plateau into a purring pussycat.

I think the idea of self-sex was practiced on me when I was three or four years old. It is vague and cloudy now, but I recall a small sensation of pleasure, and I knew that I must not tell anyone about it. There was a middle-aged man—he might have been forty years old. We were alone in the house, and he stood me between his knees and did something with his hand. I liked what he did, and then forgot about it. Is this why I have usually preferred older men?

At the orphanage, girls who wet their beds were segregated in a separate dormitory. It was a chamber of horrors consisting of iron bedsteads with lumpy straw mattresses, a stench that seeped through the corridors and into the other dormitories, about forty frightened insecure girls, and a matron who visited the ward when you least expected her, to sniff out the offenders who could not control their bladders.

For a brief period I was an occupant of this dreaded section of the school. I don't remember wetting my bed as a young child. Perhaps I did. It might have been considered usual for the very young children. But when you were transferred from the kindergarten section to the main school, bed-wetters were treated with disdain by the lucky girls who could hold their water, and as criminals by this particular witch of a matron, who punished her prisoners with the back of a hairbrush laid on the bare bottom with a heavy hand.

For several years I had wet my bed occasionally and gotten away with it by pretending to be ill and remaining upstairs while the rest trooped down for breakfast. There were always a few spare beds in the dormitory, and I would quickly change my wet mattress for a dry one. Inevitably I was caught and ignominiously sent to the dreaded dormitory. I went to bed every night praying that my bed would be dry when I awakened in the morning. I would force myself to wake up, and, like a sleepwalker, drag myself to the bathroom. But even then, my bed was sometimes wet when the bell rang at six o'clock in the morning to get up, dress, make the beds, and line up to go downstairs for breakfast.

When I heard the footsteps of the matron on her deadly mission, my heart turned over while my stomach flip-flopped in agony. I did not want to be beaten. The idea terrified me, and yet there was some exciting anticipation, waiting for the heavy hand to descend on my quivering buttocks. Afterward, thinking of it, I became rather stimulated, and a feeling of excitement permeated the area of punishment. I hated it, and yet there was this strange feeling connected with the beating.

I could not understand this, but sometimes when I was reading, I thought of the matron and the hairbrush, and the thought was not unpleasant. Was it the attention? They say that with neglected children, any attention, even a beating, is better than being ignored. Or was it that the pain inflicted was so close to my sexual organs?

Of course, I have learned that the inflicting or enduring of pain is sexually pleasurable for many people who do not enjoy normal sex. But I have never been among them, thank God. Yet there must be some corner of my unconscious that reacts pleasurably to pain, although I have never wished to inflict pain.

The rich Irishman, Sir Robert—all he wanted from me was to pinch his nipples. "Hard!" he begged as I touched him tentatively. I tried to pinch harder, but my stomach revolted.

I was alone with a well-known member of the British Parliament on his small boat off the south of France when he suddenly ripped off a shoe, pulled down his pants, and begged me to beat him on his bottom. "I can't," I shouted. When he pleaded, I said, "This is so distasteful to me that if I started I might not be able to stop." Whereupon he masturbated in front of me, apologized, cleaned himself up, pulled up his pants, and took me back to Cannes.

Exercise is another substitute for sex. I knew a Norwegian who was a marathon runner, and he told me that when he was in training he had no thought of sex; he was too tired.

I have been a great exerciser in my time, and I still walk all over New York City and London. I was such an exuberant walker that after crossing a road and coming within about three feet of the sidewalk, I sometimes took a flying leap, ballet-style. The legs aren't quite up to that now, but I still have so much energy that I have to walk it off, especially when there's no man in the picture. After walking five miles or so, I am glad to sit down, and I have less desire for sex. Not until I am rested.

I have never wanted to play golf, because it does not tire you enough, and today they use those little golf carts. If you really want to exhaust yourself so that the longing for sex is not pounding in your brain, I strongly recommend tennis or squash. Because I was so interested in sex and it is not always available, or I did not want the man who wanted me, I became an ardent tennis player, and in the years of my marriage to my inadequate first husband, a champion squash player. After an hour or so of the latter I was completely exhausted and unable to consider any other form of physical activity for the rest of the day and night.

At one time I played tennis every day. I wanted it good and quick and played mostly with pros, whom I paid for the half-hour or the hour, with the result that even today my style is superb, although I cannot run too much. I don't have to; I can place the ball and let the others run.

In London I was a member of Queen's Club, where I learned to play tennis and squash. I have always had a keen eye for a ball, and I soon became fairly good at both. At one time I was a whiz at Ping-Pong. In the days when people traveled to New York by boat, I was the women's champion on the Atlantic, coming and going. When Scott Fitzgerald rented a house on Edward Everett Horton's estate in Encino, California, we had a Ping-Pong table and a strong lamp for playing at night. I spent my weekends on the tennis court with various people—not Scott—for about three or four hours a day. When Scott and I went to Santa Barbara and stayed at the Samarkand, where they had two courts, I played with the pro for an hour, then had a swim, and felt fine—after resting for a few hours.

Without the exercise I would have wanted sex all the time and would have been too much of a good thing for any man, except perhaps a boy of eighteen. The exercise relaxed me, brought the blood down from my head. It made me feel well and took my mind off everything else, including work, love, and sex.

I used to ride horseback a great deal, but that was something else. Riding, plopping up and down on your vital area, can make you feel sexier, although in my case it did not, because I was always afraid of the big beasts, and they knew it. A horse a child could ride would make it his business to try to throw me off. I was always glad when the ride was over and I was still in one piece. One time I was not; I was thrown, and suffered severe injuries. I had become more confident, riding a gentle horse. The bridle paths had some low fences, and the horse practically walked over them. I felt I was superwoman. Then I rented a horse from a local stable and jumped over a higher fence, or rather *I* did, the horse didn't, and I suffered a broken wrist, two fractured ribs, slight concussion, and a speck of dust in my eye, which hurt the most. There was certainly no thought of sex as the ambulance carried me off to the hospital.

I did not ride again until I was living in California with my young children, and we rode old horses Western style with a big pommel to hang on to. Even then I was glad to get off, as I am to touch ground when I am in a plane.

With no honest-to-god sex after my third divorce how could I fill the gap? What else did I have a compulsive need for? A father? A mother? A home. My delight when I bought the house in Beverly Hills had lasted longer than any orgasm. The pleasure was with me all the time. I experienced the same delicious sensation as when I had, many years before, stepped over the narrow threshold of my first home with Johnny, a small apartment in London, four flights up. I said "I love my home" more often than I said "I love you," although I always said "I love you" in the delirium of sex with other men. The lack of a home in my childhood had burned a scar deep into my unconscious. That coupled with the lack of good food as a child in the orphanage would be as lingering in the crevices of my mind as sex.

As soon as my divorce was final, I decided to make some changes in the structure of my house. The

Spanish-type home was built in the early twenties when the style was popular. The red-tiled roofs, the stucco walls, the high, beamed ceilings, kept the house cool in summer and warm in winter, but Spanish was now considered old-fashioned. English fake Tudor was popular. My house could never be like that, but I could square off the round Spanish arches and hide the enormous beams that hung from the ceiling like a gloomy forest of large celestial trees. It would keep me busy, occupy my thoughts, draw an asbestos curtain over the lack of a man in my life.

My last husband had been careful about spending money. When I had wanted the outside of the house painted, he had wasted hours arguing with the painter. What did a few more dollars matter, I thought, listening to the bargaining. I have always believed in allowing the other person to make a profit. This was how the Rothschilds had become rich, I read somewhere. They got out in time to leave something for the next man. I was embarrassed by the conversation, and later called the firm and said, "Go ahead on your estimate." My husband was annoyed.

Now I could again spend my money as I liked. I had seen a false ceiling below the beams in another Spanish-style house. I had never quite liked the curving stucco fireplace. I had it changed into a gray brick fireplace with a dark gray slate hearth. I would have liked to redo my bathroom, which was rather small, but the total cost after buying new cream-colored draperies for the living room and painting the walls a pale antique apple green would be too costly. I had spent ten thousand dollars, and after the costly divorce I could not afford more.

I was almost hysterically happy while the alterations were in progress. It was a mess with sheets over the furniture and the carpet, and buckets of wet plaster everywhere, but I felt I was accomplishing something. If you had asked me then what it was, I could not have told you. The main benefit was that I was too busy to be unhappy, my thoughts too occupied to yearn for the physical presence of my husband. My work, the children, and the changes in the house gave me no time to brood.

In the last months of my third marriage—in 1956—I had planned to send my children to schools in the East, to spare them from the quarrels I was having with their stepfather. The reason for sending them away no longer existed, but they wanted to go, and I could not stop the momentum of their departure. I vowed, and told my daughter, who became anxious as the time approached, that somehow I would find a way to follow them. This had been at the back of my mind during the alterations to the house. It was now more valuable, and I could get a higher price. I thought that perhaps I would sell it and live and work again in New York.

When the painters and builders had gone and the house was quiet, there was a blankness in the days and weeks. The house was gloomy without the children and intolerable when the housekeeper decided to leave. She wanted to be in a home where there were children who would appreciate her delicious cookies and cakes.

A year after the divorce was final, I put the house up for sale. I had made some money in 1958 on my book *Beloved Infidel,* written at frantic speed after the separation from my husband. Everything I did then was immediate. There was no time to think or to change my mind. I would leave Hollywood. I might have stayed if I had not sent the children away.

With all the changes, the house looked new and beautiful. I had been there since 1947, twelve years. The children had spent their childhood there. But I convinced myself that I must find another home. Not only was I lonely, but I was afraid of my children flying across the continent for every vacation. If anything happened to them, there would be no reason to live.

A week after I put the house on the market, I changed my mind. The house was my blood and flesh. My mother's womb. I felt safe within the walls. I had a feeling of satisfaction every time I opened the front door with my key. The down payment of $15,000 had taken every cent I had in the bank. Now it was all paid off. Why should I leave it? But I was restless, the house was too big for me now, and the woman who came in to clean and cook went home at the end of the day to her family. I was lonely and frightened when I heard sounds in the night.

If I could have been interested in another man, it would have been possible to live there without my children. But I did not want to marry again, although at the various functions I attended to gather news, from force of habit I kept an eye open for a possible new husband. It was a remote chance, and I was afraid of another marital disaster. No, I will sell the house, I decided. I will live nearer my children, somewhere within driving distance of their schools.

Why is it always a buyer's market when you decide to sell your house? It was three months after I signed the contract with the agents in 1959 before I found a buyer. I received a good price for the house, fifty percent more than I had paid twelve years previously. Today it would be worth at least $150,000.

The frenzied packing kept me running all the time, throwing out cherished bits and pieces collected over the years. I saved the good furniture. By the time it arrived by van on the East Coast, I must find another house in which to put it. It was summer, and while the various escrows were going through, I decided to take the children to Europe for a month. On the way, we saw a house in Connecticut, I gave a deposit, and left on the same day for the airport. It had been very stimulating. Who needed a man?

In London we stayed with Trevor Westbrook, the father of the children. He lived in a mews house in Belgravia and had gone to a great deal of trouble to make the visit a success. His young second wife had left him for a man in Australia. He had liked being married, and thought of remarrying me. I had been difficult, but good in the lovemaking department. He gave me the biggest bedroom, which he had just repainted. He bought white satin sheets for me. The smell of paint caused my face to swell up. I hate satin sheets and tore them from the bed in a frenzy. I was a real bitch. I want plain cotton sheets, I told him. But they had to be the best. But not satin, for heaven's sake. White satin was better than black. But not much. Did I want an affair with him?

He was disappointed, I could see that. But he made no move in my direction, except when I had been to Elizabeth Arden in Bond Street to have my hair done and get a facial. "You look marvelous," he told me. We were in my bedroom, where he accompanied me to make sure everything was all right. He squeezed the breath out of me. "My hair, my hair," I yelled, breaking loose. It was easy enough to put him off. The Englishman cannot bear a rebuff.

It might have been relaxing to have gone to bed with him. He was the father of my children, and it would not make much difference. But it might. He might feel he had a claim on me, or I on him.

Trevor, hoping to soften me up, paid me three years back child support, in cash. When he had withheld it after my third marriage I had not asked for it. As I could not take the money back to America because of the monetary laws, I went on a shopping spree at Harrods with the children, and spent one thousand pounds on clothes for us, and some gold and ruby cuff links for Trevor. We practically lived at Harrods. It was glorious and gave me the same sort of satisfaction as when I furnished a house or ate expensive, exotic foods. Or had a wild night with a man. It was almost the same—expending greedily, being surfeited. I took the children to Westminster Abbey and the Tower of London, and on a weekend in Stratford-upon-Avon, where Charles Laughton was playing Bottom in *A Midsummer Night's Dream*. We met him after the performance, and he invited us for supper at the house he had rented nearby with his wife, Elsa Lanchester.

A demon was driving me. I had to keep moving, and after a week I invented an excuse to leave—I must write some columns on the Continent; my work was always a convenient handle. It had been a strain. Our children, Wendy and Robert, had found it difficult to communicate with the quiet man who was almost a stranger.

We went to Paris, where the head man from the TWA office took care of us, then to Rome, which was like a hot furnace, and to Vienna, where I bumped into my New York millionaire and his bride. I took them to the Prater, high up on the big wheel, so high you can see into Hungary. She claims I ruined her honeymoon because she is terrified of heights. So am I, but she is worse.

I wrote columns in all the cities where many films were in production. It was the beginning of the end for Hollywood, which in ten years would be almost a ghost town as far as moviemaking was concerned. I was the rat who always left the sinking ship. I was always ahead of the event. I left England for the United States shortly before the empire started to sink, and I deserted Hollywood for New York just before the big downward spiral. I left New York for London before Americans found it the most fascinating city in which to live.

Now where? We bought a map. Ah, Venice. The Jimmy O'Tooles lived in Venice. They had asked me many times to visit them there.

Jimmy and I had met in Hollywood, introduced by Johnny Shaheen—they had been in the OSS during the war, and Johnny was in Hollywood to act as technical adviser for an Alan Ladd film glorifying the daring exploits of the OSS volunteers who had parachuted into occupied territory. Johnny was quite poor when I met him on the set. Today he owns most of the oil in Alaska, among some other properties, and is one of the richest men in the world.

I liked Jimmy, and he was fond of me. He had paid me his highest compliment by nicknaming me "Poodle." The O'Tooles always have a small gray poodle and always call him Michel. Michel is now the third. He has his own song, which the orchestra in the lounge of the Danieli plays when he trots in complacently with his master and mistress.

I telephoned Jimmy from our enormous room at the Imperial Hotel—Stalin had slept there, and Hitler before him. Our three beds were lost in the vastness. The bathroom was almost as big, with huge windows and

underfloor heating. The food was exquisite. I had developed a fine taste for luxury. I must never be poor
again. Or in love again.

Jimmy was delighted to hear from me. He is one of
the great Irish charmers of all time. "You'll stay with us,
of course." "No, I'd rather stay at a hotel; with two
children we'd be too much for you." He agreed, charm-
ingly. He would get me two rooms at the Royal Danieli.
"And I'll meet you in my gondola." He would make
the visit something we would always remember. He did,
although it started badly.

There was no restaurant on the overnight train, and
when we stopped at a station in the morning, everyone
got out and bought rolls and coffee from the vendors who
were wheeling their wagons up and down the platform,
doing a booming business. We settled back in the train.
In a few hours we would be in Venice.

"Venice-Mestre," called the conductor. "Come on, kids,
this is it," I said, and rushed them onto the platform.
As the train disappeared, I realized we were not in
Venice. Why was I always in such a damned hurry? Why
hadn't I asked someone? The platform was almost deserted and there was no Jimmy, no water, and no gondola.

My children asked, "Where's Jimmy?" and were disgusted with me when I explained that we had left the
train too early.

"We'll get a car," said mother, feeling like an ass.
It was not far, the next station in fact. I told the driver
to take us to the Venice station, hoping that Jimmy would
still be there. But he had waited for the last passenger
to leave the train, and concluded that we had missed it
or were flying in. He returned to his house behind the
Ponte Della Salute, and his wife upbraided him for getting
things mixed up.

I hired a gondola and was relieved when the gondolier
knew where the Royal Danieli was—my knowledge of
Italian was limited to three words: *stazione, macchina,*
and *amore.*

The sun was shining brightly on the water. It was a

magnificent sight—gondolas filled with tourists; factories on the edges of the canals; alongside, barges, crammed with bottles and machinery; the faded old palaces; the big water buses; the small motorboats zipping through the water; the Grand Canal, opening out into a fairyland. Where has this been all my life, I asked the blue sky. The children were just as amazed and enchanted.

"Mr. O'Toole has been telephoning," the concierge, Mr. Vicari, informed me. "We have your rooms. Mr. O'Toole is waiting for your telephone call." Mr. Vicari was an amazing man. Nothing was too difficult for him. My daughter lost her wallet twice on the water buses, and each time he found it.

I called immediately and explained. Mrs. O'Toole forgave her husband. They came to the hotel and took charge of us for the rest of our stay, showing us all the wonders of Venice—the fabulous San Marco square; the beautiful Byzantine church; the four bronze horses erected by Napolean in the days of conquest; the clock with the figures; the lions of Venice guarding the square; the Church of San Rocco—I return there whenever I am in Venice to look again at Tintoretto's marvelous huge crucifixion painting; Murano, to see glass being turned into tumblers and exquisite forms; the seventh-century church at Torcello; and Harry's Bar and the Cipriani Hotel opposite. We saw a wedding party on the water, and a somber funeral, with the cortege on the boat and the priest in front chanting prayers. Jimmy rented a cabana for us on the Lido, and the children had water-skiing lessons and we swam in the warm Adriatic. The sun shone nearly every day, and even the thunderstorms were exciting—loud peals of thunder, jagged white lightning, and enormous black clouds.

For the first time since the divorce, I was content. This was wonderland. "Why not stay?" Jimmy asked. A friend of his was going away, and her apartment could be rented for a month. A marvelous cook went with the apartment. When I heard that, I took it sight unseen. The cook could not speak English, but the cooking needed no translation. I gave a series of luncheons for the O'Tooles and their friends whom I met on the Lido. But, like most of the things I rushed into, there was a problem. We had not reckoned on the mosquitoes. My daughter's face was a mass of red bites. Every morning new blotches were added. I was bitten, but not as badly. Only my son was immune. We decided to leave the apartment on the mosquito-infested Lido and return to the Danieli in Venice. Except for the swimming and water-skiing, the Venice mainland was more interesting.

Unable to make the middle-aged Venetian housekeeper understand that we were not absconding, that I would pay her wages for the month, giving the money to Jimmy to give to her, we waited until she left for the afternoon and crept out, staggering under thirteen pieces of luggage. It was a short walk to the Excelsior landing stage, where we took a motorboat to the Danieli. We laughed all the way, for no reason at all, only that we were on the move. The children had caught my restlessness. Money did not matter; just keep moving. Don't think. Live only for the moment. It was a relief not to think ahead.

The time came to return to America, to the new home in Connecticut, which had been painted during the month we were away. A maid I had employed in California when the children were small preceded the furniture by a few hours. When we arrived from Europe late at night, the furniture was still in packing cases. I called the estate agent who had sold me the house. He found me sitting on the bare floor in tears, the maid trying to undo the cases and the children rushing from room to room and out onto the two acres of lawn. (The lawn was the chief reason I had bought the house. After the small gardens of Beverly Hills, it was like having my own estate.)

There was so much to do, and I had to write my Hollywood column as well. I rehired Jonah Ruddy, my former assistant in Hollywood, to send me the news. It was a strain, writing a Hollywood column in Westport, but I was too busy to worry. Curtains and carpets had to be made, new furniture bought. Some of my treasures had been broken in transit, and I had to see the insurance people. Buying a car was another task. My life was crowded with trivia, and there was no time or inclination to look for another man.

When I finished decorating and furnishing the house, everyone agreed I had done a marvelous job. In my early years I had no taste in this area at all. Wherever I lived, the rooms always looked like hotel rooms. But now I was expressing myself—white walls, French blue coverings for the settee, and a blue-flowered print on the armchairs. My collection of books, most of them given to me by Scott, filled the shelves of the small library. My daughter's bedroom was a replica of hers in Beverly Hills; Wendy hated change. My son was more like me; he enjoyed making a clean sweep of the past and starting all over again.

When it was all finished, I sat back and surveyed my pretty house with the pretty rooms and said, "I love my home." But when the children were away at boarding school, I was unbearably lonely. More and more frequently I took the plane to Los Angeles, where I stayed in a hotel. In April, feeling the warm sun on my face and neck, I said to myself, "If someone were to offer you a job here and said it was on condition that you have to live in this beautiful Beverly Hills, wouldn't you jump at it?" I had not enjoyed the long winter and the late, cold spring in Connecticut. I could not spend another winter in the East. All the years in California had thinned my blood. I must have a home in California again. I rented a furnished apartment on the south side of Wilshire Boulevard in Beverly Hills. I bought a new bed—my beds are scattered all over the world—a typewriter, and expensive linens.

From an apartment, the next step was a house. I had to sell the house in Connecticut to have another house in California. I would have to be much richer to afford the upkeep of two big homes. My son was delighted when I told him of my plans. My daughter was depressed: just as she was getting used to the house in Connecticut, she grumbled. But they were both pleased when I told them that their new home in Beverly Hills had an Olympic-size pool.

A woman saw my Connecticut house on Tuesday. She brought her husband on Thursday, and on Monday I had a check for the full amount, less the agent's fee. I moved eight times in ten years, always making a profit on the house. "You should be in real estate," my friends told me. Each time there were curtains and carpets to buy, auctions and sales to attend. My furniture went from coast to coast four times in all. Whenever the last article had been bought and the last workmen had gone, I had a compulsion to move. I was happy as long as I was buying and furnishing the house. That excited me, as the men I had known had excited me at the beginning. Then the affair, like the house, had become humdrum, and I wanted a change. Except with Scott, I had usually wanted to be somewhere I was not, and with someone else.

I made endless trips to the East to see the children. That was the main reason, but the flying and the change in time was exhausting, and I did not have time to think about my private life with no man in it.

I was pursued by a succession of men of all ages. One man fell in love with the photograph at the head of my column and tracked me down wherever I went, even to London. He alarmed me, and I reported him to the police. But the other men I led on to keep in practice, then backed away. I quite liked Arthur Cameron in Beverly Hills, with his big house, swimming pool, and tennis court. I played tennis and swam with him, but when he wanted to sleep with me, I burst into tears. This alarmed him and put him off. If I did not want any problems, neither did he. But he was surprised at the weeping. I was amusing and to have reached my position as a powerful columnist, he figured, a girl would have to be tough.

I had not wept much during my last unhappy marriage and divorce. Now, the slightest mishap brought the tears. But I never stayed too long anywhere to weep too long. The journeys, the packing, the work, and the nonstop buying and selling of houses had me spinning. I put the same eagerness into this way of life that I had previously put into my search for the Man. It was a different kind of orgasm, but for the same reason, to experience sensation, to be spending, money or sperm. Not to be still. Not to think. To be courted, even if it was only a salesman who was selling me carpets, or draperies, or furniture. It was being with people who wanted my favor. It was wanting and being wanted.

I made new friends, people who were not connected with my work. It was refreshing to talk about something else. I met a couple who own the Ranch House restaurant at Ojai in the mountains near Santa Barbara, and when I was very restless I drove there eighty miles to have dinner with them, and back to Los Angeles the same night. The food had something to do with it—four-star caliber.

My children were delighted to return to California for vacations, and to swim in the big pool. But while they were getting used to having a house with their own pool, I was getting tired of it. The alterations and furnishings were finished—months of turmoil. When I had the fireplace enlarged, the man fixing it had asked, his head up the chimney, "Is it true that your ex-husband has a yacht?" I had not answered. Would that marriage haunt me forever? When he came out of the chimney, his look querying, I replied, "No, he does not." There was some comfort in talking about him, because in spite of the trouble Stanley had caused me, I sometimes wished we were together again. I missed the comfort and pleasure of a man in the house.

In the early 1960's, making the excuse that the constant flights to New York were exhausting, but mainly because I missed being near the children, I rented an apartment in New York and put the house with the pool in the hands of a capable real-estate woman, who sold it within a few weeks. All of my houses sold quickly, because I made them attractive. I learned something new each time, what to do, what not to do, new color combinations, more daring schemes. The furniture I bought usually had

a two-day route, one to my home, one back to the shop.
I could never imagine how the furniture would look until
it was actually in the room, as I never knew what a
man was like until I went to bed with him. After many
changes, the furniture would finally please me. My New
York apartment was exquisite. I spent $12,000 fur-
nishing the two rooms. Everyone admired it, but it was
too small for my children. I had rented it while I still had
the house with the pool in California. But now that that
was sold, I took a house in the country, Connecticut
again, something I had sworn I would never do because
of the mosquitoes in the summer, the caterpillar blight in
the spring, and the freezing temperatures in the winter.

I sold the new house after a year, and rented a three-
bedroom apartment in New York, and also bought a flat
in London. I was happy to go back to my roots. My
first husband was pleased, although he died before the
contract for the flat was signed. I was never lonely in
London when he was alive. He was always available,
and I missed him, especially in Hyde Park, which he
always said was "our" park.

Again I was busy, attending auctions in New York
and dashing through the swing doors into Harrods in
London to find furniture for the new homes. They would
be the prettiest of them all, I vowed somewhat hysterically.

The deal in London was completed by mail—lawyers
there taking their time to close a contract. I arrived in
London on a cold December day, flying at night to get
there in the morning to go straight to Harrods to buy
a settee and two armchairs. I had bought one of their
very best beds at a huge price, something like five hundred
dollars, which was already in the apartment. I still have
it. It is marvelous. It takes me in its arms and holds me.

Nine A.M. in the furniture department at Harrods: "I'll
buy this settee and the armchairs," I told the attentive
salesman, "if they can be delivered to my home before
six o'clock today." He checked and came back beaming.
"You're in luck." I now wondered if perhaps they
were too large; my apartment is tiny, I told him. I gave

him the measurements. No, he did not think they were too big.

When I saw the three men staggering up the stairs to my flat, I thought, "Oh, my God, they are too big, and if I don't like them, how will they get them down again?" The settee and two matching armchairs took up most of the space in the small living room. I tried arranging and re-arranging so I could get to the big desk I had also bought under the same condition, that it would be delivered before six. I called a helpful friend, and she came over and suggested putting the settee flat against the longest wall. There was no place for the armchairs. "They looked smaller in the shop," I wailed. In any case, I did not like them. They were covered with a heavily embossed cream brocade. How could I have bought them? You must never transact any kind of business until forty-eight hours after a long plane journey, I'd read somewhere. If only I would take things more slowly.

After a few days of knocking myself on the furniture, I called Harrods and said to the salesman, "I think you had better take back one of the armchairs; then perhaps I will have room to move." Two days later: "Please," I begged, "take back the other armchair; I still have no room to move." When I telephoned him a few days before Christmas, he groaned, "Not the settee!" But it was the settee. The great thing about Harrods is that they will always take back what you don't like. I once bought a mahogany dining table from them, and I had to return to New York before they could pick it up. When I returned, four months later, I telephoned them, apologizing, and they took it back and credited it to my account.

The little flat was charming but small, and after two years—two years is usually my limit—I decided I needed a larger place in London. I was walking to the Knights-bridge Post Office, and a pretty blond woman was standing by the white door in the center of five two-story houses. I glanced inside, the sun was streaming through, and I gasped, "Oh, how pretty." "Would you like to come in-side and see the rest," the blond lady asked. She had just finished converting the house, she told me over a cup of tea, new central heating, marvelous mirror-lined bathroom, an enchanting cloakroom with a wash basin she had found in Venice, an exquisite navy blue tiled kitchen with a white plastic patterned ceiling. She had knocked down the wall between the dining and the sitting rooms and installed a slender marble fireplace. I asked immediately to buy the house.

"But I've only just finished it," the lady protested. Adding, "I have bought the house at the end, because it has a garage. I can sell you *that* house without the garage. I also have a small house in Kensington which I have just put on the market now that this one is finished. Would you like that?" "No," I insisted, "I like *this* house. I want to buy *this* house." Well, she had three houses, and she had to get rid of two. She and her husband also own a beautiful sixteenth-century house in the country with a marvelous garden—I saw it later and wanted to buy it: masses of flowerbeds and a beautiful lawn. Why anyone with a house like that would want to live in a city, even London, I cannot understand.

"I'll have to ask my husband," she stalled. It was too fantastic, a woman coming in from the street and offering to buy her house. She did not know that houses had become my substitute for sex, for my lover, and further back in my unconscious, for my mother. I went after houses with the blind tenacity of an Elizabeth Taylor tying down a man.

I gave many deposits for many houses in London and the British countryside. The best part of buying a house in England is that you can get your deposit back at any time before signing the final document. I would want the house or flat, but when I could get it at my price, it was not as appealing. Just like a man that you could get too easily.

Dilly-dallying through a summer—I want it, no I don't want it—I finally bought the house because the owner was going away the next morning, and she had an offer she was planning to accept from a rich American couple. Having decided to sell the house to me, she was now anxious to sell and start all over again, transforming the house at the end of the road into the same sort of paradise.

Now I was frantic, and to make sure of getting the house, I rushed to my lawyer and gave him a check for the entire amount. I have owned this house for two and a half years. It is a jewel box, furnished with expensive antiques for which I went as far as Winchester and Somerset, and decorated in soft autumn colors—russet, browns, yellows and greens.

I picked up an ancestor at an auction to put over the fireplace, a portrait of a young lady of fashion in the eighteenth century, painted by John Hoppner. I paid fifty-eight pounds, cheap for an ancestor. The eyes remind me of my daughter.

Question: With nothing further to do for the house, will I sell it? I don't know. I am trying not to, because I love it. But the restlessness is still there, and one thing a house has over a husband, you can get rid of it without fuss—or heartbreak.

CHAPTER 13

The Most Common Substitute for Sex

Food, glorious food. I hate it. I hate being fat. I lose all my confidence as a woman when I am fat—as most women do. And yet, in the times between being in love with a man, I have eaten myself out of shape.

Which is the most important—food or sex? You could live without sex. But not without food, although we are all accustomed to eat more than we need. The child turns away when the mother tries to force "one more, darling" down its gagging throat. We are overstuffed as babies. We are praised when we clean our plates. At party time, for rich and poor, there are always lots of sticky cakes, cookies, and rich ice cream.

We are taught to love sweet, fattening food when we are too young and helpless to protest. So that when we are adults and we are disappointed for one reason or another—in work or in love—we remember how popular we were when we polished off the food as children with no other problems than trying to please our mothers. The pattern of future physical disaster is set by our mothers, who love us.

I do not smoke, I rarely drink, and when I have been nervous I have thought I would go out of my head unless I found something sweet to nibble on while I work or read. Nuts. When I am nervous or tired, I have an over-

175

whelming desire for nuts that makes me scrape the almonds from the tops of cookies, or if I am in a cocktail bar, grab every nut within reach. I always hate myself afterward, and, satiated and nauseated, cannot understand the compulsion that nagged and nagged until my hand started reaching almost by itself.

It is the first nut or the first piece of candy, as they tell you in the Weight Watchers' classes, that starts the stampede. They warn, "Don't have them in the house." But when you are happy and in control, it would not matter how much of the "illegal" food is around; you would not be tempted. The alcoholic, when he is on the wagon, can watch his companions drink liquor, and he will not be tempted.

When Scott Fitzgerald was not drinking, it did not bother him at all when other people were drinking. When he was sober, he disapproved of drunks. After he took that first drink, it was impossible for him to stop until he collapsed. Then the thin chain which kept him from going beyond the point of no recall pulled him back to the realization that he must stop, for a while, anyway.

Food is like drink or sex. The more you have, the more you want. Men who have sex regularly can get an erection when they are eighty. Less passionate men who are faithful to their wives can peter out in their forties when the excitement has evaporated from the marital bed. Food, sex, and liquor create their own appetite. Cut down on any one of them, and the desire is lessened.

In recent years, since my last divorce, I have not wanted sex as much, although I am still on the alert for a possible man who would be satisfactory as a companion and a lover, not necessarily in that order; it would depend on how good he was at either.

At the moment, I am on one of the innumerable diets, which is an indication of my hopes for the near future. When I am nibbling my head off, I am not looking for a man. I am not looking for anything except self-pity. I won't buy new clothes, I won't go out at night. I sit at home watching television, wearing a comfortable dressing gown, stuffing myself with crackers or cookies. It is too much effort to squeeze into one of the dresses I buy in my thin periods. I am now down to almost normal weight. Watch out, men!

I would like always to be as slender as the rich women I see in society. Here and there you see a fatty, but mostly they are pencil slim. They look marvelous in clothes—so many of the top designers are men, or rather homosexuals, and they design their best clothes for the women who look most like boys. I could never look like a boy, even when I am most thin.

I was skinny as a kid, but looking at a photograph of myself when I was seventeen, I realize that I have always been on the round side. Perhaps I was always looking for a man. I have mama-size breasts. There is no way of hiding them, although when the rest of me is thin, they are not so noticeable.

They were a problem when I was on the stage. It was the fashion then for women to look like boys, flat-chested and short-haired. I compressed my abundance into a tight bodice that hid the curves but loosened some of the muscle. When, in the late 1930's, breasts were allowed to be natural again, I had to hold myself up high or they would have seemed to droop.

The uplift bra was a godsend for women of my generation who had to flatten their breasts to be in the fashion. The strapless bra in the 1940's was one of the great blessings for women who wished to seem to have upstanding breasts. Instead of straps, there was steel to support the sagging bosom.

I once tried to weigh my breasts on my bathroom scale. I lay on the floor and put a breast on the scale, but it did not seem to weigh more than a few pounds. I would put them at ten pounds apiece. Some women have operations to reduce the size of their breasts. I would never do that, and I would never have my face lifted either. I do not believe in tampering with nature, beyond wearing a wig when I can't be bothered—usually when I am overweight —to get my hair fixed for a function.

In the daytime I wear hats. My halo headgear is almost as famous as Queen Mary's toques and Bea Lillie's pill-boxes. My halos give my face height and make it look thinner. They also suit me, and fat or thin, I want to look seductive when I am lunching with important publishers. It works. The other day I had a handsome, youngish publisher almost in my lap; his kiss when we said good-bye lingered for seven seconds—I counted in my head. It was the hat, I am convinced, and the fact that I had shed a few pounds.

If you want to be attractive to men, slim down, and if you want to know about diets, ask me. I have tried them all, and there is only one that works, willpower, or you could call it self-hypnosis. Like everything else, sex included, it has to start in the head, *your* head.

It helps to have a goal. I am dieting now because when I finish this book, I am not merely going to wish for another man to be important in my life, I'm going out to find him, and to get him, I must be confident of my charm as a woman. And you cannot be confident as a woman when you are wearing a Lane Bryant size twenty. I am at my best in a twelve or fourteen. No one makes pretty clothes for anyone bigger than this.

When the A line was popular, fat women thanked God. The fashion lasted for several years; then, inch by inch, the waist was back. There was no hiding the fact that you did not have a waist, that your top went out and never came back until too late.

I was always hoping for a magic pill so that I could eat all I wanted and remain thin. "Have they got one yet?" I would ask my doctor, who would smile and shake his head. Why can't someone invent a pill that will eat up fat as fast as the food goes down, or one to kill your appetite without making you nervous. The Romans had their vomitoriums, but there has to be a better way than throwing up, which makes you feel ghastly. There should be a simple remedy for the people who get fat with every bite they eat.

Doctors warn us that extra weight is dangerous. To an insurance company, thirty excess pounds is as good, or rather bad, as having a leaky valve in your heart. But all they can advise is going on a diet, without curing the cause of why you overeat. That is why the health farms and the various weight-watching organizations are only of temporary value.

I saw Raymond Burr the other night on television; he was a guest on the *Andy Williams Show*. He was gigantic. I had not seen him in person for a few years, and I could not believe what I saw. I put my glasses on to be sure. He was just as heavy as when he first came to Hollywood and was cast as the villain because he was too fat to be the leading man.

When he signed to star in the Perry Mason series on TV, Raymond went on a killing diet and lost more than a hundred pounds. He looked good in his clothes—he bought a whole new wardrobe—but there was a lot of flab underneath, as I learned when I playfully punched him in the stomach to see if the new thin man was real. My fist went in several inches, and we were both embarrassed. Now all the weight is back again. You don't notice it when he is sitting in his *Ironside* wheelchair, but he looked like Man Mountain Dean when he was cavorting with Andy.

You lose it, then gain it back, and this is dangerous. It is better, doctors say, to stay at the heavy level rather than go up and down. This weight Yo-Yo killed Mario Lanza. He would eat himself into hideous overweight, then go on a strenuous diet and lose the weight, then celebrate with a mad eating rampage again. Why?

Mario was a singer and actor, and I have learned that singers and actors are very insecure, as women feel insecure without a man. When I first heard Ezio Pinza singing the songs from *South Pacific*, I thought a man with a voice like that must be confident always. I was wrong. Ezio was out of the show with a psychosomatic sore throat as much as he was in it. Raymond Burr has all the money he will ever need from his two series. Why should he have the compulsion to eat so much? Perhaps because he has no new goal to aim for. Perhaps because he is a bachelor —no woman to undress for. It works both ways.

Rod Steiger's weight goes up and down. He is so proud when his clothes hang loosely on him, he holds out the top of his pants to show you how many inches he has lost, and then I see him walking down the King's Road in London, hoping to look like a hippie, the space between his stomach and his pants gone. Rod admits to being insecure. When he finishes one picture, he wonders whether anyone will offer him another. This is incredible for such a fine actor.

Shelley Winters is happy when she is able to stay on a diet. Or rather she was. Now she does not seem to care. She is accepting the pounds as part of her personality, the way Kate Smith never seemed to care about being so heavy. But Kate obviously did care, I learned when I was lunching with her in New York a few years ago. She was on a diet of one good meal a day, and she had lost twenty or maybe thirty pounds. Kate is a strong-minded woman and does not appear to have any psychological hang-ups, but it seemed to me, when I saw her recently on television, that she was as plump as she had ever been.

Elizabeth Taylor loathes me when I mention in my column that she is overweight. Everyone else mentions it, and she is unhappy when they do. With Liz it is sheer love of guzzling. No one could accuse her of not having a good sex life. But who knows? I am always suspicious of those who keep talking about sex. They usually don't do much. Elizabeth has been at her fattest since her marriage to Mr. Burton. Their idea of happiness was to eat, drink, and be merry. In the past year, Richard has cut down on the drinking. So has Elizabeth, who always copies her men. Having seen himself on a television show and realizing how much weight he had gained, Richard also cut down on the food. His wife followed suit, and she became beautiful again. Richard has been faithful to Elizabeth, so they say. He does not have a chance to be otherwise. She never let him out of her sight. Wise woman.

But I am different. In the first place, I never put a chain around a man. If he wants another woman, then he does not want me, and I let him go. And when you see me fat, you will know that it is because I let the last man go, that my life does not contain my own special man. I deliberately put on weight after my last divorce. I did not want to be attractive to any man. I wanted a breathing space before I fell in love again. And then it becomes a habit to overeat.

Food is the most primitive form of comfort. Sex might be ahead of food for young men and women—if they are normal, they are on fire for sex most of the time—but for some women, especially as they grow older, and if they are alone, the compulsion to eat too much is an everyday problem. When they force themselves to diet, they get depressed.

More women commit suicide when they diet than at any other time. Marilyn Monroe was dieting when she took an overdose of pills. The insecure girl found comfort in eating and drinking, but she loved to show off her body, and she could do so only when she was slender.

Judy Garland, the second lost lady of all time, lost too much weight in too short a time. One month she was heavy, the next, thin as a rail. I bumped into the skinny Miss Garland at a theater one evening and asked enviously, "How did you do it?" "That you will have to find out for yourself." Her laugh was rather cruel, I thought.

But I have always known how to be thin. Cut down on food. "Stop eating," Lauren Bacall said to me when I was moaning about my weight. But unless you are in a hospital, you must not stop eating. I went to the hospital in Philadelphia where you stay in bed and drink weak tea and dietetic soft drinks. I was there for ten days and lost twelve pounds.

Fasting makes you very clear-headed. My brain was dancing on the ceiling after the first two days. I have never thought so clearly in my life. After the first forty-eight hours, not eating was no problem, and it was lovely weighing myself every day and seeing the pounds go. But with the first solid food, the weight came back, and the fasting caused my works to go on the blink. It was a week before I could go to the toilet properly.

With due deference to the doctor who invented this method of losing weight, it is not the right way. For women and men who are dramatically overweight, but not for the woman who eats because she does not have a man in her life.

There was one glorious time, a few years after my divorce, when I shed all the weight I had accumulated—about forty pounds. It was wonderful buying skimpy little dresses. By holding my breath, I could even get into a size ten. When you lose weight you are never satisfied. You want to lose more and more.

It took me three and a half months to lose the weight, and I was never tempted to eat fattening foods, not even when I was in Spain and had to wait until eleven P.M. for my dinner. I did it by myself, without visits to the fatty groups or diet doctors, although the diet was based on some previous visits to Dr. Morton Glenn in New York. I lost twenty pounds on the doctor's diet, but then it came back. I needed a shock to my vanity to make me follow his rules without having to visit him once a week and be weighed. In any case, I was two thousand miles away in California.

I had been to a cocktail party at the Universal studios. Ross Hunter was starting a picture with Lana Turner, and he invited the press to meet his cast. I had trouble finding a dress to fit me; the only possible one was bursting at the seams.

The late Cobina Wright, who was never fat in her life, although she had her troubles, saw me and gasped, "My God, Sheilah, you're as fat as a . . ." While she was searching for the word, I supplied it. "A pig," I said, trying to sound funny. She nodded, and I smiled a horrible smile.

I was too depressed that night to do anything but feel sorry for myself. How had it happened that I was as fat as a pig? The next morning I stood on the scale, which I had avoided since the divorce. A hundred and sixty-seven pounds. My pre-divorce weight was between 124 and 128 pounds.

The time had come. The fat was ruining my life. What man would want a woman who was as fat as a pig? My friends had been telling me that I was overweight; I was too pretty to be overweight they said. For some reason, a remark like this makes you eat more. And yet my friends, my good friends, did not despise me for being fat. I despised myself. There is something gross, undisciplined about a man or a woman who has become fat.

Russell Birdwell, a great publicity man, tried to shame me into losing weight. "Why can't you diet?" he asked. "Even little starlets can diet, why can't you?" Now I would diet. I would follow Dr. Glenn's formula, and I would do it without help.

I girded for the battle. I told the greedy imp in my brain, "I do not want food as a substitute for sex. I am not hungry." I was living at the beach, and when the long hours at the typewriter made me restless, I walked up and down on the sand, sometimes splashing in the water. I made myself tired, and some of the nervousness subsided.

It was easier after I lost the first six pounds. I was proud of my willpower. My dresses were not as tight. I felt superior, like a child who has been promised a trip if she does well at school. As each pound disappeared, the dieting became exciting. There were not so many holes in my stomach, demanding to be filled. And yet I was eating well.

Breakfast was half a grapefruit without sugar, a slice of dry toast, an egg or one and a half ounces of cottage cheese, a vitamin pill, and sugarless coffee with milk. Black coffee has always made me nervous, and I never drink coffee after two in the afternoon, or I would not be able to sleep at night. They have a marvelous substitute for coffee in Europe—Café Haag; it tastes like the real thing, but the caffeine has been removed. Bloomingdale's in New York sells it under the label of Calma.

In midmorning, exactly between breakfast and lunch, I had a cup of homemade chicken broth, with two Trisquits, which I was not supposed to have, but as I lost the weight anyway, it did not matter.

Lunch was the hardest meal. Only three ounces of fish, meat, or fowl and one-half cup of a green vegetable or salad, or a thin slice of dry bread. With tea or coffee. The liquid filled me up so that I did not crave more food.

At the exact center between lunch and dinner, I indulged in the equivalent of half a cup of fruit. Oh, how I looked forward to that. It was all right to make it a half-banana, Dr. Glenn had said, although most diets said no bananas at all.

Dinner: a cup of broth or tomato juice—usually I skipped this because I retain water, and the diuretic pill made me feel ill; then six ounces of fish, meat, or fowl, lean of course; two vegetables, a half-cup each; a half-cup of fruit; and tea or decaffeinated coffee. At bedtime I drank a glass of skim milk. I took it hot as they do in England, and it helped me to sleep.

After a month I could have skipped dinner entirely, but I was eating to live. I felt extremely well. I could walk faster. I could run again, without the heavy load I had carried in my body.

It was heaven to see the pounds fading. I was writing a book, *College of One,* and I had always excused the fat with, "Oh, I get terribly nervous sitting for hours typing." But I was more clear-headed now, and the book was coming along beautifully. I took some chapters to the editor of *The Sunday Times* when I was in London, and came out with a contract to supply two installments for ten thousand dollars. I was confident in my thin state: I took off my coat—fat women always keep their coats on. I was wearing a thin suit, and I looked twenty years younger; the old magic was working and the newspaper editor didn't have a chance.

Well, how did I gain it back? It was Christmas; I weighed 127 pounds and felt I could conquer the world. But the waiters at my favorite restaurant in London shook their heads at my thinness and the meager food orders and said I did not look as well. "I feel well," I told them happily. They were used to more face, that was all. I would never again get fat. Once more I belonged to the human race, and men whose eyes had glazed when they saw me were now telling me I was very attractive. There were suggestions of sex I had not heard for several years.

No matter what I ate, I continued to lose weight. I even became somewhat worried. I did not want to get too thin. I had seen skeletonlike women in various sauna and health clubs, and if you had to make a choice, the fat ones were more attractive.

The small hot mince pies at the Caprice restaurant in London were delicious. I could afford to eat two. No gain. Next time I had three small mince pies. By the time I returned to New York, I was eating well again, and when I weighed myself, there were five pounds more of me. This would never do. I must stop. Five pounds would be easy to lose. But I had lost the willpower that had made the dieting so easy. My will was in my stomach instead of in my head. I did not gain back all the weight I had lost, but it was still too much.

Now I have again lost weight. Thirty pounds in three months; only four more to go. I swear I will never put it back on again. It is willpower—no fattening foods—aided by a small pill recommended by doctors in Europe that is not stimulating and has no bad side effects. My magic pill. I have to remind myself that it is time to eat. Oh, heavenly bliss. I am again wearing the form-fitting clothes of five years ago—just on or below the knee in today's fashion.

I knew a film director who lost one hundred pounds by eating less of everything. He has kept them off. Food, he pontificated, should not be eaten in company. Food and drink were associated with happy, laughing people. Food should be eaten alone, and then we would eat less, he believed. Try telling that to the solitary secretive eater. Like telling the solitary drinker. Dear George, that is when a person eats or drinks most, when he or she is alone. And you have to become a bore with your disapproval of friends who are eating themselves into the grave.

At one of the gatherings of the fatties, I made a speech stressing the reeducation of the taste buds. Food must not be connected with being a "good girl." You are a good girl if you avoid the foods that make you fat. The women who capture the great matrimonial prizes are slim. But it is no use being thin and nervous. Get a man, and you will have the willpower to eat sensibly. You will not grab at the food and eat it as though it is your last meal. One thing is sure. It is easier to diet when you are not worried, or overly excited, or too depressed. Try to aim for something in the middle, on an even keel.

Make sure you are happy with your work. If you are straining at a job, whether housework or in an office, wishing you were doing something else, you will eat more, especially sweet things. Do not believe the skinny people who say they eat anything they like. Look at what they are eating. There will be an absence of starch, and rarely a dessert. "You must find out what is troubling you, what makes you an oral personality," I told the fatties. "Why you still have the characteristics of a child, of which being greedy is one. Find out what makes you toss in your bed—alone—at night. Why you feel so guilty. Is it really justified? You are no worse, and perhaps no better, than anyone else. Don't get overtired. Be rested. Be calm. Then dieting will not be so difficult. The need for the comfort of food will recede. Take a tranquilizer and a man. Then soon you won't need the tranquilizer."

Oh, the diets I have tried, but unless there was a man to appreciate the new thin body, they were useless and did not last. I have followed the five-prunes-a-day diet. I lost three pounds. The next morning I was ravenous, and I ate everything in sight. I would have picked it up from the floor. I have been to all the health farms—Maine Chance, the Golden Door, Buxted Park; fine for a rest and to lose a few pounds, but it all comes back under the stresses of life, particularly for a woman without a man.

I have been on five hundred calories a day. The weight goes, but returns when you start eating again. I have been on the drinking man's diet. You can eat fat, butter, cream, all the meat, fish, fowl you want, with no calorie-counting, but few carbohydrates.

I was with the multimillionaire Ralph Stolkin at the Bistro in Beverly Hills. He told me he had lost ten pounds on the drinking man's diet. "I'll start right now," I promised him with my usual haste. He ordered a large portion of caviar. Even without toast it was still delicious to gorge on my favorite food. After an enormous steak I was so full I could barely swallow the string beans. I could even have one small potato, but I didn't want it. Sanka with cream, and I was completely satisfied.

I had a glorious time. In four days I shed five pounds. Then the retina of my right eye became detached, and I was rushed to the hospital for an operation. It was a coincidence, of course, but I always associate the drinking man's diet with a detached retina.

Women without men are usually nervous. Don't keep it in. Explode when you are angry. If you keep it bottled up, you will be forced to diet on milk and slops to cure the ulcer. I will never get an ulcer. I say what I feel at the time I feel it. I weep when I am sad. I laugh when I am happy. I am usually very healthy, even when I am fat. My emotions are still childlike. I have tantrums when I am frustrated, and am generous and giving when I have my own way. But I am working on being an adult. I am intelligent, and that is why I have survived. I have been careful never to be too educated. I know enough, I have read enough, but not to the exclusion of living.

Don't seem too intelligent around men. Women are brighter than men, and the bright ladies hide their learning under a facade of sweet helplessness. Make the brutes work for us. They are better at drawing water and hewing wood than we are. The important thing is to have a man, even if you just like him. Pleasing him, you will please yourself. Everything will fall into place—your irritability, your nervousness, and the food. You will have no desire to overeat. You will have no need for an injurious sex substitute.

CHAPTER 14

The Unconscious

I needed a change. My life in New York had settled into a smooth routine—work, play, sex. I was tired of listening to the problems of my friends, getting involved, giving sympathy and advice that became worthless as the problems continued. I wanted some problems of my own. I wanted a new scene, new work, a new man. Change.

As I do so often in my life, I made a clean sweep. Leave New York. Get a job in another city. Find a new man. On December 24, 1935 I transferred the rest of my New York lease to a young man from Los Angeles. My apartment was furnished with what I had regarded as my precious things from England, but as soon as I made up my mind to leave, I lost interest in them. My tenant brought in some things of his own. A small oil portrait of a man in a red cloak—it brightened up the whole room—and a gun, which I found in a drawer when I came to pick up the rest of my clothes. He was a nervous man, his family was rich, and to the day he died, aged thirty-five, he was afraid of being kidnapped. He had come to New York to recover from his broken engagement to Anita Louise. Her photographs were all over the apartment. His family had a large house in the Los Feliz district in Los Angeles. Their seventy-foot living room featured an organ and a ten-foot-high stone fireplace which I saw when I spent my first Christmas in Hollywood with them.

My column appeared all over the country. I had power. I was courted by the most courted people in the world, the top stars and executives of the Hollywood film industry.

"Be sure you don't accept mink coats from directors," my new boss warned me. What a delightful thought! Would anyone really want to buy me a mink coat? I would not accept, of course. But if I fell in love with a star or a director and he fell in love with me, surely that would be quite honest. In reality, stars and directors were as spoiled as columnists, and did not scatter money around except for exceptional services rendered, although I was sure that Louella Parsons did not buy her own mink coats; I heard stories of the fabulous Christmas presents she received—jewels, paintings, furs, and expensive items of furniture.

I was determined I would not be misled into praising a film or a person. I metaphorically put myself into a fighting position to ward off the would-be corruptors—an unnecessary gesture. In all the years I worked in Hollywood—my first column appeared early in 1936—I received only one piece of jewelry, a gold brooch, the gold spray slashed in the center with a row of small emeralds, from Howard Hughes, whom I had known in New York casually, running into him at various cocktail parties. I had not been attracted to him, nor he to me. But he was now producing pictures in Hollywood, and he believed in the power of the press. It was Christmas, and it was better to have them on your side than against you.

When a Hollywood columnist traveled anywhere, Mr. Hughes, when he controlled TWA, usually sent her in a car to and from the airport, and his executives all over the world were alerted to the fact that So-and-So was on the plane. I soon accepted this as my due and became rather arrogant. If the car was not on time, I staged a small tantrum. When I visited Janet in New York in May, a few months after I had packed up and left, she complained gently that I had "gone Hollywood." It was my attitude of superiority and of expecting people to jump for me, and to listen to me with rapt attention, Janet explained. I had not been aware of the change, but promised I would watch it.

In spite of the new acquaintances in California, Janet was still my best woman friend. I missed her, and I missed the activity of New York. Not a girl to sit around moping, I bought a pale blue Ford and joined the Beverly Hills and the Westside tennis clubs, where I played tennis with George Murphy and his wife, singles with Robert Taylor, and doubles with Gilbert Roland. I swam in the blue Pacific at Malibu and in the Santa Monica pool at the beach home rented by Cary Grant and Randolph Scott, and felt lonelier and more of an outsider than I ever had in my life.

Some of the actors and directors tried to "make" me. Errol Flynn appeared at the door one evening, and I sent him packing. I had never fallen for the "wolf" type, and they were in full cry. I was the pretty new girl in town, but with my job I had to be careful. I had to maintain a good reputation. The young man who had rented my apartment in New York warned me, "Be careful with the Hollywood actors. Ninety percent of them have clap or syphilis." Years later I told this to Bob Hope, who has a good eye for a pretty girl, and afterward whenever we met he remembered the story and roared with laughter.

I was restless and longing to be loved. But at the beginning, all I had were dreams. The sex in my dreams was more exciting than anything I had ever experienced in real life. I had had them before, during times without sex, but these were different. They were fantastically exciting, peopled with Hollywood's most attractive men. I dreamed I was in bed with Cary Grant. He was playful and gorgeous, flashing and dashing. I awakened as I was having a fantastic orgasm. It had been so real. I had a special feeling for Cary after that and wrote about him glowingly in my column, but strangely, I never wanted to have a real-life affair with him. I would have liked to dream of Gary Cooper, but he never came into my dreams. In real life I thought him the most desirable man in Hollywood. Oh, what lovely times I have had with Frank Sinatra and Marlon Brando. As recently as a few nights ago I dreamed that Marlon was holding me in his arms and gently undressing me. I was very excited and somewhat worried. I wondered whether he realized I was older than when we had first met while he was starring on Broadway in *A Streetcar Named Desire*. It did not occur to me in the dream that he too was older. He looked young, and I was thankful that I had been dieting. When Frankie makes love to me, I am always glad that we have patched up our long-standing quarrel. In real life I detest them both. But in my unconscious I love them.

I dreamed about Mickey Rooney, who was then a cocky young man just emerged from adolescence. We were in my big bed, and I was fondling Master Rooney. "Oh, Mickey," I said, "I can teach you so much," and awakened instantly. Mickey Rooney! "I must be sex-starved," I said to no one in particular. Mickey Rooney! But Ava Gardner was to find him sexy, Judy Garland was in love with him, and Elizabeth Taylor found him charming. My unconscious had discovered his secret.

I was always dreaming. I had several each night, and remembered the last one on awakening. Some that were exciting or frightening I never forgot.

I can remember my first dream. I was two years old, sitting in my crib, which for some natural dream reason was in the middle of a quiet road. A man with a sack over his shoulder passed the crib, then came back, picked me up, put me in his sack, and ran off with me. I still shudder when I see a tramp with a sack over his shoulder. "If you are bad, the tramps will take you away in their sacks." I vaguely remember the threat.

When I was an actress, and for years and years afterward, I often dreamed I was on stage—the curtain was up and the audience in place, and I could not remember what I had to say or do. I would improvise wildly and wake up in a sweat.

When I was first in New York working as a journalist,

I nearly always dreamed about my next day's assignment. Sometimes I succeeded brilliantly in the dream, and I felt powerful and godlike, yet anxious, because in the dream I knew I was asleep. When I failed, I was lost and unwanted, people shunned me. Awakening after failing came as a great relief. I rarely failed with an assignment. I could not afford to. I had established a myth of invincibility, or so I thought. Did anyone really care whether I succeeded or failed? I cared, and that was enough. The tension I brought to each reporting assignment took possession of my unconscious, and the brain could not rest.

An actor friend told me of his recurring dream. He was tied to the end of a kite and floating in the sky. Apparently this dream signified that he was searching for his penis.

I had several recurring dreams. In the most frequent, I was in a narrow passage with high glistening wet walls on either side. It was dark, and I was compelled to keep walking. Coming toward me was a dark shape, sometimes in a black cloak, and I knew it was a man who was coming to kill me. Inexorably we were face to face, and with a roaring explosion I awakened. I was terrified; my heart beat fast. Was I repeating the experience of birth? Sometimes, in the same narrow passage, horses were galloping out of control toward me and would have trampled me with their hooves if I had not pressed flat as a leaf against the damp wall until they were gone. Horses, you may know, are a sex symbol.

Another recurring dream that always upset me concerned my teeth. I dreamed they were falling out, or they were loose as I touched them with probing fingers. Sometimes they dropped into my hand, one by one. When I awakened I immediately felt my teeth and was immensely relieved to find them still firmly in my mouth. Friends who have similar dreams believe teeth have something to do with sex, that they are another sex symbol. For a woman it is fear of losing her unnatural aggressiveness.

Another dream I often have, particularly when I am tired, is missing my plane or train. Every conceivable obstacle gets in the way. The driver does not know where the station is. I don't have the money for the fare. The airport official sends me to the wrong gate, I have to run frantically to find the right gate, and when I awake I am still anxiously searching for it.

One dream terrified me, because I am not sure it was a dream. It began with a shapeless form standing at the foot of the bed. The cloudiness gradually disappeared, revealing a tall man with piercing eyes. Perhaps the father I had never known? The first time this happened, in the early time of my first marriage, I awakened Johnny, screaming, "There's a man in the room," and dived under the covers. I had the dream—or was it real?—again when I was working in New York.

It was more frightening than my "dead" dreams. When I dreamed I was dead, I accepted it as inevitable, although what a relief to wake up and find I was alive! At the beginning of the war, when the air raids were devastating London, I dreamed I was running on a street brilliantly lit with bomb flares, and Hitler himself, laughing madly, was hanging out of the cockpit of a low-flying plane gunning me down. These are the dreams I cannot forget. The pleasant dreams vanish, except for the sex dreams, before awakening.

I missed the trimmings that went with a real-live man. I must find one. I had been so busy with the new job in Hollywood and so determined to make it a success that I had not put out my sex antennae.

Now, driving to the studios, driving back home, when I read the trade papers, when I ate, all of the time, I thought about sex, mainly imagining myself in the arms of Gregory Peck, who always flirted with me. He narrowed his eyes and looked meaningfully at me through the slits while I asked him questions. I became confused and forgot what I was saying. I would almost have an orgasm. Just imagining Gregory Peck making love to me was enough to turn my loins into warm liquid.

It was no dream. I was lying on my stomach in the king-size bedroom of the beautiful home of one of Hollywood's important directors. He had made his name with a poignant war film just before the talkies arrived and ruined so many careers. Because he was articulate and intelligent, he was successful in the new medium and became very rich.

I met him after attending the Santa Anita races in a party that included Paulette Goddard. One of Paulette's best friends had been linked romantically with the director. At the time she was in Philadelphia visiting her relatives. Paulette was married to Charlie Chaplin and lived nearby, but, not in the mood to go home right away, she suggested, "Let's stop and have a drink with ——," naming the director. There was a Filipino houseboy who made the drinks and produced some lightly fried shrimps with a pungent red sauce, who then sat in another room softly playing a guitar. It was like the distant tinkling on the piano in my school when the teachers were having a party. The faraway sound was comforting, the sort of sound you would hear if you lived at home with a family.

Paulette looked at her watch and jumped to her feet. "My God! Charlie will wonder where I am." She was gone in a flurry of good-byes and a sharp look at us both. I wondered afterward whether she had arranged it with the director. There were some men who found me desirable but were afraid to make the first move, as I learned years later. I was a powerful columnist, and if I did not respond, they thought I might write nasty things about them and their films. This meeting with the director had been managed so smoothly that it could mean something or nothing.

I felt a bit strained at first, but after another long drink and more fried shrimps, and with the Filipino boy playing the guitar in the background, my shoulders relaxed, and I smiled, listening to the director sing very hauntingly, "Summertime, and the living is easy." "Summertime" was my favorite song from *Porgy and Bess,* next to "There's a boat that's leaving soo-oon for New York, come with me sister, that's where you belong." Why was that song so sexy? Certain songs always arouse me sexually. When he sang "I've Got You Under My Skin," he was sitting very close to me. The scene had the quality of a dream.

I cannot remember how he got me upstairs. I think he was showing me over the house, and said something like, "I want you to see the plans for the new house I am building. I'd like your opinion." The plans, as it happened, were in his bedroom. He spread the plans—large sheets of blue paper—on the bed and explained what all the white lines meant. It was another language for me. How satisfying it must be to build your own house and have it exactly the way you want it. How I would love to be married to a man who would have such a magnificent house.

It was to be on the very top of the hill, overlooking and dominating the homes of Sam Goldwyn and Fred Astaire, and even looking down on "Pickfair," which Douglas Fairbanks had built for Mary Pickford, where she still lived, with her third husband, Buddy Rogers.

"Would you like me to massage you?" the director asked, kissing me. "I love massage," I confided dreamily. "Lie on your tummy," he commanded, and I obeyed. He started with my neck. "Very tight," he murmured, and bent down to kiss it. I had not realized it was tight. "Do you like a hard massage or a soft massage?" he asked solicitously. "I don't really care," I murmured into the pillow.

"You'll be more comfortable without the dress," he said, and gently unzipped it and pulled it out from under me. It took him a minute to undo the hook and eye on my bra, which I hugged to my front. He was now massaging me all over, while managing to remove most of his clothes. We made love, and it was delicious, just like a dream, only better, because he was still there when I opened my eyes.

What a stroke of luck! A rich director who said he loved me, who was building his own home and would change whatever I suggested—a bigger dressing room for me, more closets, a larger swimming pool. "It is perfect, I wouldn't change a thing," I murmured. We were back to the plans. "You will live in it with me," he said tenderly. Was he proposing? And would I say yes? You bet I would. The singing, the drinks, the shrimps, the plans for the house—I was sure I was already in love with this kind, considerate, gentle, rich man.

I would be his wife, a top Hollywood hostess. All the stars, including Gary Cooper and Gregory Peck—I supposed I would have to invite their wives—would come to my dinner dances. I had attended a dinner dance at the home of the Sam Goldwyns on New Year's Eve, and every star and director of importance had been there. I was standing next to Mr. Goldwyn on the stroke of midnight, and he had kissed me with more than the usual passion reserved for a complete stranger. I would make sure that Gary Cooper was next to me at midnight, and he would kiss me passionately. What was I thinking of? Of course, I would be kissing my husband.

I awakened abruptly from my daydream. As a gossip columnist who wrote about these important matters, I knew there was a steady girl friend in the director's life. "What a pity," I said, returning to the reality. "What a pity that you have a girl. Isn't her name Kitty?" He looked slightly uncomfortable. "Oh," he said, "that's all over, that's why she is with her family in the East." "Oh," I said, and smiled winningly at him. There were no obstacles. It was full steam ahead.

I saw him every evening for weeks, and was very happy when he said, "I love you. I want to marry you. Please say you will." Would I? Hold it. No mistakes. Managing to put a shade of seriousness into my wide smile, I said, "You are sure it is really over with Kitty?" "Yes," he was sure. "I'll meet her train when she comes in; didn't I tell you she is coming back on Friday?"—it was now Wednesday—"I'll tell her all about us." He saw the slight cloud in my eyes. Was it necessary to meet her if the affair was over? "I'll tell you what I'll do," he said with resolution. "To set your mind at rest, I'll buy you an engagement ring." I was embarrassed. He must not think I doubted him. "Oh no," I protested, "I don't need a ring to prove that you love me. We can get it afterward."

It was my second mistake with him. Like so many of the rich men I had known, the director was very careful with his money. If he had invested a large sum in a ring, he would have followed it in person and married me. But it would not have been a success, because in addition to his thrift, the director was also an incurable hypochondriac. During the weeks of our association he had sometimes telephoned me at three in the morning to complain of feeling ill.

"I can't sleep. Will you come over and sit with me until I fall asleep." "What is wrong?" I had asked, somewhat pettishly. I needed my own sleep for the day ahead. He felt ill, that was all. "But you look so well," I had blundered. This had been my first mistake. No one had told me that a hypochondriac hates to be told he is in blooming health. I had not sympathized with him. I was not going to be a mother again. It was not as though there were anything the matter with him. With his career, all that money, and me, he should be the happiest man in the world, I thought, irritated. Ah, if only I had all that money, I would never imagine I was ill. I would have a marvelous time. I'd know how to use my money. I'd be happy. But strangely enough, the rich people I know are usually unhappy, worried about imaginary problems and ailments.

It was the end of 1936, a time of the year which I have always found sad. I had my first serious operation the day before Christmas. I lost an important radio show a week after Christmas. In 1955 I had started to film a grueling television series shortly before Christmas and robbed my children of their holiday fun. In 1940 Scott Fitzgerald died on December 21.

I had expected to spend Christmas and the New Year with the director. I waited in vain for a call, and afraid that something was wrong—perhaps he was really ill this time—telephoned his home. He was skiing at Lake Arrowhead, the Filipino boy told me. I called Paulette, who was, I knew, at the Lake Arrowhead Hotel. She confirmed my fears; yes, Kitty was with him. She felt sorry for me, but she had thought the affair with Kitty was over, and after all, her first loyalty was to her friend.

The Filipino brought me Christmas presents from the boss—a navy blue cashmere sweater, a book, an enormous box of candy, and a flimsy expensive nightgown from Juel Park's exquisite lingerie shop on North Beverly Drive. I lingered over each one and wept. I had been sure he would telephone and send his car for me.

I read of his marriage to Kitty in the *Los Angeles Times*. They had flown to Europe for the honeymoon. When they returned he called and asked me to lunch with him at the Beverly Hills Brown Derby. I prepared angry speeches, which remained unspoken. What was the use? He was only slightly uncomfortable. Perhaps he thought I was not in love with him. That must be it. Or did he suffer from amnesia? But he soon proved he was not a victim of the latter.

"We went to Garmisch-Partenkirchen," he told me with only a shade of embarrassment. I had been to Garmisch with Johnny soon after I had left the stage. We had loved the quaint little town at the foot of the mountains with its narrow stream flowing through the main street. I had danced with my husband and the handsome young Bavarian men every night at the Post Hotel, while the beer flowed and the concertinas played. After our divorce I vowed that if I married again I would go to Garmisch for my honeymoon. When the director had asked me to choose the place for our honeymoon, I had insisted on Garmisch.

What a bastard, I thought, looking at his complacent face. But I faced the fact that I had not really been in love with him. It was a dream in my conscious mind. In my unconscious I was not in love with power and money. I was in love with love. I had been in love with the plans for the new house, the shrimps, the exotic drinks, and the idea of being rich and important and enjoying a life of leisure. I had seemed too self-sufficient. I had not catered to him, and perhaps I had gone to bed with him too quickly.

CHAPTER 15
Fantasia

Fantasies have always been an important part of my life. After reading *Daddy Long Legs* in the orphanage, I daydreamed that a rich trustee would adopt me, send me to a good finishing school, and then marry me. After leaving the school, I imagined—usually on the top of open buses—that I would be a great writer, or a great painter, or a composer. I could almost hear the applause. And the money I would make! First it was a thousand pounds a year, a great deal in those days, but with all I planned to do with it—one expensive project was to buy my mother a house at the seaside with a nurse and a housekeeper—it soon spiraled to three, four, and even five thousand pounds a year. Spending all that money was delicious!

Later my fantasies turned to sex. When I rode with a handsome instructor from the Ojai Inn—a lovely bungalow hotel in the valley of the Santa Barbara Mountains— I fantasized about riding our horses to the top of the mountains, dismounting, and making love on the soft earth. We did go to the top, and we did dismount, but it was only to give the horses a rest while we admired the view. Some years ago I had some sessions with a psychiatrist in London and afterward imagined him doing all sorts of sexual things to me. Supposedly women always fall in love with their psychiatrists, but I had also convinced myself that he was in love with me. I questioned him about it and was somewhat deflated, if relieved, when he laughed and said, "Don't be silly." You don't really expect your fantasies to come true.

At one time I had thought I'd rather die than live without having a man in my life, but it was not as difficult as I had imagined. There was always the easy satisfaction of masturbation, the comfort of food, and the fantasies. Constantly I thought about sex. Without a man to love, the idea of sex went to my head. Lovemaking was always in my mind. I had been too busy making actual love in the past to be obsessed with it in my thoughts. It was something new and quite exciting, rather like my dreams.

I discussed this with a former lover and learned that men have more fantasies than women, but they act them out—at least Americans do. The Englishman, having been repressed from birth, needs his fantasies for masturbation. Or sometimes a case erupts in the British papers, an important man caught with his pants down—literally —picking up a man in a public lavatory, sexually molesting a child, or discovered in a raid, strung up by his wrists, his bottom a mass of welts from a severe beating. The British men go in for beatings more than the Americans.

Because American men act out their sex fantasies, there are more men in American prisons than women. And more women in mental institutions than men. When a man has a fantasy about killing or rape, he usually finds a way to do it. A woman, afraid of the consequences, fantasizes instead, and sometimes goes mad in the process.

Beatings and rape are the favorite fantasies for women, I learned when trying to understand the behavior patterns of my life. Exciting in my fantasies, but I did not want it to happen in real life. Two men in Hollywood had tried to rape me, and I had not enjoyed the experience. The first was an actor—blond, sensual, his Nordic ancestry mixed with black. I was interviewing him at his luxurious home in the Pacific Palisades. We were sitting together on a low couch when he told me I was beautiful, grabbed my notebook and pencil, threw them away, and in one fast practiced motion was on top of me. I clawed at him and managed to twist my legs so that he could not get inside me. His orgasm ruined my skirt. The sticky stuff never came off. He was not ashamed, he said, no sir. He had wanted me ever since he saw me in the MGM commissary. He had wanted to make me, but more satisfactorily than this. "I could have given you pleasure. Why did you struggle? I wanted to give you a good time. Ah, well"—he yawned—"next time."

The other rape was attempted by a plump vice-president of an advertising agency with an office in Hollywood. Advertising men were important. They could make you rich with a radio show or a television show, and I had gladly accepted his invitation for dinner. Afterward, he drove into my garage, where he grabbed me and tried to scramble on top of me—a very awkward maneuver with the steering wheel and his own plumpness in the way. Another ruined outfit. I was furious. I could forgive the attempt—they all tried in their various ways—but it was my most expensive dress. I wore it to impress him, and not all the cleaning in the world removed the stiffness of the white-of-egg-like substance from my black satin dress. When I was sixteen and working as a skivvy in Brighton, I had occasion to visit a dentist, and he had tried to rape me in the chair, which was tipped back, and quite awkward for him as it shifted from side to side and went up and down, but not in rhythm with his orgasm, which landed on the only decent dress I possessed. I never saw him again, and I have never forgiven him.

And yet, in my fantasies, rape was a major happening. In fact, it was my favorite fantasy. It was sometimes my last husband who raped me, but usually no one I knew— strangers, dark-haired men with frowning faces. Sometimes a group of men put me in the middle of a close circle and two men held me down while each man took his turn. Was it rape if you enjoyed it? Should I let them know I was having orgasms? No, the whole idea of rape was the unwillingness of the woman. But how could they get inside you unless the wetness induced by desire made it possible? But some women were torn and bleeding after being raped. I shuddered at the thought. It would be easier to cooperate as long as they did not kill me for destroying the fun.

And yet sometimes I wanted to suffer. Why? What had I done that merited punishment? Why did I feel guilty and in need of suffering? (The only way I could go on a diet was by telling myself: "You must suffer.") Had I wanted my mother to die? Definitely not. Had I been wicked? I don't think so. I was somewhat of a liar, but all women are. They have to lie to get what they want. It was only in my fantasies that I enjoyed suffering. In my unconscious I wanted to be hurt, but that did not explain everything. When I had been left in the charity school I had fleetingly thought it was because I was not worthy to live in a real home.

"How old does a woman have to be before she stops having fantasies?" I asked a close friend in mock despair. He told me the story of the Spanish women in a village conquered by the Moors. The soldiers herded the women into a room, tied themselves to benches, and told the women to do whatever they liked with them. There was an old woman standing next to a girl of twenty, who said to her, "Not you, surely; just say you will do nothing." The old woman looked at the girl sternly and said, "War is war. Do not interfere." Oscar Wilde claimed that the tragedy of old people is that they remain young. As I grow older I find this true. There is no age limit to the desires of sex, in fact or in fantasy.

Some men have the fantastic notion that there are teeth in a woman's vagina. I heard this story from Paul Newman. "There was this girl who married a mama's boy. On their wedding night, the bride undressed quickly and got into bed. Her bridegroom took a long time in the bathroom, and when he came out his eager wife told him to come to bed and make love. 'I'll come to bed, but I won't make love,' he said. 'Why not?' the surprised bride inquired. 'Because my mother told me that women have teeth in their vaginas, and I'm afraid you'll bite off my penis.' She laughed. 'No, that's not true; look. You see,' she said, spreading her legs, 'there aren't any teeth.' He drew a long breath and gasped, 'My God, your gums are in terrible shape.' "

The fantasy of being killed is very common with women. I sometimes die in my dreams, but my fantasies never go as far as wanting to be killed. And yet I put myself in danger constantly, in my fantasies and in real life.

I have often thought of being tied up, but I am frightened when I read of men who tie women, rape, and sometimes kill them. Surely the conscious was the true indication of what I really wanted. No, the unconscious is supposed to be the real barometer of your desires.

Not long ago a young American in London wanted to have an affair with me. His talk was always suggestive when we were alone, and I would look around hastily, warning him with a "sh-sh," but he continued with his innuendos, his eyes and mouth moist. The young American was in his early twenties, and I could have been his mother.

Driving me home after dinner one evening, he told me of a strange, beautiful woman from the south of France— a true story, he claimed. Each night she was bathed in perfumed water by a maid and led into her bedroom. Several strong, naked men appeared, and she was spread-eagled on the bed, her hands tied to each side at the top, her legs in a wide inverted V fastened at the bottom of the bed. Two men sucked her nipples; the other, between her legs, ate her hungry vagina. When they could endure it no longer, they each made love to her while she was still bound moaning with the torturous pleasure.

I allowed the man to tell his story in full the first time, and it excited me, although I did not let him know. When he wanted to repeat the story on subsequent occasions, I laughed and refused to listen. If I had, I might have been tempted into an affair with him, and I did not want to be in bondage to any man again, especially a very young man who probably would treat me badly. But when I was alone and feeling restless, I thought of the woman tied to her bed, and it was enough to give me an orgasm.

Occasionally I fantasize about a man pointing a gun

at me. The gun looks vaguely like a penis, and a bullet is exactly like a penis—in miniature. The terror that puts all the senses on the alert, the shot that is like the explosion of an orgasm.

I sometimes thought of a burglar attacking me. Once in Westport my house was robbed, but I have never caught a burglar in the act. Thank God. I am sure that if it really happened I would be too terrified even to scream. I am sure any thought of sex would flee! But it is a fact that a woman's most frequent fantasy is about being killed! Women who walk down dark streets late at night are, in their unconscious, asking to be killed. As are the women who go home with the strangers they pick up in bars. In real life I would never bring a stranger into my home, although I do in my fantasies.

Muriel Spark's book *The Driver's Seat* is about a girl who deliberately chose a stranger to murder her, with the understanding that he can make love to her dead body. I disliked the book, although I enjoyed *The Prime of Miss Jean Brodie,* by the same author. That was a story I could understand—a teacher obsessed with her pupils, almost in love with them, a repressed woman getting her kicks by making her girls "the crème de la crème" and trying to turn them into fascists. Was that sexual? Perhaps. The ruthless use of power over the helpless individual is rape in its way.

After seeing *Born Free* I had a vague fantasy about lions. What would it be like to be made love to by a lion? Poor Elsa returned from her runaway nights with her shoulders torn and bleeding from the claws of the lion mounted on her back. I'd cut the claws, I thought. But would it be pleasurable? I have never seen a lion's erection. Monkeys in the zoo, yes; they are always playing with themselves, and dogs were always licking, smelling and scratching. I had seen dogs in the East End streets trying to mount a willing bitch. When the bitch was in heat, they succeeded in penetrating her, and the only way to separate them was to drench them with cold water.

I have heard that some women like Pomeranians because they have long tongues to lick their vaginas. Is this true? It is mostly old ladies who have Pomeranians. Do they want their pussies licked by a dog? I cannot imagine it, but apparently the weirdest things happen in sex.

Lions are important in the world of bizarre sex. A psychiatrist told me that many women as they lay relaxed on the couch in his office tell him of their desires to be eaten by a lion. I could tell him with my hand on my heart that I had never envisaged such a dreadful fate, not in my conscious, my unconscious, nor deep down in the lowest layer of my prehistoric inheritance. To be eaten by a cannibal would be bad enough, and I had never had a fantasy about that. As a child I had been terrified reading a book about cannibals, although I did wonder about the taste of flesh. It would depend, I supposed, on the age of the person being eaten. Hearts, livers, and kidneys appeared to be the same in their varying sizes, and I liked them from the fowl and four-footed worlds, but the idea of eating the human counterpart made me gag.

I have been told that what you hate most you want most. I am afraid of being injured in a car accident—this is one of my great fears. Does this mean that I want to be mangled in a car? Death is the final escape, but I do not want to die, and no one I know wants to die, unless they are very ill or insane.

I am a day girl, awakening very early in the morning, feeling that something wonderful is going to happen. Even after the unhappiness I suffered from the break-up of my third marriage, I was happy on awakening—until I remembered. But I had my children to live for to keep me sane. I have never thought of suicide. Except in my dreams or fantasies, I have never envisioned my own death. I am curious about what each day will bring. Until I had my unexpected eye operation, I believed I was omnipotent, immortal. I was sometimes depressed, but more often hopefully optimistic. I am healthy in body, and the fantasies which induce orgasms relieve the pressures in my life when there is no man I like to love me.

I was working in my study. On the grass outside, two cats were playing the love game. It was fascinating to watch the female, so like the human woman in heat. After some rough-and-tumble playing, the female dashed away —not too far away. She stopped suddenly, all hunched up, four paws together, and looked over her shoulder to make sure the male was still there. He had stopped when she did, but when she ran off again, he scampered after her, never quite catching her. The play went on for more than an hour, until the female allowed herself to be caught. What yowling! But it had been exciting to watch, and I was stimulated and found it difficult to return to my typewriter.

The horse figures frequently in women's fantasies. Is it coincidence that most of the paintings and drawings in my home are of horses? In mythical times horses raped women. The minotaur, part bull, part man, was an important figure in Greek legend. The head was of a bull, but the rest of the body was a man's, with the sex appetite and huge genitals of a bull. Some of the earliest paintings and sculpture show a horse with a man's head. I dreamed of galloping horses in the narrow, high-walled passages. I did not want to be trampled or raped by a horse; I had been terrified as they rushed past me. But apparently my unconscious yearned to have a horse for a mate.

Women who ride horses frequently have orgasms as they bounce up and down, their legs outstretched over the saddle. Some find sexual excitement in pulling on the reins to make the horse's mouth bleed. Do men beat and spur their horses for sexual stimulation, I wonder.

I've found that the horse-loving men and women are usually virile and interested in sex. They use strong language while riding, and make passionate uninhibited love in the evening, refreshed after a hot bath and excited after the hard ride. The young and middle-aged members of the hunt are often promiscuous. They have to have sex, and it doesn't matter with whom. The hunt itself can be interpreted sexually—the dogs devouring the fox, like the vagina consumes the penis.

On my several hunting ventures I've been too busy hanging onto the restive horse to think of sex. On one occasion I insisted, in spite of being thrown over a jump, on following the hunt, and inevitably came to grief. Perhaps this was my unconscious desire to be killed? I'm always eager for adventure, no matter how dangerous.

Once I went down the dangerous Cresta Bob Run at St. Moritz, sandwiched between a team of famous brothers. The sled ahead of us had gone over the top, and we had to wait for the track to be cleared. My eyes were tightly closed all the way down, but I could hear the harsh scraping noise as the heavy toboggan rocketed from side to side on the narrow slope. When the terrifying ride was over, I could barely stand up. In recounting this experience, I said it took two years off my life. Two years! I could have been killed.

In my early twenties I had taken a ride in an open two-seater plane with the earl, recently qualified as a pilot. Afterward his instructor had taken me up and looped the loop over the clubhouse. I was frozen with fear. When we were upside down, the pull of gravity was terrifying. Why did I do it if I did not have a hidden wish to be killed? I am nearly always afraid of flying, and yet I fly all over the world on my various assignments. I often wish that planes had not been invented, but I use them because time is always important. Whenever there is heavy turbulence, I vow I will never fly again. But I always do.

Once fearing that the next flight would surely be my last, I returned from England on the *Queen Elizabeth.* I was seasick for five days, and the long voyage was like a slow death. If a helicopter had come along, I would have begged for a rope.

One summer I took my children by train to Sun Valley, thinking it would be a novel experience for them. Instead they found it boring and dirty. They were delighted to step into a fast, clean plane for the return journey. Most of the people I know are afraid of flying. Then why do we? Do we all have the death wish?

The most uninhibited woman I have known is a rich Park Avenue Englishwoman. She's a size forty-four, but when I questioned her about her fantasies, she replied, "I have never had a fantasy in my life. I have sex whenever I want it. Right now I am having affairs with three men. They are always young. Why have a middle-aged or an old man when there are so many young men around who want to have an affair with an experienced woman?" Perhaps she is right. Why fantasize about young, virile men, when you can have them in the solid flesh? I might have a go if I could find an interesting young man, or a young man who was a good lover. Alas, they are rare.

CHAPTER 16

Sex Is Wasted on the Young

I was lying on the beach at the Outrigger Club in Honolulu, half-asleep, when I heard a group of teen-agers discussing sex. They had been romping around and were now having what they regarded as a serious conversation.

"I did it five times last night," a male voice boasted. I kept my eyes closed. The eavesdropping promised to be illuminating.

"Only five times?" a girl scoffed. "That's nothing. The real test is doing it eight times in one night." There was no mention of love, passion, or even enjoyment. Sex was only a test of physical endurance. Wham bang, a badge of virility. Eight times? A girl can have thirty orgasms in one night by masturbating. But this is not my idea of sex.

For the young of today, sex is like going to the bathroom. You must do it to remain healthy and happy. Too many divorce pleasure and love from the physical act. Sex without love is not too satisfactory. "I love you" is sweeter to hear than a thousand "Fuck me, fuck me's." Eighty percent of today's young people are completely promiscuous. They don't care who the partner is, as long as there is one. Girls go in groups to one or two boys who will make love—in this case "screw" is the better word—to all of them, then zip up the unisex pants and leave, wondering why it had been so urgent and was now nothing.

Casual sex for the young in the so-called civilized countries has reached a point where a British minister is advo-
cating "ultramodern" camps where young people can be
promiscuous.

Why is this new way of sex only for the young? If we
are determined to do away with the illusions and mysteries of sex, why not include *all* age groups? According
to Swinburne, lust is more honest than love. It is certainly
less complicated.

In my own experience, sex meant little in terms of
gratification until I reached my mid-twenties. It is the same
for men. What do they know about making love until
they have been in love?

Young people today are mixing religion with desire.
To worship a good leader—Jesus or Moses or Buddha—
gives the young a passive leaning post. In California the
stickers on the jalopies state "Honk for Jesus." It's certainly better than honking for drugs or for the dirty hair
and clothes favored by the hippies. (I rather like the
long hair—you get used to a style—but is there a law
against washing it?) Does making love on a mystical
cloud, in a religious trance, or following the dictates of
the medieval game of tarot, enhance the sex experience?
I doubt it.

A boy I know is only now, at twenty-five, beginning to
realize what sex is about. A year ago he married a girl
two weeks after they had met. He moved in with her the
day they met, leaving his previous female roommate without a good-bye. Now he follows his wife's mystical religious beliefs. Before his marriage he would have laughed
at the tarot cards; now his life is ruled by them.

His initiation into sex began when he was a fifteen-
year-old student at a fashionable co-ed boarding school
in the East. In his senior year there was some trouble with
two fifteen-year-old girls, and he was expelled. Before his
marriage he was responsible for several abortions. There
would have been one more, but the girl lost the fetus on
the handlebar of her motorcycle. The old, the young, the
virgins, the experienced, were all grist to his cock-a-doo-
dle-do.

Dutifully his father warned him that he could get into serious trouble with the girls who were under eighteen. His mother, engrossed in her acting career, had some suspicion of the sex life of her son, but she was rather pleased with his prowess. Most of the sons of her theater friends were homosexuals, and she was grateful hers was not. Once he brought home a sixteen-year-old girl and had sex with her in his mother's bed.

The evidence was on the sheet, and the bed was clumsily remade. "Why *my* bed?" she wailed at her grinning son. "It was bigger than mine," he replied. His impudence made her laugh. She had always been a permissive parent. Her own upbringing had been very strict. She knew little about sex until she married, and it took her several years to learn to enjoy what her generation still quaintly call making love.

She adored her son, but there was no communication between them. She felt awkward and embarrassed when they were alone. Frantically she searched for subjects to discuss with him, but only in rare moments could they let down the barrier and talk naturally. Only recently has she learned that communication is a two-way channel. She has forgotten the first principal of successful acting—there must be audience participation, you must bring your audience into whatever you are doing or saying. Otherwise, it is a solo monologue in a vacuum.

Once they were sitting quietly together—he talking, she silently memorizing some dialogue for a new show. Suddenly he confessed why he had broken off with the last girl.

"She always wanted to be on top of me. The man should be on top of the woman." The mother's attention was jolted back to his conversation. She wanted to keep him talking. It was an unexpected moment of communication. But then she made the mistake of explaining that it is sometimes the masculine girl who enjoys that position in sex. The boy clammed up, mumbled something, and walked away.

He had brought the girl to her parties. He had seemed so devoted to her, always holding her hand or kissing her, oblivious of other people. This happened with all his girls —complete devotion, then nothing. The mother usually felt sorry for his callous treatment of her sex and wanted to call the girl and commiserate with her, but her loyalty to her son stopped her.

The young have taken the excitement out of sex. Their attitude is too casual. There is no build-up. When I was a girl, we teased our boyfriends and saved the final act for the marriage bed, although if I were a girl now, I would not.

Now I think that if a young couple believe they are in love, they should go to bed and learn how they are as sex partners. This gives them the chance to see how their bodies harmonize. If the boy has a cold skin and gets goose pimples, it can put you off, although he might improve with time, and you have to be in love to be willing to give him the time.

Nowadays they don't have the time. It's off with the old, on with the new, on with the endless search for instant sexual gratification.

The safety of the pill has naturally resulted in promiscuity. But the pill is not always safe. Abortion, legal or otherwise, is an unpleasant ordeal, often leaving the girl depressed and wondering if she will be able to bear children in the future. Neither is a shotgun wedding the ideal solution.

The rise of venereal disease among the young is frightening, even though today there is less shame in going to your doctor for treatment. But not everyone does, and before they know they are infected, they may spread the disease around to the whole neighborhood. One London swinger, the daughter of a titled landowner, infected most of the virile men in Chelsea, Mayfair, and Belgravia. The tarts have more or less been driven off the streets in London, but they have their own methods of attracting the customers—from their cars, and with provocative gestures behind lighted windows. It was safer in the past, when the prostitutes were licensed and given frequent checkups. Prostitution is legal in many rural counties in

Nevada. But the incidence of venereal disease is higher in Las Vegas and Reno, where it is illegal.

It is interesting to note that today's ladies of the night are usually young and pretty. They have to be to compete with the young amateurs who are in bed at least once every twenty-four hours with a new male, seeking to satisfy an insatiable need. It's like biting and chewing but never swallowing.

If the rampaging members of women's liberation groups really want to do something for their sex, why don't they campaign for licensed male brothels where a girl can pay to have a go (this is real equality) without the danger of contracting syphilis or gonorrhea? Burning bras and girdles is ridiculous. Whistling at men on building sites is absurd. You can't reverse nature. It is the male prerogative to do the whistling, and always has been.

Nearly every play (except for some of the Greek), every opera, every ballet, every book, until very recently showed the man in control of the woman, or despised because he was not. God made Eve from Adam's rib, which is next to his heart. I wish I could believe this.

In the animal world the male body is more beautiful than his mate's. The broad shoulders, the narrow hips, the strong firm legs of a healthy man—no wonder Michelangelo's best sculptures and paintings were of the male form. And small wonder that this creator of beauty was a homosexual.

Young people today learn about sex early. One small girl informed her mother, "Today we had a lesson in sexual education." She was only eight, and her surprised mother asked, "Did you understand it all?" "Oh, yes, all of it, but, Mommy, what does 'male' mean?"

I remember that Scott Fitzgerald was reluctant to let his daughter attend too many dances when she was fifteen and sixteen. "You will be blasé and won't enjoy them when you are eighteen," he explained to the disappointed Scottie. In the same way, if you have experienced too much sex without love before you are twenty, you may become satiated and cease to enjoy it fully when you are older.

When I was twenty-eight, a young man said to me, "A woman is most attractive when she is thirty." I had been slightly worried about the imminence of that milestone, and his words gave me comfort. He was right. My whole life was aglow in my early thirties. I really enjoyed sex, and I enjoyed being in love.

The Aga Khan, once every mother's dream for her daughter, did not take a young girl for his bride; he married a divorced woman in her thirties. Jackie Kennedy married Onassis when she was thirty-nine. Even Richard Burton was truly in love for the first time in his life when he married Elizabeth Taylor, at that time a ripe thirty-two.

A woman knows how to handle herself better in bed and how to make the man and herself happy when she is no longer in the awkward flush of youth. She is less shy as she gets older. She knows how to keep the man in suspense until the right moment. She has learned what makes him tick, and knows how to make the most of *her* attributes.

Experience is the teacher. Experience blended with intelligence, which today's young girls don't seem to possess in the area of sex. They make themselves too cheap by giving themselves to every male who wants them, and to some who don't, and are treated cheaply. In spite of the strident utterances from some of the homeliest women I have ever seen on a dais, girls still want to get married. Every girl I know has told me she hopes to marry "someday." "Someday" often can be interpreted "as soon as possible." The marriage ceremony is a man's legal affirmation that he loves you and is prepared for the responsibility of raising a family and taking care of you. And no matter how today's girls sneer at old-fashioned marriage, they want this security.

CHAPTER 17

The Gay People

Some of my best friends are gay. In the world of the arts and on the periphery there are many disoriented, tormented, and often hysterical people who are neither men nor women. There are so many homosexuals that a girl would be lonely if she consorted only with men who had no problems on the score of virility.

I am glad I was born normal. I have never wanted an affair with a lesbian. I have always loved men. There was never room for a woman, although there almost was one time with a close friend, Edith.

Edith's daughter had been approached by a woman counselor at summer camp. Edith had found letters in the toilet bowl, where her daughter had unsuccessfully tried to dispose of them. They were filled with endearments from the counselor. Edith was very distressed and asked my advice on how to break up the relationship. I was indignant. The counselor should be exposed. She was a danger to her young charges.

"Take your daughter away where she cannot be with her," I advised. I could not think of anything else, and was worried that I had given the wrong advice. I was afraid that if the girl were prevented from seeing the woman, she would want her more.

At fifteen, the girl was dressing in masculine style—

severely tailored jackets, trousers, shirts, and ties. She looked like a caricature of a grown-up lesbian. Edith was distraught. She could not bear to have a lesbian daughter. She loved men passionately, and once had tried to kill herself when deserted by the man she loved.

While her ex-husband had left the bulk of his money to his daughter, there was six thousand dollars for his former wife. Edith decided to use this money to take her daughter to Paris. She wanted the girl to see the usually unattractive lesbians of Paris in their squalid clubs. I was doubtful of the scheme. What if her daughter fell in love with one of them? But it worked. They were in Paris for six months, and when they returned the girl was so feminine that she would not walk on the sunny side of the street because the sun might hurt her complexion. All her clothes were fluffy to the point of absurdity. But her mother was ecstatic. She had spent her entire inheritance, but had saved her daughter from a dreary life.

But Edith had become curious about lesbians, what it was like to be a lesbian. She decided to find out. On a train journey to Chicago, we shared a bedroom. From the top berth, Edith asked in a sleepy voice, "May I join you in your berth?" "No," I replied. Whatever was Edith thinking of? Perhaps she had not meant anything. But later, while I was dressing in my hotel room, Edith entered, suddenly clutched me, forced me backward onto the bed, spread my legs, and her lips grabbed my vagina with great sucking sounds. I vigorously tried to push her away. But she was like a leech. She would not let go. As she continued, I became angry and shrieked, "Go away, for God's sake!"

Afterward I wondered what would have happened if I had allowed her to continue. I might have had an orgasm with a woman. Heaven forbid! I hope no one will say, "You were afraid because this is what you really wanted." I've been told that woman have a tendency toward lesbianism, especially as they grow older. God, please don't let this happen to me. I might think of it in a fantasy, but never in real life. At least, I don't think so.

I saw less of Edith after that. I did not want a repetition.

It was embarrassing. What if I got to like it? Lesbians had such a difficult life. No, I don't want that. Edith and I remained good friends, and after her daughter married I always stayed with her in New York when I visited from Hollywood. There was never another attempt. She had only wanted to understand what her daughter had found so thrilling.

My English friend on Park Avenue talked continually about sex. I rarely talk to another woman about sex—although in the early days of my friendship with Edith we had discussed our men at great length. For me, sex is a private business. The Englishwoman was on a continual diet of sex. If she wasn't doing it, she was talking about it.

But she really liked women. The nonstop affairs with young men were to convince her unconscious that she preferred men. I realized this when a famous international actress was performing her one-woman show on Broadway. There were rumors that the actress was a lesbian. Since she had never made advances to me, I don't really know. I had two tickets for her show, and on an impulse gave my friend a treat, asking her to come with me. Afterward we would meet the actress in her dressing room.

My companion was in a high state of excitement. Her laugh was louder than usual. She clutched at my arm, and I could smell the sex. My God, I thought, I hope she won't pounce on her in the dressing room. I was sorry I had brought her.

During the show she applauded every number wildly. The actress smiled in our direction, and she went wild with joy. Backstage, I thought she would explode with suppressed frenzy. When the actress told us she was going to Washington for her next engagement, I could see the woman making a mental note of the hotel where she would be staying. Was the actress leading her on?

Going home in the taxi, the Englishwoman raved about the beautiful actress. She dribbled spit in her excitement. She was eternally grateful to me, she claimed, for giving her the great experience of meeting that wonderful woman. I was not surprised when the Park Avenue apartment was empty the following week. She was in Washington. She

reported calling on the actress, who had been most gracious to her. I did not ask for details, and she did not
offer them.

While the woman talked endlessly about the men she
slept with, she made no mention of her affairs with women.
I had heard stories of a woman in London who was paying
the Park Avenue bills. Why should she, unless there was
something going on? Sometimes the woman canceled appointments at the last minute, and people knew that her
English admirer was in town.

Eventually something went awry with the relationship.
My friend, who had previously been very extravagant—
going to East Hampton in the summer and Florida in the
winter, and flying to Rome or California for Christmas—
was no longer visiting those expensive places. She was
looking at the prices of things before she bought, and when
presented with a bill for ninety-five dollars at 21 for a dinner for four, she was shocked. In the past she had been a
frequent patron, picking up the tab with barely a glance.
Obviously her generous allowance had been drastically cut.

In Hollywood I knew a woman film agent who was
openly a lesbian. She was big and fat like my New York
friend, although more sensitive. She had always been fat,
one of those grotesque children almost as wide as she was
long. Her mother died when she was born, and her father,
an important state official, was ashamed of his freakis'
daughter. When they walked in the street he made hი,
walk far in front so that no one would know she was nis
daughter.

Like many other unattractive girls, she had suffered
when boys ignored her, preferring the slim, pretty girls.
The rejected freaks turned in desperation to their own sex.
They became lesbians because they had the same sex urge
as the pretty girls and they might find a misfit girl,
whereas they would never get a man unless he was a
homosexual.

When I met her in Hollywood, she was in love with a
woman who had been deserted by her rich husband. Her
ambition was to be a film star, and the fat woman took on
the role of agent and lover. They slept together in a big

double bed with no shame, no concealment. When the woman returned to her husband, they remained on friendly terms, and the agent found another lover.

The agent admired me and was always trying to kiss me on the mouth when we met or said good-bye. Her futile attempts were humorous. I liked her. She was outgoing and wanted the best for her clients, mostly young talents. She was always telling me I would go far, that I was a fine writer, and that I was wasting my talent doing a column. "You should be writing books or film scripts that I could sell for you. You are too good for the stuff you have to write for the Hollywood column. If you will let me handle you, I can make you rich and famous."

I was not sure what she meant by "handle," and I said nicely, "No, thank you." It became a game with me never to let her kiss me on the lips, always to turn my cheek at the kissing second. She realized that she was being rejected, but there was always the chance that one day I might break down.

This woman in California is tne only person I ever knew who was openly a lesbian. The Park Avenue woman was a lesbian, I was sure, but she would never admit it, not to me, anyway, because she wanted to keep my friendship. She talked only about the men. But why was she always making suggestive remarks to me?

I had not had sex with a man for a while, and I wondered what it would be like to have an affair with her. I imagined her naked. I'd heard reports that before I knew her she had hostessed an orgy. The British loved them, once they could be induced to relax. It could work for the Americans, too. The best way to achieve this was to make them take their clothes off. Once they were naked, they would be rid of their inhibitions. Psychiatrists have been known to do this with tense patients. Tallulah Bankhead had tried it when she first came to London. Guests arriving for supper were usually greeted by a naked Tallulah, and some of them stripped and frolicked around. Sir Francis this, Lady that—all in the nude.

A friend gave me details of the orgy on Park Avenue. "When I came in, she stopped me and said, 'You'll have to take your clothes off. It's that kind of a party.' " He was intrigued, and he obliged. He did not tell me what happened at the party. Probably not too much except loud laughter and giggling. But whenever I thought about this woman, she was always nude when she greeted her guests at the door.

She was the strongest woman I had ever known, a brunet Amazon. An exercise maniac, she walked for miles all over New York. Horses were her passion, and she rode whenever she got a chance, competing in all the important horse shows. On horseback she was as statuesque as an officer in the Queen's Guards. I felt like a wobbly beginner beside her, although I had been proud of my ability to jump small fences.

I was sure that there was a dildo in her apartment, and while I was able to fantasize about it, the thought of actually using it made my flesh crawl. I made excuses and gradually stopped seeing her. She had been a stopgap, someone to go to movies with, someone to be with after my last divorce.

The first famous homosexual I knew was a young playwright whom I met when I was on the stage. I found him attractive. Even knowing that he had no interest in women except as friends—his closest friends were women—I could have fallen in love with him. Homosexuals do not like women who are attractive to men, and the playwright was barely civil to me.

Quite often homosexuals are fairly normal in their early manhood. One well-known homosexual actor has several children and a happy marriage. Suddenly there was a spate of rumors about his association with young men. Oscar Wilde had four children, and there was no doubt of his homosexuality. A man could change in later life, although the seed must have been there.

When I was being courted by the young bloods who had attended Eton, Oxford, and Cambridge, they often talked of the seniors who had buggered and beaten them. Some anxious well-heeled parents sent their sons to school in Switzerland rather than risk a homosexual in the family. Most of the young men forgot what happened at school and university after they had their first affairs with women, but some of them who had domineering mothers hated women and were homosexuals into old age, when they were no longer sexually potent, and the lover usually became a companion and heir.

It hurt me when an attractive man preferred other men to women. I became depressed when I was with them. A famous homosexual maestro in New York married, much to my surprise. When I had met him in the home of a former opera singer, he had with him a beautiful young Greek boy sitting quietly by his side, in the same way that a dumb blond sits by the man who is keeping her. Are these people under orders not to say anything? Or are they intimidated by the company in which the men who are supporting them move with such ease? It is probably the latter. The kept boy is usually ignorant and a whore, entering the relationship for monetary reasons. If he were intelligent, he would earn his way with more satisfaction than he gets from being an aperture for a homosexual, although very often they get to like it, especially if the partner has a large penis.

I know a French singer who had lived with several women before becoming the lover of a famous musician. He was bisexual; he could make love to women as well as men, and was married twice to well-known women. Both marriages were failures. He is an opportunist and he married for money and position. One of the women in his life assured me that he was very good in bed. Bisexual lovers, I have heard, are often better with women than the heterosexuals.

I met him just before he married a famous writer. We were the musician's guests at an after-theater supper at the Caprice restaurant. While the conversation around the table hummed, the musician was whispering to me, "It won't be a success, I've told him. Why don't you try to convince him?" "No," I whispered back; "if this is what he wants, you can't break it up. They seem to be in love."

After his marriage, the singer did not give up his association with the musician. He might need him again. The musician had made him a star and would always be his friend. The divorce was costly for the singer and the musician. The wife could have ruined them both with her revelations. The threatened disclosure of his homosexuality gave her financial security for life.

The film maestro liked me—a situation which worried me. I feared I had lost my appeal for normal men. Nevertheless, it was a relief to have as a friend a man I did not have to fight off. He trusted me, and I was careful never to use a story that concerned him or his handsome protégé without first checking it with him. He always told me the truth, or nearly always. He could be spiteful, and when he disliked someone, told the most horrible stories about them. He claimed to hate a New York woman columnist. He informed people she was a sponger, always trying to get money from him, even sending her bills to him. But I was always sure he was in love with her as much as he could be with a woman.

He was always kind to me, and sometimes a great help. He was the confidant of many of the top stars in London and Hollywood, and when he gave me a story, which he did often, I could depend on its accuracy.

I thought I liked him because of the scoops he gave me and the stories I heard from the important people who wandered in and out of his apartment at cocktail time. It wasn't until he died that I realized I had liked him because of his great kindness, to me and others. The scoops did not matter as much as he did. I wished I had known this when he was alive. Perhaps I could have helped him.

Actually I did in one way, because I was his sounding board for all the shows he was writing, and for those he chose for his protégé. Occasionally I stayed with him on my visits to London. On one visit he asked me to read a show he had optioned for his protégé. He waited anxiously for my opinion. "Did you like it? Would it be good for——?" I thought it would be very good. "The problem," explained the musician, "is that whoever does the show must do it first on Broadway. But he does not want to spend six months in New York. Larry [Olivier] will be appearing there in a play, and he does not want to compete with him for the attention of the critics." "But the two shows are completely different," I protested. I was tired, and edging my way toward my bedroom. The musician followed me step by step as I walked backward. "Do you think he should do it?" he persisted. I was now at the door of my room, and opening it stealthily behind me. He was still coming forward. His face was an inch from mine, and I almost caught his nose in the door closing it, vowing silently I would never stay there again, and thinking how I hate homosexuals. But I did not really hate them. It was only when they were as emotional as women that they irritated me, or if I was exposed to too many of them at one time.

On a visit to London, I was given a letter of introduction to a debonair British lawyer by a mutual friend in Hollywood. Peter was rich, successful, and urbane. His clients included the best names in the world of entertainment. He liked women, but not sexually.

He gave a dinner party for me at the Mirabelle. The guests were carefully chosen by him to be helpful to me in my quest for news.

Whenever I came to London, he entertained me elegantly. He was delightful, knew everyone, never betrayed a confidence, and was adored by most people. "What a marvelous husband he would make," I thought. If only he were not queer. I did not realize this until he invited me to his country home, where the young man of the moment was installed. Otherwise I might never have guessed. He did not have the usual mannerisms of the homosexual—none of the poised little finger or the hand on the hip, as the singer had when he was drunk, and the musician always had.

I was shocked when the Englishman committed suicide by shooting his brains out. It was not like him to be so messy. He was so fastidious in everything he did. The suicide was unbelievable. There were all sorts of stories to explain his death—that he had been threatened with, exposure as a homosexual, that he was depressed after losing an important case, that he was being blackmailed by a detective because of an unorthodox procedure in a divorce case.

I didn't believe any of it. At our last lunch together I realized that he was losing his sanity. This controlled man who was so careful of what he said when he was in public places was banging on the table with his fist and shouting, "He's a liar! He's a thief!" about the famous husband of the woman for whom he was acting in the divorce. He was obviously a sick man. I thought that being homosexual had never worried him, but perhaps it had.

I met an attractive young publisher through the lawyer during the days of his gay sanity. The young man had been married and had a son. He seemed quite normal until he suddenly decided he would be a homosexual. He went to Greece and came back with a beautiful young Greek. There must be lots of them in Greece, just waiting for rich men to find them and take them away. When last heard from, the publisher had sent his Greek boy back, and was fairly normal again. But what an extraordinary thing for a prosperous young Englishman to do!

The common characteristic of these sad misfits is their supposed devotion to mother. I had always thought they loved their mothers, until I realized that their complete dependence on them produced a fierce hatred. I vowed I would never be the kind of mother who would make her son a homosexual. I realized there was no fear of this when we were in Venice, in Harry's Bar. I looked up and saw a well-dressed man of about forty standing by the door, staring at my son, Robert, who is very handsome and was then sixteen. He was so open in his admiration that not only my son but everyone else in the bar was aware of the situation. "Is there another way out?" Robert quietly asked. I paid the bill, and we left. "Phwew!" he said with relief when we boarded the water bus.

Are there more homosexuals in England than in the United States? Once I thought so. When I was in England during the war, I argued with the writer Peter Fleming that there were more homosexuals in London than in any American city, especially Dallas. "I will take bets that there is not one homosexual in Dallas," I said with complete conviction. He laughed at my innocence. Now I have come to the conclusion that it is the same everywhere—Paris, Rome, Madrid, St. Tropez, Dallas, everywhere in the world. Men who live by manual labor and big businessmen do not seem to have this problem, although with my first husband in Germany before the war I had stumbled over the beefy degenerates on the streets and in the exotic nightclubs. Seeing *Cabaret* on the stage in New York brought the whole atmosphere vividly to life.

I do not like homosexuals. They are too much like women, with all the tricks and bitchiness of the female sex. Even when I like a homo, I am never quite comfortable in his company. They can see through me and are sometimes cleverer than I am. In particular I dislike a young homosexual writer I frequently see at parties in New York, Hollywood, Rome, or London. Like all the homosexual writers, he has a vicious pen. There is no mercy for the voluptuous women he writes about, and no sympathy for the men who love them. I am always careful to avoid these men. I can do without their claws in my neck.

There was one homosexual in Hollywood I did like. He wrote for fan magazines and was devoted to me. He would never admit, perhaps not even to himself, that he was queer. Despite his nasty comments about homos, it was obvious to everyone that he belonged to the gay group.

Although he was never seen in the company of a boy, he had all the homosexual symptoms, chiefly a vicious feline tongue when talking about people he felt had slighted him. Why, when he had written so glowingly of them, did they not invite him to their parties? He would carry on about it for hours. But in other moods he was kind and gentle and would do anything for me because I had helped him get some writing assignments. I took him to dinner a few times at Trader Vic's in Beverly Hills. The conversation was strained at close quarters, but on the phone we were easy and could gossip for hours.

Once I had a fight on television with a man who had

played a homosexual in an explicit film. I was completely out of my depth. He cut me up in little pieces, and I was raw and bleeding. I met him at a cocktail party several months later and tried to avoid him, but he made a point of talking to me. He was charming and gentle, and I liked him very much. Trying to sound casual, I asked him, "Are you a homosexual?" Although he said no, I had my doubts. Perhaps he had not wished to distress me again.

I do not like homosexuals, nor do I understand them too well. It is a sterile, unnatural act. And there are more and more of them. Actually, it isn't that there are more homosexuals, but rather that the gay people of both sexes are now coming into the open. Perhaps it is a good thing. They are human beings, and they have been afraid too long. Except for the male and female whores, they did not ask to be half-male or half-female—to be subjected to the derision of the coarse and brutal men who think they are all man or the contempt of the greedy women who use sex as coldly as a computer to get the material things they want from life.

CHAPTER 18

Deballing the Jack

The domineering woman who bullies her husband is more objectionable, in my opinion, than a homosexual or a lesbian.

The wise man will keep his woman in subjection. Give her an opportunity, and she will tell him how to eat, how to dress, how to think, what to say, and how to make love. On the other side of the sex coin, I detest the man who squelches his wife or girl at home or in public.

I overheard one of these detestable creatures several tables away in a dining car on one trip from San Francisco to Los Angeles. No matter what the woman said, he answered derisively. He was well dressed and looked and sounded as though he considered himself God's gift to the world. She was looking out of the window as the train raced through the countryside and exclaimed, "What a pretty tree." His only reply was, "What do you know about trees?" I deduced they were married. She thought the coffee was too weak. "Personally, I find it too strong," he barked. He contradicted everything she said. If he were my husband, I would have clobbered him. One day she probably will kill him.

A successful businessman husband of a former dancer friend of mine seemed to be ashamed of his wife. It was embarrassing being with them. He never stopped telling her off. When she tentatively started a conversation, he would interrupt with, "You don't know what you are talking about. Shut up!" She did, meekly. There are three daughters, one still in college. I have often wondered what they thought of their father's constant bullying of their mother. After his death, the widow put on a big show of sorrow. Perhaps she had loved him, as her sadness indicated, but more likely she was laughing inside. He left her a great deal of money, and now, living as she pleases, saying what she pleases, she is blooming.

More often, surprisingly enough, the boot is on the other foot. The woman tells the man what to do. And God help the man when the woman has the money! She will push him around until he spins off to an early grave or into the arms of a more gentle woman. The man must be the stronger. If a gorilla is mounting his partner and he sees another gorilla ambling by, he leaves the female to fight the intruder to prove who is the stronger. To the victor belongs the lady gorilla.

Weak men sometimes put their house and capital in the name of the wife for safekeeping in the event of bankruptcy. Such is the case of an American-Irishman in the antique business in Philadelphia. He is extremely generous, but his wife made such a fuss when he spent his money on lavish entertainment for his friends that he ultimately acceded to her request and put everything he owned in her name. "Otherwise we will be ruined," she insisted. The wife is French, and a number-one nagger. If he takes a drink she hisses, "Tommee!" When he is on a binge he does not listen to her. Only then does he answer back. But she convinced him that if he does not give up liquor he will soon die. He had a slight heart attack, and it frightened him. He has not touched a drop since. When they quarrel, his wife threatens to leave her money—his money!—to a home for cats. She is mad about cats, and there are always three or four on the mantelpiece, jumping into your lap, your chair, or on your head. I can take dogs, but I do not care for cats. The only live thing I want rubbing up against me is a man.

A successful career woman I know married a man who

worked as a manager in a small store. "She treats me like a butler," he confided in his diary. But she would not have dared treat a servant as she was treating him. You can always get another husband, but a good butler is hard to find. After reading his diary from start to finish—she had a key made to unlock it—and realizing how much he hated her, she did the sensible thing. She divorced him. Now, with no man to nag, she nags her children, who will undoubtedly leave home as soon as they are self-supporting.

A doctor acquaintance is in a similar fix. He is efficient and respected in his consulting room and the hospitals where he donates his time two mornings a week. But at home his diminutive wife orders him around as though he were an office boy. Peace at any price is his motto, but I sometimes want to slap her when I hear her giving him orders: "Get me this! Get me that!"

The dominant wife extends to all levels of society. While in London I attended a reception for Queen Frederika of Greece and her late husband, King Paul. As I edged my way toward the royal couple I heard their conversation. Whenever he tried to talk, she interrupted. He was a henpecked king, I realized with sympathy and shock. Now she lives in Rome, an exile.

I was complaining to a young man about a married woman who makes her husband do most of the housework. They both have jobs and should at least share the home chores. He washes up, vacuums, cooks, drives the car, runs errands. "Why does he take it?" I asked. The young man looked thoughtful and answered, "Perhaps he enjoys being dominated." That had not occurred to me, but it's probably true. Some men prefer to be dominated. They want their girl friends or wives to make the decisions. They are usually lazy, easygoing men.

Such is the case of a handsome boy who in his early twenties married an eighteen-year-old girl. They both came from affluent families. The boy had been used to a domineering mother who had always run things. He had affairs mostly with older women. Now he was hitched to a girl four years his junior. The marriage almost broke up because each was waiting for the other to give the orders.

Before the divorce they came to see me. I had known the boy for a long time, and when his wife said, "I wake up in the morning expecting him to tell me what to do," I said, "You'll have to wait a long time, then. He does not tell people what to do. He is used to being told." That was three years ago. They are still together, and I visited them recently. The wife had become the dominant partner. She was making the plans. She was being rude to his friends whom she did not like. She was telling him what to eat and what to wear. This comes naturally to a woman with a weak husband, or even a strong husband if he allows her to hold the reins.

It is a fact that many men resent women with important jobs in fields they regard as their own exclusively. They see these powerful women as a threat to their cock. They are afraid of castration or that they won't be able to get it up. Men who are secure in their masculinity are not afraid of a woman who competes with them in work or in the home.

A famed professor at Harvard is married to a physically strong woman who was an American fashion editor in Paris before she descended on Cambridge, Massachusetts, and became anathema for most viewers of television talk shows with her brash, conceited, know-it-all, positive (but frequently erronous) statements. Very few people like her. She is the loud voice in her family. While her husband sits quietly, sometimes smiling to denote that he is listening, his wife monopolizes the conversation. And when he ventures to speak, she usually squelches him with, "How can you be so stupid!" He always laughs at her feeble jokes. Why doesn't he belt her one? Why doesn't he tell her to shut up? Why? Because he likes it this way. He likes to be dominated. His first marriage failed because his wife was gentle and feminine. There is room for only one gentle person in this marriage, and it is not the wife. I saw them recently in a supermarket in Boston, and from three aisles away I heard the wife bullying her husband, who was meekly making suggestions for the dinner party they were planning for an exalted member of the Senate. People were turning around to stare and smile.

I wouldn't be too surprised if she beats him up when they are alone at home. Some men have a compulsive desire to be hurt. The masochist enslaves himself at the feet of his women. He wants to be maltreated and betrayed. I know one man who begged his wife to whip him in front of her lover.

It is usually a happy mating when a professional man marries a rich woman. She provides the comfortable home. He can work at his profession without the necessity of making money, and without the financial worries, he generally does very well. It is a fifty-fifty partnership. She has the money; he has the status. For some reason, women rich in their own right are not usually raving beauties, and some are downright homely. When she marries a man in a respected profession she is making a good bargain. He gives her a home and children, a full, warm busy life, in contrast to the life she would lead as a rich spinster.

If you are a domineering woman, be sure you find a man who is prepared to let you push him around. Some advice to men who want to be the man in the marriage: run a mile from the ambitious woman, whether she shows her power in the arts, in business, or in the home. The ambitious woman wants to grow a penis but she can't. Not all the operations in the world will give her a real penis. This kind of woman often marries a homosexual or a weak man. Then she can believe that while the man has the penis, she has the drive. All she really wants him for is to father her children. And yet the power-crazed career woman is lonely without a husband or a man in the home.

The times when I have been most unhappy were when my work caused me to act like a man. When the competition made me ruthless and the desire to have a better life caused me to walk over a few heads, the exhilaration lasted only briefly. I have learned that the women who seem the most powerful are wearing masks. When they are challenged, they fall apart. They work so hard at being powerful that they deny their real dependence on others.

This happened to a woman doctor, a supreme authority in her field. Men were afraid of her, and she never married. Somewhat late in life, she decided to undergo psychoanalysis. She confessed on the couch, "I'm frightened, because I am always wearing a mask, pretending to be strong. No one knows how weak I am."

The president of a famous women's college in America had to retire when her depression turned into melancholia. She was single and had no sex life. She was too remote even to take a homosexual husband or a lesbian lover. This woman did not choose her life. She was afraid to compete for a man with other women, even though she knew he could make her life complete.

She was like the young man with a clever sister. He did not try to be good at his studies. He would not compete for fear he could not succeed as well as his sister had done. If he did not try, no one would know whether he might have succeeded. He did not realize it, but he was deballing the jack.

CHAPTER 19

Looking Forward

I still think of sex, but not with the fervent "I-must-have-it-or-die" attitude of my youth. I have learned that sex is important only when it goes wrong, or when you don't have it. Otherwise it is a natural part of life. I am sorry for the women who feel virtuous when they are merely frigid. I would like to have another man to see me through the last exit, but it might be a nuisance always having him underfoot, or even on top. I am accustomed to leading my own life, and I do not want anyone, my children or anyone, male or female, telling me what to do. I have complete independence except for the "hoops of steel" that bind me for all time to my family and friends. This can be slavery of a different kind, but I would not change it for a thousand freedoms.

My face is fairly unlined. My hair is now a natural pale silver. No more dye jobs to lighten the color. No more long hours in the beauty parlor hoping the color will be right. "You look so fresh, so well," I am told constantly. This is because I will always be vitally interested in what happens around me and in the world. I love my work. I love the effort that goes into the writing of a book. I love projects. I am a devoted watcher of basketball and football on television—American and English style. I still play tennis (doubles) and enjoy the excitement of Wimbledon and Forest Hills. I am a better swimmer now than when I was young. An instructor at the Golden Door taught me to breathe in the water, and my daughter showed me how to do the crawl.

I can still walk almost as fast as any young man, especially on a spring day on Fifth Avenue or in Hyde Park. I'll admit to a touch of arthritis in my left knee, caused, I am sure, by the many tumbles I took on the ice at the London rinks and in Switzerland, but it's a small price to pay today for the fun and enjoyment of yesterday's ice-skating.

"And you have your memories," an admiring friend told me the other day. To hell with memories. It is today and tomorrow that are important, and it is important to keep the apertures of the mind and body open for new experiences, never to clamp down the lid and say, "This is it—I've had all there is to have." There is always something more. A new project—if it is only learning, finally, how to wait for another right man. Another man. How old was Cleopatra? "Age could not wither nor custom stale her infinite variety."

With all my experience (and I am drenched in experience), I would not like to pass away without explaining what to do and what not to do—with men, sex, and everyday living. I have not always practiced what I preach, but my mistakes have been valuable, instructing me—and you—on what to avoid.

What do women want most from a man? Sex? Money? Support? No. Tenderness. It is my belief that most women, except for the incurable nymphomaniac, would rather have tenderness from a man than anything else. Most women would almost rather have the pre-sex play and the after-sex tenderness than the act of love itself. Sex is the climax of love, but the trimmings are what remain in the memory. Mature women are in love with tenderness. I have searched for it all my life. I found it with my first husband, who was twice my age—and impotent. And with Scott Fitzgerald, who was a decade older. Tenderness is the greatest gift a man can give a woman.

Any woman can have an orgasm; she does not need

a man for it. Women have orgasms faster when they masturbate than when a man's penis is jammed inside them. Some women can have orgasms only when they masturbate. This is the danger of too much solitary indulgence. Sex without masculine tenderness is barren, sterile, even when it results in conception. The woman is relieved when the orgasm is over. She has to like the man, even if she does not love him, so that she will want to stay with him after the lovemaking. This is the advantage of marriage or of living with a man: neither of you has to get up and go. You can stay for some tenderness. The best lovers of both sexes are those who do not rush away immediately after the orgasm is reached.

You can be married and still rush away. I was planning to write the biography of a famous blond actress. Her husband volunteered information about their sex life. (I can be brash on occasion, but I would never ask a couple I did not know well—or even if I did—for details of their sex life.) I was surprised and uncomfortable when he confided in me, "She's like a tigress when she wants me to screw her, biting my face and neck. But as soon as she comes, she is completely uninterested. She goes back to reading a book or eating an apple. She does not want me around." They were divorced recently.

In the course of my conversations with the wife, it became apparent that as a girl she had been in love with her father. Everything she did as a child was to please him. The worse he treated her, the more she wanted to please him. He told her that she would never be any good at her chosen goals. She achieved both ambitions—to be a ballerina and an actress—and decided to punish her father by never seeing him again. Actually, she was punishing herself. When she was famous she went to see him, and he, realizing his power over her, closed the door in her face. She promptly had a nervous breakdown.

Thank God I am no longer looking for a father. A relative gave me an enlarged photograph of my father. I stared and stared at his eyes, which were the same shape and color as my own. "I am fascinated by my father's eyes; I cannot tear myself away from them," I confessed to a friend in New York. "His eyes are what you remember," he replied. "But I was a baby," I protested. "The first thing a baby sees and remembers are the eyes of the parent," he claimed. Actually, my father's eyes and Scott Fitzgerald's were rather similar—candid, compassionate, and looking straight ahead.

Compassion is first cousin to tenderness. I received and gave compassion to my first husband, for his infantile anxieties that had removed him from reality and made him impotent. He could not push strongly in the world of money, and he was unable to push strongly in the world of sex. I wonder now, if I had been less capable, would Johnny have been less impotent? Capable women can frighten a man who can be impotent with one and a good lover with another.

Women who need psychiatric treatment are usually single, widowed, divorced, or childless. A woman who is married or living with a man and is having regular sex with a man who cares about her does not have the problems that a psychiatrist might solve. Are these emotional cripples ever completely cured?

I have a friend I have known for thirty-five years. When I first met him he was tortured with numerous problems. He was having sessions with a psychiatrist every day. Now he goes only occasionally for a brush-up. He is still a mixed-up kid, although much improved since I knew him as a young men. At the age of forty, he married a woman five years older than he was. She had a daughter of twenty, and his mother—a brilliant pianist—was aghast. He, however, seemed genuinely happy with his new family. Then, one day he took all his money from the bank, hid his car, and disappeared. The wife blames the mother for breaking up the marriage. I blame the psychiatrist, who had not completed his therapy.

There are good psychiatrists and bad ones. And the latter can do great harm. I knew a couple in California; he was a professor at Stanford; she worked for a doctor. They seemed happy, but something compelled her to consult a psychiatrist. After many treatments, her confusion led her to discard the man she thought she had loved.

That was five years ago. She now lives by herself and is desperately lonely. He married again on the condition that his new wife never visit a psychiatrist!

Psychiatrists can tell you only what is wrong and why it is wrong. But they cannot wave a wand and pronounce you cured. You have to cure yourself. If you are a confused person who goes to a psychiatrist, even though you realize all the causes of your malaise, you will not be strong enough to cure it. You can learn about yourself and probably will be better after a long period of treatment, but I doubt whether you will ever be completely cured.

With the turmoil of the absolute necessity of having a man now in the past, I am finding happiness in my writing. I do not consider myself a great writer, but I am competent and have always been a keen observer of human nature. I am constantly questioning. What makes him do that? What influences in the past have molded her into the image of today? Why is it easier for men to make easy love to certain types of women, and vice versa? In both cases, it is easier to make love to a man or a woman if you are not trying to make an impression. This is why men seek out prostitutes, and why women marry stupid men, although the clever woman never lets him know it.

The passionate woman does not count the cost. She gives generously. She asks for nothing in return. Her attitude is, this is as much fun for me as for you. But when she is older, when the heat has cooled, she might wonder whether she had not been too generous. She may have nothing to show for her sexual extravagance. I now believe that passion should sometimes be curbed, although I never curbed my own. I think a woman should watch out for her future, although I never watched out for my own.

I believe that a woman can get all she wants by judiciously using her femininity. And this I did, sometimes with calculation. The art of being a woman is the same principle as that of karate and judo and all the Oriental hand-to-hand combat—remain soft and pliant, then step

aside, touch him at the right moment, and he falls flat
or his face. That is the philosophy of the Oriental woman. She is feminine and yielding; she looks up to hei
man and is revered by her husband and children.

The secret of being a desirable woman is that while
everyone may guess that you spread your legs, they can
1ever prove it from your demeanor. Alfred Hitchcock is
always seeking this quality in the women who star in his
films. The lady in the bedroom, the whore in the boudoir.
Keep the man guessing. Nothing is more of a come-on.

Never introduce your boyfriend to your best woman
friend. After Scott died and I was in New York trying
to rebuild my life, a sympathetic friend I had known
in California invited me to have dinner with her and the
man she was living with. He called me the next day. I
was lonely and agreed to have lunch with him. He never
went back to the other woman. I would feel more guilty
if I had not lost this man to a woman friend who lost him
in turn to a woman to whom she had introduced him.
Sometimes you just have to lock them up. Let him meet
your predatory friends after he is safely hooked into matrimony. Even then, you have to be careful. There is
always the "other woman" lurking in the shadows, ready
to pounce on what you had thought belonged to you. A
few words mumbled over your head does not give you
permanent possession. Not even if you are a member in
good standing of the Wives' Club.

There is so much I can tell women. I am an expert
on the impotent man. Sometimes it helps to go down on
him when he is impotent for one reason or another—
money troubles, lack of confidence, getting older, too
much to drink. I tried this with Johnny, but not all the
suction from a thousand female lips could raise that limp
organ into more than a feeble erection which wilted as
soon as I stopped the boring act. I had quite liked it when
he had done it to me, but I never really wanted to do it to
any man. Although sometimes I did.

In the early days with the earl, we spent a weekend
in Paris, which was a more romantic place then than
now. He took me to some haunts where the waitresses

were nude. We drank a magnum of expensive, bad champagne, and when we came out, the taxi driver said, *"Tableaux vivants?"* The earl nodded, and I imagined we were going to see a "feelthy" film. But this tableau really was *vivant*. Live. Nuns were toying with each other on stage—not real nuns, of course. One of the nuns lifted up the skirt of another, who was sitting on a chair, and disappeared under the voluminous black folds. To judge by the heaving and groaning of the sitting nun, she was being sucked into an orgasm. It had been exciting at first, but then nauseating. I begged to leave.

Looking back, I believe that while men like women to go down on them, and vice versa, women do not enjoy fellatio. They are reluctant to do it, except as a last resort to make his penis erect. They would rather excite him manually.

A woman told me that her lover always made her suck him off, and when his sperm flooded into her mouth she usually gagged. But she loved him and did it to please him. Sperm has a strange odor, rather like sour castor oil, although not quite as thick. A man's penis secretes a lubricant, smegma. If the penis is not washed regularly, the odor is sour and fetid. The taste of the vagina is rather like salty fish. You know the story of the blind man who passed a fish shop, raised his hat, and said, "Good morning, ladies."

Why does lovemaking usually take place in the dark? Perhaps because the couple can imagine they are making love to whomever they fancy. But if you love the man, the fact that he is loving you, that he is pouring his life into you, is the greatest aphrodisiac of all. Let the others have their oysters and their Spanish fly. Nothing, in my experienced opinion, can equal the act of sex with a man you love. It makes every nerve in your body aware of the pleasure you are receiving. I could never again have an affair with a man unless I loved him.

Nothing can be done if the man's penis is permanently disabled in his mind, but when it is nervousness that makes it difficult for him to perform, all that is usually required is a few coarse words to bring the blood from the nead to the penis. You become the free-wheeling prostitute of his dreams. You are inferior, and the fear of not getting a hard-on will disappear.

I knew a hippie who said, "You are still inhibited unless you can crap on a toilet in the middle of a group." I am not inhibited, or rather I don't think I am, but I doubt whether I could ever go to that length to prove it. Proust was excited about the smell of urine. He expounds on it at great length in one of the volumes of *A la Recherche du Temps Perdu*. Perhaps because of the association with bed-wetting days in the orphanage, I have never found the odor of urine conducive to sex. The sweat of a man is different; it is very sexy.

I have often wondered why some of the homeliest women get the handsomest, nicest husbands. Perhaps, like the Avis car, the second best has to try harder. Men are so simple that they are taken in by a girl who seems genuinely interested in them, so that her looks don't matter as much as her adoration and efforts to cater to his whims. And when you get used to a person, you don't know whether he or she is handsome or homely. You just know if you like, dislike, or are indifferent.

Take the case of the Negro for whom the starlet left the film producer. I had thought the Negro ugly in his early pictures. He had thick lips, tight crinkling hair, and you saw too much of the whites of his eyes. Later, when he became a familiar and famous face, he seemed good-looking, and I could quite understand why the girl had fallen in love with him.

Anouk Aimée—how did she finally rope Albert Finney? They were in love. Previously Anouk had seemed to be in love with that perennial lover, Omar Sharif. But it was the real thing with Mr. Finney. She was so sure of her feelings that she gave a statement to the press that they were engaged. Mr. Finney had been married once and did not wish to rush into matrimony again. After the publicity, he was furious with Anouk. The marriage was off, although they continued to see each other. Anouk won him back with the same doglike devotion that Elizabeth Taylor uses to get her man. She abandoned her film *Justine* because, she told me, "I wanted to be with Albie." She was with him on the set all during the filming of *Scrooge*. They were quite open about living together in London. She cooked for him and cared for him as a wife would. Marriage was the natural conclusion.

When he's soft he's hard, and when he's hard he's soft. This precept needs no explanation from me, except to assure you that a woman can get practically anything from a man when he desires her, and practically nothing when he does not.

Should a girl take the initiative in sex? Not openly. Men back away from a woman who pursues them. It turns them off. You can bring a man to bed, but you can't make him perform unless he finds you sexually attractive. But I learned early in the game that I could make a man interested in me even if at the beginning he was not. Just thinking about sex made me desirable. He could see it in my eyes, on my mouth. My state of heat cried for attention. I knew when the man was hooked—the look, the lingering, the compliments, or just the way he said hello.

No matter what women's liberation advises, a lady cannot—or rather, should not—come right out and say, "I want you," unless she knows for sure that the man desires her. You have to lead him on, but not be too easy for the kill. A woman can fake an orgasm (I have, many times, to make the man feel that he was satisfactory as a lover), but a man cannot fake. It has to be there, visible to the eye, hard to the touch.

Men by nature are the hunters, although in the lion family it is the lioness who makes the kill. When she does, she knows that her first duty is to her master and her children. She must feed them first, and everyone is happy, as they are in the human family. The woman must feed her children and her man and she will have much more than the scraps for herself.

Women sometimes bring home more of the spoils than the man. She may have a better-paying job, but she must be careful to underplay her superior earning power, and give the impression that the man's work is more important, that he is looking after her, that he is in control of their sex life, that she needs him—which she does. He is the king, and while the queen is very important, the game is over if the king is checkmated.

In the prepermissive days, the educated woman was often a vinegary skinny female who went in for learning as a substitute for marriage and children. There are still some spinster headmistresses around to give this some credence. Many of the younger teachers of today are married. But it is true that the higher the academic degree, the less likely she is to get a husband, and the less likely to hold him. A B.A. or even an M.A. is okay, but don't go for the Ph.D. until after you have gone for a husband. The silliest girls get married all the time. The intelligent ones sometimes frighten the man.

Some women prefer making love on top of the man. She can manipulate his penis to give her more pleasure. There are men who enjoy letting the woman do the riding, although they find it difficult to have an orgasm in that position. Turn and turn about is a more fair arrangement. I have rather liked being on top. It is easier on the stomach.

I nearly died during the birth of my second child, and the doctor thought it inadvisable for me to have more children. He measured me for a diaphragm. I was rather small, and the rubber contraption was a junior size. I went to his office to try it on. "You do it like this," said the gynecologist, squeezing the diaphragm between the thumb and finger of his right hand. "You bend it, then insert it." I took the diaphragm from him rather gingerly. I squeezed it, and it flew across the room.

I tried again, but I could not get the required grip on the thing. "Ah, well," I said brightly. "I'll just have to be careful, won't I?" I was. The egg must not rendezvous with the long wriggly things that men ejaculate by the million with each orgasm. Nature, so lavish, was determined that one of them would hatch. It was up to me to see that none of them did.

It took some of the fun away from fornication, having to be so careful. I acceded to the doctor's suggestion that my tubes should be tied up. "Not cut. You might want more children; then we can blow them open. Think of all the fun you can have now," he said jovially. I was awake during the minor operation, and managed a wan smile. It is too late to have more children now, but there is the great joy of my granddaughter and possibly future grandchildren.

Today's nubile women have the pill. In my heyday, it was the man's responsibility to make sure the girl did not get pregnant. If he did not have the sheath—"the French letter," they called it in England, and *le manche anglais* in France—he withdrew his penis in time to splatter sperm on her body.

Many women today use the coil, but it sounds horrible to me. I heard of a case where the coil traveled into the girl's stomach, necessitating an operation. As for the diaphragm, it is only half-safe. If it shifts to the left or right, it could result in pregnancy. Abortions are now legal in enough countries that a girl who becomes pregnant unwillingly can lose her predicament without much trouble. But it is still a nuisance. And the menopause is a bore, with the hot flashes and occasional irrational behavior.

But it is the journey, not the arrival, that matters. The women who settled early for security have a dull life. I never settled for that. I always took chances. I always felt that tomorrow would bring something stupendously exciting. I always yielded to a new experience. I still do. It is still a full life. Whether good or bad I wouldn't know, but when you have had fun on the way, you can settle into a new skin with a certain complacency. Never say you have had it. Anything can happen.

I am now in a state of warmth rather than heat, but I have not given up looking for the ideal mate. There must be one more in the barrel. Perhaps an intelligent businessman, or a writer, or an amusing admiral or general, or an uncomplicated man with a pension and a nice house in the country. Someone who will not demand too much—talk, occasional sex, understanding, tenderness and long walks in the woods or on the beach to round off a life that has been full and interesting, if not always happy, from the time that I discovered sex and used it, knowingly and unknowingly, to get what I wanted. If *I* could do it, you certainly can.